Woodworking with Sheet Goods

Handyman Club Library™

Handyman Club of America
Minneapolis, Minnesota

Woodworking with Sheet Goods

CREDITS

Tom Carpenter
Creative Director

Mark Johanson
Book Products Development Manager
Handyman Club of America

Dan Cary
Photo Production Coordinator

Chris Marshall
Editorial Coordinator

Steve Anderson
Senior Book Production Assistant

Kam Ghaffari, Mark Johanson, Chris Marshall
Writers

Marti Naughton
Series Design, Art Direction and Production

Kim Bailey
Photographer

Tom Deveny, Jon Hegge, John Nadeau
Project Builders

John Drigot
Technical Illustrations & Project Design

Bill Nelson
Creative Consultant

Photo Credits:

Pages 6-7	*APA-The Engineered Wood Association*
Pages 10-11	*Willamette Industries, Inc.*

ISBN 1-58159-040-7

7 8 9 10 / 05 04 03

Handyman Club of America
12301 Whitewater Drive
Minnetonka, Minnesota 55343
www.handymanclub.com

Contents

Introduction **4**

Base Cabinet **34**

Wall-hung Cabinet **44**

Plant Stand with Storage **54**

Sailboat Sandbox **62**

Sheet Goods Cart **72**

Entertainment Center **80**

Hallway Bookcase **92**

Play Table & Chairs **100**

Walnut Writing Desk **110**

Desktop Console **118**

Corner Booth **126**

Changing Table/Dresser **140**

Country Cupboard **150**

INDEX **158**

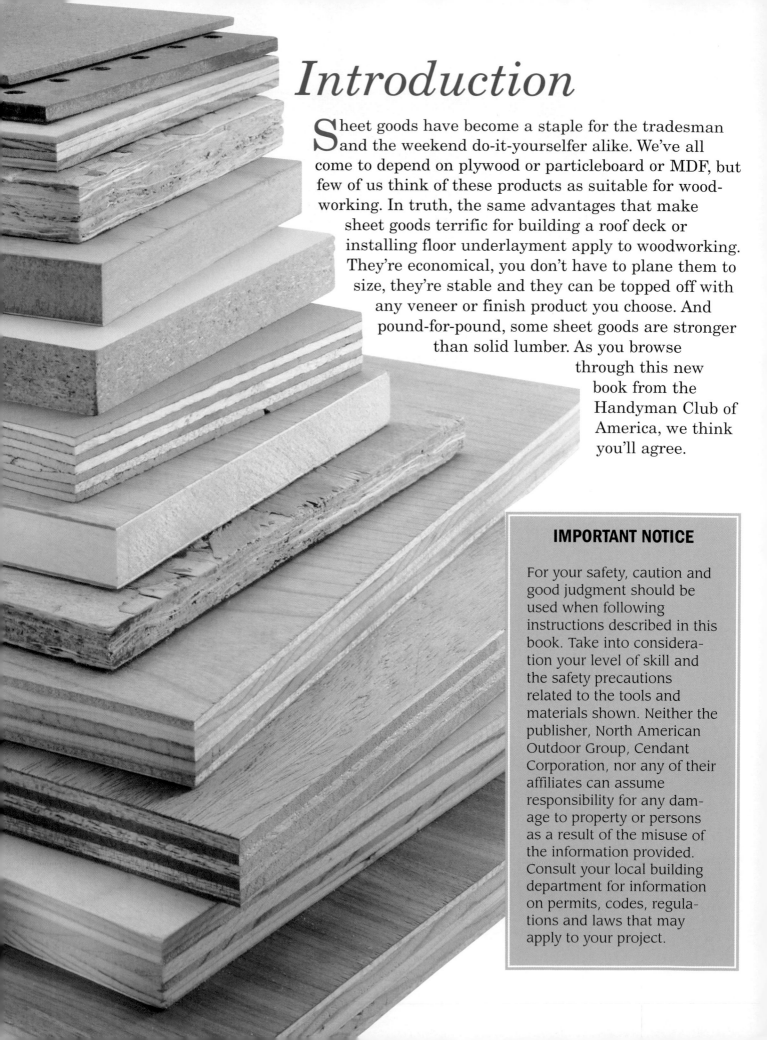

Introduction

Sheet goods have become a staple for the tradesman and the weekend do-it-yourselfer alike. We've all come to depend on plywood or particleboard or MDF, but few of us think of these products as suitable for woodworking. In truth, the same advantages that make sheet goods terrific for building a roof deck or installing floor underlayment apply to woodworking. They're economical, you don't have to plane them to size, they're stable and they can be topped off with any veneer or finish product you choose. And pound-for-pound, some sheet goods are stronger than solid lumber. As you browse through this new book from the Handyman Club of America, we think you'll agree.

IMPORTANT NOTICE

For your safety, caution and good judgment should be used when following instructions described in this book. Take into consideration your level of skill and the safety precautions related to the tools and materials shown. Neither the publisher, North American Outdoor Group, Cendant Corporation, nor any of their affiliates can assume responsibility for any damage to property or persons as a result of the misuse of the information provided. Consult your local building department for information on permits, codes, regulations and laws that may apply to your project.

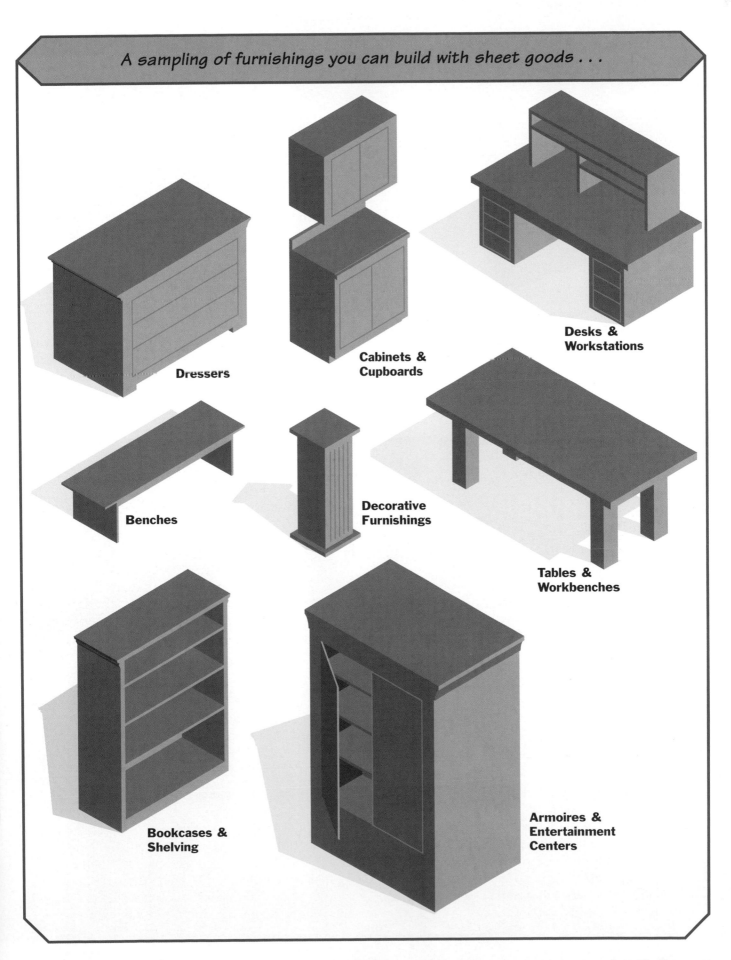

Dressers

Cabinets & Cupboards

Desks & Workstations

Benches

Decorative Furnishings

Tables & Workbenches

Bookcases & Shelving

Armoires & Entertainment Centers

erhaps no building material has brought about greater changes in the way building tradesmen work than plywood. Originally developed for use as decking and subfloors, plywood quickly gained acceptance in the years immediately following World War II, where it was ideally suited for the mass-production demands that accompanied the post-war housing boom. Due to its ease of use and versatility, plywood soon found its way into the lumberyards and building centers, where it was instantly popular with weekend do-it-yourselfers as well.

Initially, nearly all plywood was fashioned from sheets of softwood veneer—primarily, pines and fir. By orienting the wood grain of each laminated sheet so adjacent sheets are perpendicular, the product was able to withstand greater stress than construction lumber of the same thickness. In addition, it was (and is) more dimensionally stable. The only real drawback to plywood was aesthetic: scarred with plugs and cracks on the outer faces and filled with voids on the edges, it simply wasn't much to look at. But since its arrival on the market, new grades of plywood with hardwood face veneer and a range of core options have essentially elimi-

Plywood is manufactured in several thicknesses, using many different materials and processes to create the core, but ¾-in.-thick laminated veneer-core plywood with smooth hardwood veneer faces is the type used most frequently for woodworking projects.

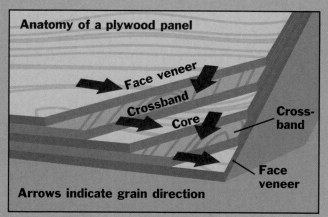

Traditional veneer-core plywood gets its strength from the perpendicular arrangement of the wood grain direction in alternating plies. The grain in the veneer on each face always runs lengthwise.

Manufacturing plywood

Although it is only within the last 50 or 60 years that plywood has become a common building material, the concept of face-gluing multiple sheets of thin wood together to create a panel is centuries old. Naturally, the process has become more sophisticated as various mass-production manufacturing processes have arisen. The end result is an inexpensive, versatile building material that makes efficient use of our dwindling forest resources.

Logs are peeled of bark, steamed or soaked, then trimmed to just over 8 feet in length before they're chucked into a rotary veneer slicer. The slicer shaves the log into long, continuous veneer ribbons. Softwood veneer for the core and crossbands is sliced to a thickness of .1 to .25 inches. Face veneers generally are sliced to about .03 in. (1/32). The rotary slicer can produce up to 600 lineal feet of veneer per minute.

The plywood manufacturing process starts with the selection and separation of suitable logs. The logs are peeled of bark, cut to length, then usually soaked or steamed before being mounted in a rotary cutter that slices them into sheets of veneer. The veneer sheets are dried, trimmed, sorted,

nated this drawback. Today, plywood is a favored working material for many designers and builders of fine furnishings, and it has become a standard for use in building custom cabinetry.

Most lumberyards stock furniture-grade plywood in several thicknesses and with a few face veneer options (pine, red oak, birch and maple are the most common face veneers). Lumberyards and wood products distributors carry or can order plywood with dozens of additional veneer options. For ease of use and economy, look for 2 × 4-ft. and 4 × 4-ft. "handy panels."

Plywood thickness guide:

Thickness (nominal/actual*)	Uses
¼ in. / ⁷⁄₃₂ in.	Back panels, drawer bottoms, frame-and-panel inserts
½ in. / ¹⁵⁄₃₂ in.	Small cabinet carcases, drawer sides
¾ in. / ²³⁄₃₂ in.	Structural components, large cabinet carcases, solid doors, drawer fronts, face frames, stretchers

* Actual thickness varies by type and grade: read grade stamp or take measurements to find individual panel thickness.

Sheets of green veneer are fed into a dryer for the curing process that reduces their moisture content to about 5%. The dried sheets are sorted and graded, then glued, heated to about 270°, and pressed into plywood panels under as much as 200 pounds of pressure per square inch. Then the pressed panels are sanded, graded and trimmed to size.

plugged or patched if needed, glued, then arranged by hand into multiple-ply "sandwiches" with cross-directional grain. The sandwiches of veneer are hot-pressed into plywood, some grades are sanded, then each panel is individually graded and stamped.

Plywood core types

The most common plywood core types are: *(A) Combination core* (wood veneer and composition board) has smooth surfaces and holds screws well; *(B) solid core* (MDF) resists warping and has smooth surfaces: good choice for tabletops in low-moisture areas; *(C) veneer core* has all-wood plies with alternating grain direction for light weight and high strength; *(D) lumber core* plywood is made by bonding face veneer to edge-glued strips of solid lumber; very rigid, good screw-holding capability, but has less dimensional stability than other core types.

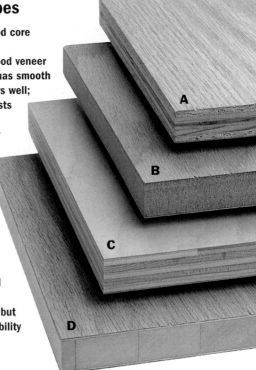

Special-purpose plywood

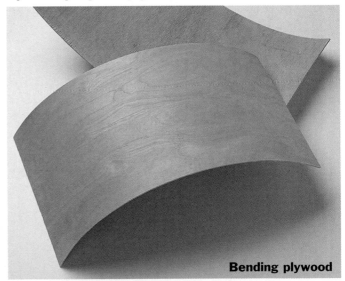

Bending plywood

Exterior-rated plywood

Bending plywood has a single-ply core (often lauan plywood) with face veneer (maple is shown above); some types have multiple plies laminated with the same grain direction to allow flexing; Exterior-rated plywood is made with water-resistant glue and is used for cabinetry in high-moisture areas; choose panels with one *B* or better face.

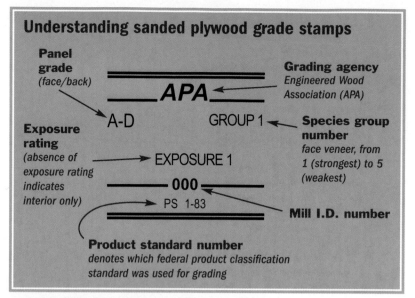

Understanding sanded plywood grade stamps

Panel grade (face/back)

Grading agency Engineered Wood Association (APA)

APA

A-D   GROUP 1

Species group number face veneer, from 1 (strongest) to 5 (weakest)

Exposure rating (absence of exposure rating indicates interior only)

EXPOSURE 1

000

PS 1-83

Mill I.D. number

Product standard number denotes which federal product classification standard was used for grading

Every sheet of plywood is stamped with grading information. On lower-grade panels, such as exterior sheathing, the stamp can be found in multiple locations on both faces. Panels with one better-grade face are stamped only on the back, and panels with two better-grade faces are stamped on the edges.

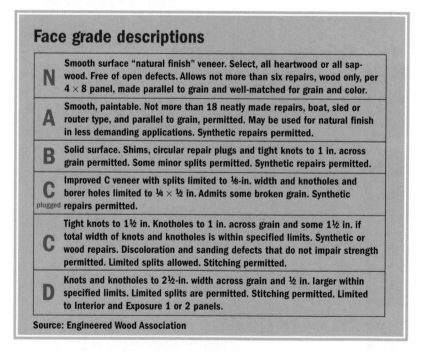

Face grade descriptions

N Smooth surface "natural finish" veneer. Select, all heartwood or all sapwood. Free of open defects. Allows not more than six repairs, wood only, per 4 × 8 panel, made parallel to grain and well-matched for grain and color.

A Smooth, paintable. Not more than 18 neatly made repairs, boat, sled or router type, and parallel to grain, permitted. May be used for natural finish in less demanding applications. Synthetic repairs permitted.

B Solid surface. Shims, circular repair plugs and tight knots to 1 in. across grain permitted. Some minor splits permitted. Synthetic repairs permitted.

C plugged Improved C veneer with splits limited to 1/8-in. width and knotholes and borer holes limited to 1/4 × 1/2 in. Admits some broken grain. Synthetic repairs permitted.

C Tight knots to 1½ in. Knotholes to 1 in. across grain and some 1½ in. if total width of knots and knotholes is within specified limits. Synthetic or wood repairs. Discoloration and sanding defects that do not impair strength permitted. Limited splits allowed. Stitching permitted.

D Knots and knotholes to 2½-in. width across grain and ½ in. larger within specified limits. Limited splits are permitted. Stitching permitted. Limited to Interior and Exposure 1 or 2 panels.

Source: Engineered Wood Association

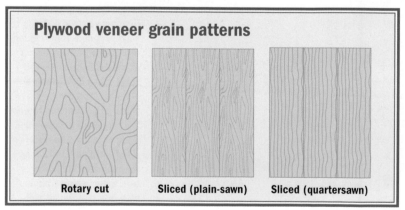

Plywood veneer grain patterns

Rotary cut   Sliced (plain-sawn)   Sliced (quartersawn)

Selecting plywood

Choosing the right plywood for your project is an important task that can get complicated pretty quickly. In addition to the various core, thickness and face veneer options, you'll also need to make a decision on the plywood *grade*. Despite the fact that trade-association sponsored plywood grading systems are clearly established, their application isn't always universal. This can complicate the task of ordering plywood, and can lead to costly miscommunication. Basically, there are two grading systems in use today. The one most people are familiar with is administered by the *APA (Engineered Wood Association,* formerly the *American Plywood Association).* The *APA* grade stamps (See Illustration, left) are found on sanded plywood, sheathing and structural (called *performance-rated)* panels. Along with grading each face of the plywood by letter (*A* to *D*) or purpose (for example, *sheathing* or *sturdi-floor),* the *APA* performance-rated stamp lists other information such as exposure rating, maximum allowable span, type of wood used to make the plies and the identification number of the mill where the panel was manufactured.

Many hardwood-veneer sanded plywood panels are graded by the *Hardwood Plywood and Veneer Association (HPVA).* (The grading organizations are trade groups whose stamps are used only by manufacturers who are members of the respective group.) The *HPVA* grading numbers are similar to those employed by *APA:* they refer to a *face grade* (from *A* to *E)* and a *back grade* (from 1 to 4). Thus, a sheet of plywood that has a premium face (A) and a so-so back (3) would be referred to as *A-3* by *HPVA* (and AC by *APA).*

When ordering some species of hardwood plywood, you'll find you have more than one option for veneer grain pattern. Most plywood has *rotary-cut* veneer (See photo, page 6), which is the most economical type. But for surfaces that more closely resemble solid hardwood, look for sliced veneer faces that have strips of veneer, usually less than 1 ft. wide, that are laid edge to edge. The strips may be *plain-sawn* (also called *face-sawn)* or *quartersawn.* If ordering from a mill, you can specify that the veneer strips be applied in the same order they're cut from the log.

Common face veneers for plywood

When using plywood to build woodworking projects, the species and quality of the face veneer are critically important to the final appearance of the project. For most projects, choose a product with an "A" grade hardwood veneer face on at least one side. Some of the more common wood species available for face veneers are shown here (without finish applied).

Clear pine. Species varies by geographic location; generally plain-sawn, sliced face veneer; cost is usually at least double the price of standard fir plywood with one *A* face. *Recommended finishes:* orange shellac or clear topcoat; light to medium wood stain; can also be used for decorative painting techniques, such as pickling and colorwashing.

Mahogony. Both Phillipine and Honduran mahogany are available at better lumberyards (Phillipine mahogany is shown here); generally rotary-cut veneer; Phillipine varieties are inexpensive to moderate; Honduran is moderate to high. *Recommended finishes:* mahogany (red/purple) wood stain with hard, glossy topcoat.

Birch. A very versatile veneer that can be stained to resemble most major wood species; has subdued, but occasionally interesting grain figure; normally rotary-cut veneer; cost is inexpensive to moderate. *Recommended finishes:* wood stains of any color range with clear topcoat; frequently used for painted projects.

Cherry. If your goal is to build a woodworking project that doesn't look like it was made of plywood, cherry veneer plywood is an excellent choice. Usually plain-sawn, with sliced veneer strips; because color varies dramatically from sapwood to heartwood, hand-select panels after careful inspection. Cost is moderate to expensive. *Recommended finish:* Dark natural wood tone is better left unstained; protect with clear topcoating product.

Walnut. Another good choice for projects intended to look like they're made from solid hardwood. Most walnut plywood veneer is American black walnut, plain-sawn and sliced. Cost is moderate to expensive. *Recommended finish:* Avoid dark stains; light walnut or mahogany stain can create richer wood tone. Apply clear topcoat.

Oak. Red oak (shown, right) is perhaps the most widely available hardwood plywood. Usually rotary cut, although sliced veneer is also available. Inexpensive to moderate. White oak plywood is costlier, but has a lovely golden cast and can be purchased with quartersawn veneer (a good choice for Mission style furnishings). *Recommended finishes:* light to medium wood stain (oak or walnut) with clear topcoat.

Maple. A popular hardwood plywood that is relatively easy to locate. Light wood tones makes it a good choice for contemporary projects. Rotary cut in most cases. Cost is inexpensive to moderate. *Recommended finishes:* Can be tricky to stain due to dense wood grain; topcoat only for a light appearance. A good choice for painted projects.

For wood-working, particle-board is used almost exclusively as a substrate for plastic laminate.

NOTICE

Particleboard and MDF usually contain urea formaldehyde resins that continue to emit low levels of formaldehyde gas for at least six months as they cure. People with high sensitivity to chemical vapors should limit the number of composite panels added to a room at one time. Always wear a particle mask or respirator as required and provide adequate dust collection and ventilation when cutting or shaping these products.

Particleboard has developed a dubious reputation over the years, perhaps in part because it is used so extensively in the manufacture of low-grade, knockdown furniture that's mass-marketed through discount store chains. While it certainly has its limitations in woodworking pursuits, it also possesses several unique qualities that might make it just the right sheet goods choice for your next project—particularly if the project includes a counter or tabletop. Particleboard is very dimensionally stable (it stays flat and isn't likely to be affected by wood movement issues); it has a relatively smooth surface that provides a suitable substrate for plastic laminate; it comes in a very wide range of thicknesses and panel dimensions; and it is inexpensive. In addition, particleboard makes efficient use of wood chips that might otherwise be wasted, helping to conserve forest products.

But particleboard does have some drawbacks: it lacks stiffness and shear strength; it has poor screw-holding ability; it degrades quickly when exposed to moisture; it's too coarse in the core to be shaped effectively; it's heavy; and it's made with bonding agents that release potentially dangerous or irritating chemical vapors.

In some woodworking applications, particleboard can be used for purposes other than as a substrate for plastic laminate. It is used occasionally to build carcases and doors for light-duty cabinets in low-moisture areas, and it is often employed as an inexpensive shelving material (although it tends to sag as spans get longer).

Manufacturing particleboard

Particleboard is made by using heat and pressure to fuse wood chips, shavings, resins and bonding agents into dense, continuous panels (up to 2¼ in. thick) that are trimmed to standard panel dimensions. The wood ingredients on better grade panels are distributed so the larger flakes and chips are at the core of the panel, and the finer shavings and sawdust are closer to the faces. This arrangement increases the stiffness and strength at the core, while creating surfaces that can be sanded to a reasonably smooth texture.

In some cases, admixtures are included in the particle board recipe to create special-purpose wood panels. Among them are fire retardents and exterior-grade resins for moisture resistance.

Because the wood particle used to make particleboard can be as large as ¼ in., the finished

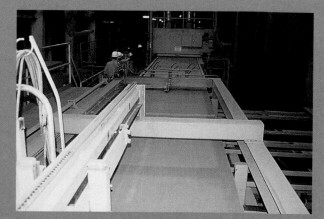

Particleboard moves along a conveyor belt from the sander, past the blow bar (which checks for delaminations) and to the stacker, which stacks the boards into units.

product is generally coarser and less dense than other types of composite board, such as medium-density fiberboard (See next page).

MDF

Medium-density fiberboard (MDF) is quickly becoming the industry standard for many woodworking and carpentry activities that involve sheet goods. It's similar to particleboard in constitution, as it's created by hot-pressing wood fibers and resins into dense sheets that are trimmed to size. But the main difference is that MDF is formed from wood and wood pulp that has been pulverized into individual wood fibers, rather than chips or flakes. The individual fibers fit together much more tightly than odd-shaped chips and flakes, creating a smooth, dense material that can be edge-shaped with a router. The difference between standard particleboard and MDF is a little like the difference between concrete and mortar: Mixed with large aggregate, concrete surfaces and edges tend to exhibit popouts and voids, whereas mortar mixed with fine sand is smooth on the surface, edges and throughout.

The smoothness and density of MDF make it a good substrate choice for veneered projects: the rougher surface of particleboard and most plywoods do not bond as cleanly with thin wood veneer. You can even laminate layers of MDF to create table legs and other structural components that can be veneered or even painted. MDF is also increasing in popularity as a trim moulding material.

Like particleboard, MDF does not have a great deal of stiffness, and tends to sag if not adequately supported. It also tends to be fragile around the edges, swells and degrades from constant moisture contact, and it does not hold screws well (although coarse-threaded wallboard screws can be reasonably effective). If you are using it to build structural project parts, try to use mechanical knock-down fasteners wherever possible, and don't skimp on the wood glue. MDF costs a little more than particleboard, and is comparable in price to construction-grade plywood.

Medium-density fiberboard (MDF) is growing in popularity as a veneer substrate, paintable surface and as a raw material for moldings.

Composite board thickness

Unlike most plywood, which is typically undersized in thickness by 1/32 in., composite boards such as particleboard and MDF are manufactured within .005 in. of their nominal thickness. When designing your woodworking project, be sure to use the actual thickness of sheet goods, especially on finer projects with little tolerance for error.

Manufacturing MDF

The process of forming MDF begins with the heating and grinding of white softwood until it is broken down to individual wood fibers no more than 1/8 in. in length. The fibers are coated with resin and (in some cases) additives and formed into a mat that's about 18 in. thick. The mat is hot-pressed at about 350°, using 350 pounds per square inch of pressure to compress it to finished thickness (from 1/4 to 1 1/4 in.). The continuous webs of MDF are cut to rough size then loaded into cooling racks (See photo, right). Then, the sheets are sanded lightly, cut to finished size, inspected and given appropriate grade stamps.

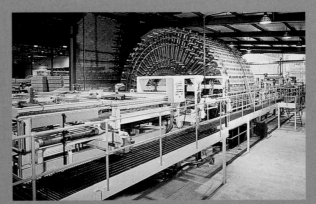

Cooling wheels are used to cool composite panels (both MDF and particleboard) as they begin to dry and cure after hot-pressing. The cooling wheel lets air circulate across both faces of the panel before it is processed further.

Melamine is a very popular sheet goods product for making shelving and building European-style cabinets. Generally fashioned with a particleboard core, most melamine boards have two faces that are surfaced with thermofused melamine. It offers the advantages of plastic laminate while saving you the trouble of applying the laminate yourself. Thicknesses range from ¼ to ¾ in. Stock colors at most lumberyards and building centers generally are limited to white, gray, almond and sometimes black. Other colors may be available through special order. The panels are oversized by 1 in. in each dimension (a 4 × 8 sheet is actually 49 × 97 in.) because the brittle melamine has a tendency to chip at the edges during transport. Plan on trimming fresh edges for your project.

The brittle surface and particleboard core are not friendly to screws or nails—the best fasteners to use when working with melamine board are knockdown styles (See page 19).

While most melamine board is surfaced on both faces, it is available with the melamine bonded to only one of the faces. The other face is left bare so you can apply laminate of a different color or style if you wish. Particleboard with one face veneered and the other surfaced with melamine, called *mela-quinella,* can be purchased for cabinetmaking (See photo, left).

Melamine board is faced at the factory with melamine laminate. The thermofusing process used to apply the melamine creates a much stronger bond than you can achieve with plastic laminate applied at the job site with contact cement. (and saves you the trouble of doing the laminating). It also reduces the number of seams.

The two faces of mela-quinella

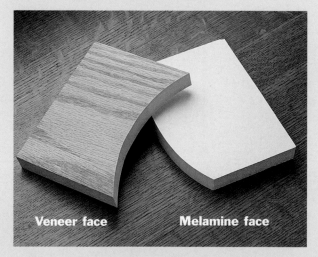

Veneer face   **Melamine face**

Designed mostly for cabinetmakers, mela-quinella is a hybrid between melamine and veneer-faced plywood. One face is finished with hardwood veneer, and the other face is coated with thermofused melamine intended to face inside a cabinet carcase or drawer. The veneer can be stained or topcoated to match the rest of the cabinets and face frames, while the melamine surfaces are ideal for cabinet interiors because they're bright and easy to wipe clean. The core is usually MDF or particleboard.

Cutting melamine board

When cutting melamine board, as when cutting plastic laminate, the main goal is to avoid chipping the fragile laminate by using a blade that produces minimal tearout. Blades designed specifically for cutting laminate are the best choice (See photo below), but if you'd rather not spend the money on a specialty blade, any plywood cutting panel blade will do (these blades are distinguished by high tooth counts and minimal tooth set). When using a table saw, pass the material through the blade with the good (laminate) side facing up: when using a circular saw, cut with the good face down.

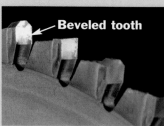

Beveled tooth

Laminate cutting blade: beveled teeth score surface of laminate to prevent chip-out from cutting teeth.

Miscellaneous sheet goods

The universe of sheet goods is growing larger all the time, with new-and-improved and special-purpose products constantly added to manufacturer inventories. Most of these products have little application in woodworking, but some, when used creatively, can provide an interesting or unique touch to your project. A few of the more useful types are shown here.

Textured plywood. Designed to be used as exterior siding, textured pine plywood can be used as a back panel on open cupboards, or even as a cabinet carcase material on informal projects. The channel-groove surfaced plywood shown here is readily available with grooves that are either 4 in. or 8 in. apart. Rough-sawn and brushed textures (with or without kerfs or channel grooves) can provide interesting surfaces for rustic or Country style projects.

Glue-up panels. Fashioned from strips of solid pine, these panels offer the benefits of solid wood: superior nail and screw holding, and ease of sanding and shaping. They do not require edge-taping or filling. The strips are finger-jointed together at the ends and edge-glued into ¾-in.-thick panels sold in a variety of sizes, ranging from 12 to 30 in. wide and 36 to 96 in. long. As a woodworking material, glue-up panels cost more per square inch than most plywoods, but are cheaper and more convenient to use than solid lumber. Higher-end versions are made from strips of select clear pine that are laminated together to increase thickness, finger-jointed to length, then edge-glued into prefabricated panels.

Tempered hardboard. Hardboard is used in woodworking mostly to make inexpensive panel parts that will not have high visibility: drawer bottoms and cabinet backs are two of the most common usages. It also makes good templates and patterns for project parts you may want to duplicate many times or make again in the future. Tempered hardboard (avoid the softer, non-tempered hardboard) can also be used as a bending plywood in areas that will not receive high stress or be exposed to moisture. It can be used as a veneer substrate in low-stress areas.

Perforated hardboard. Known commonly as "pegboard" or "perfboard," perforated hardboard is simply hardboard (tempered or untempered) that is machined with ¼-in.-dia. holes every 1 in. on-center. For woodworking applications, perfboard may be used as a back panel material for cabinets that require ventilation, but its main use is as a drilling guide material for locating shelf-pin holes in cabinet sides and standards.

Sheet goods are awkward to handle, especially if you're trying to carry them yourself. With denser products weighing in excess of 100 pounds (4 × 8 sheet), they can cause considerable strain on your body. The best advice for handling sheet goods is: never try to move full sheets by yourself. But for those occasions when no help is available, there are a few tricks and devices you can employ to make carrying sheet goods less risky to the objects around them and to the general health of your muscles and back. Specially-designed carts, like a rolling sheet goods cart (See photo, left) and a sheet goods dolly (See photo, next page), allow you to move the panels easily around your shop (although loading the panels into the devices can be tricky). There are also a number of handling aids, mostly shop-built, that can function like a third hand to help improve your grip and balance when carrying (one of these is shown in the photo at the bottom of the next page).

Storing sheet goods requires some care and planning. If left unchecked, it doesn't take many sheets of plywood to overwhelm your shop or to cut off access to any other building materials stored behind them. If you have the floor space and will be storing the panels for more than a few days before using them, laying them flat on a hard surface is the best method. This reduces the risk of warping that can occur when panels are stacked on edge. If you must store panels on edge, avoid leaning other objects against them, and stack them so they are as close to vertical as you can get them without risk of falling over. Slip scrap wood beneath the bottom edges to protect them from ground contact.

A rolling sheet goods storage cart is one of the handiest additions you can build for your workshop (See project plans, pages 72 to 79). The cart allows you store many panels in one convenient spot, where damage is less likely. And because it rolls, you can use it to transport the sheet goods to your work area. Shelving, bins and an upper shelf create storage for dimension lumber and larger cutoff pieces.

How much does it weigh?

Type	Size	Weight
Veneer core plywood (softwood face)	¾ × 4 × 8	65 to 70 pounds
Veneer core plywood (hardwood face)	¾ × 4 × 8	55 to 60 pounds
MDF	¾ × 4 × 8	105 to 110 pounds
Particleboard	¾ × 4 × 8	90 to 100 pounds
Composite-core plywood	¾ × 4 × 8	80 to 85 pounds
Lumber-core plywood	¾ × 4 × 8	55 to 65 pounds

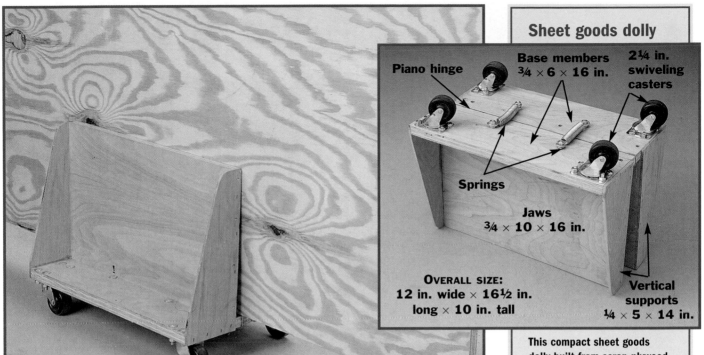

Piano hinge

Base members
¾ × 6 × 16 in.

2¼ in. swiveling casters

Springs

Jaws
¾ × 10 × 16 in.

OVERALL SIZE:
12 in. wide × 16½ in. long × 10 in. tall

Vertical supports
¼ × 5 × 14 in.

This compact sheet goods dolly built from scrap plywood actually uses the weight of the sheet goods to pin themselves between the jaws of the dolly. The two halves of the dolly are held together with a piano hinge that flexes downward from the panel weight, drawing the jaws together. When the panels are removed, springs mounted on the undersides of the base members open the jaws up again for easy loading access of the next sheet goods "passenger."

Design by Michael Guimont, a Club Member from Princeton, Minnesota.

Sheet goods tote lends a hand when carrying panels by yourself

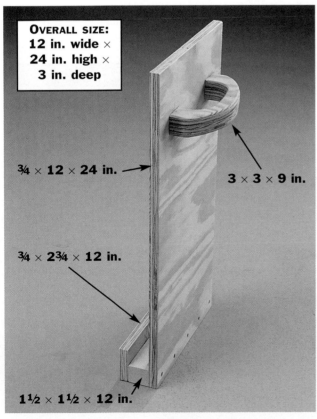

OVERALL SIZE:
12 in. wide ×
24 in. high ×
3 in. deep

¾ × 12 × 24 in.

3 × 3 × 9 in.

¾ × 2¾ × 12 in.

1½ × 1½ × 12 in.

Although some types of sheet goods can get quite heavy (over 100 pounds for a 4 × 8 sheet), the real problem with carrying them by yourself is that they are awkward. Unless you're a retired pro basketball player, you probably have a difficult time spanning the distance from edge to edge with your arms, and you won't find many handles on a sheet of MDF. The shopbuilt tote shown here is one of many handling aids that can help you get a better grip on bulky sheet goods. To make this tote, you'll need: a 12-in.-long piece of 2 × 2, and two pieces of ¾-in.-thick plywood (one 2¾ × 12 in., the other 12 × 24 in.). Sandwich the 2 × 2 between the plywood pieces as shown, and join them with glue and 1½-in. wood or wallboard screws. Then, make a handle by face-gluing two pieces of ¾ × 3 × 9-in. plywood, then cutting out the handle shape with a jig saw. Center the ends of the handle on the back of the larger piece of plywood, 3 in. down from the top, and attach with glue and four 1½-in. screws driven though the plywood and into each handle end.

Build a table extension the same height as your table saw table and position it on the outfeed side of the saw. A simple table extension can be made with a 2 × 4 table base and a plywood or particleboard tabletop. Bond a piece of ⅛ in. thick tempered hardboard to the plywood tabletop, using construction adhesive. The hardboard provides a smooth, slick surface that's easier to slide stock across than plywood.

Clamp a straightedge cutting guide to your sheet goods stock when cutting with a circular saw. To support the cutoff piece, lay the entire panel across two or three scrap 2 × 4s and set the cutting depth of your saw blade so it will cut about ¼ in. into the 2 × 4s. Be sure you allow for the correct distance between the outside of the saw foot and the edge of the blade—make a test cut in scrap first and measure the distance from the kerf to the straightedge.

Cutting sheet goods

Cutting full sheet goods panels down to size is a task some handymen wouldn't wish upon their worst enemy, but with a little patience and the right tools and techniques it becomes manageable—even if you're working alone. When cutting on a table saw, make sure the panel is supported on both the infeed and the outfeed sides of the saw. An extension table or tables or adjustable roller stands can be used for this purpose. Make sure the panel is steady and square against the saw fence before starting your cut. Set the saw blade so it projects ¼ to ½ in. above the top of the panel, and feed the panel through using steady, even pressure. If a helper is available, station him at the outfeed side to guide the workpiece, but make sure he doesn't pull the workpiece through the blade: that's the job of the person on the infeed side. If cutting with a portable circular saw, make sure the panel is steady and secure, and always use a straightedge cutting guide.

Panel cutters: Big performance (with a small footprint)

Panel cutters are high-performance, precision tools designed specifically for cutting sheet goods. The two guide rails allow you to track the integral circular saw through the cut safely and accurately.

If you do a lot of work with sheet goods (and don't already own one) a panel cutter probably is at the top of your wish list. Designed to fit against a wall, the panel cutter cuts 4 × 8 sheets on a vertical plane, compared to cutting a 4 × 8 sheet on the flat, where you'll need a clear area at least 6 × 10 ft. for a circular saw, and around 8 × 20 ft. for a table saw. The panel saw is also the safest way to cut sheet stock: because the saw is mounted to the guide rails, there is no chance for kickback. The panels are fed into the panel cutter framework on rollers. The adjustable guide rails are calibrated to an end line so you can set the desired width of the panel you're cutting by locking the rail down at the appropriate spot (the same way you set a table saw cut by clamping down the saw fence). Then you simply engage the saw and lower it down through the cut.

The main drawback to panel cutters is their price. Costing roughly the same as a good cabinet-style table saw, you'll need to work through a lot of sheet goods to justify the cost of the tool.

Circular blades for cutting sheet goods

There are many specialty blades available for cutting sheet goods with a table saw or portable circular saw. The common characteristic they share is a high number of teeth per inch and a minimal tooth set. Some blades, like laminate cutting blades, have beveled teeth to reduce chip-out (See page 12), as well as a skip-tooth design that creates a cleaner cut by removing waste wood from the kerf area more effectively.

Plywood cutting blade: 10-in., 200-tooth blade cuts through veneer-core plywood with little chip-out or tear-out. Do not use for particleboard or MDF: steel blade points will dull quickly.

Laminate cutting blade: 10-in., 60-tooth, triple-chip grind, carbide-tipped-blade is recommended for cutting plastic laminate and melamine board.

Carbide cross-cutting blade: 10-in., 60-tooth, alternate-top bevel grind, 7° hook angle blade is recommended for plywood, particleboard, MDF and general crosscutting of hardwood and softwood.

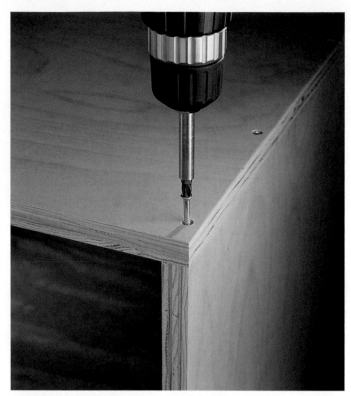

The basic butt joint is the workhorse of sheet goods joinery. Butt joints should be reinforced with wood glue and fasteners. Here, countersunk wood screws are driven to reinforce the joints between two plywood panels. You can also use biscuits, dowels, pocket screws or mechanical knockdown (also called ready-to-assemble) fasteners. Mechanical fasteners generally are not used with glue.

Joining sheet goods panels is a slightly different exercise than joining solid lumber. Many types of panels cannot be effectively machined to create such common woodworking joints as mortise-and-tenons, finger joints or dovetail joints. Neither are they particularly capable when it comes to holding screws and nails (although some are certainly better than others). When using veneer-core plywood, for example, you can often get away with making glued butt joints that are reinforced with wood screws (See photo, left). MDF and particleboard generally hold nails better than screws, but as with plywood the glue will be doing most of the holding. You can increase glue surface by using dado, rabbet or dado/rabbet joints (See below). You'll have more luck machining dadoes and rabbets into better quality sheet goods.

Due to the ineffectiveness of typical woodworking joinery, mechanical fasteners often are used when building projects with sheet goods. Known generically as "knockdown (KD)" or "ready-to-assemble (RTA)" or "European" hardware or fittings, mechanical fasteners are two-part pieces of hardware that rely on pressure on the opposing parts to make a joint. These fasteners have the added advantage of allowing your project to be easily disassembled and reassembled.

Woodworking joints commonly used to join sheet goods

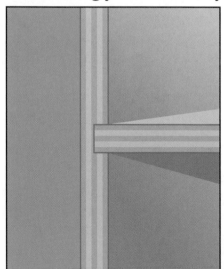

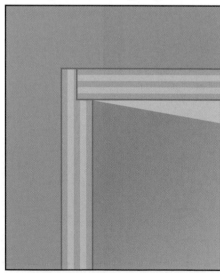

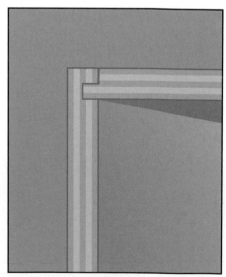

Dado joint is used mostly to join fixed shelves to cabinet sides or shelf standards. When using ¾-in.-thick panels, the dado should be ¾ in. wide by ⅜ in. deep—never cut a dado more than halfway into your stock. Dadoes are usually cut with a router and straight bit, or on a table saw fitted with a dado-blade set.

Rabbet joint is cut into the end or side of a panel to house the top or bottom panel of a carcase. Rabbets also are cut around the inside of a back opening to create a recess for the back panel. A router with a piloted rabbet bit is the best tool for cutting rabbets. Or, you can pre-cut rabbets into the individual panels before assembling the carcase.

Dado/rabbet joint creates an interlocking joint at the top or bottom of a cabinet carcase. The tongue created when you rabbet one panel fits into a ⅜ × ⅜-in. dado cut into the other panel. In addition to the extra strength created by the interlocking nature of the joint, the dad/rabbet also strengthens a joint by creating additional surface for gluing.

Common mechanical fasteners (shown in cross-section)

Minifix brand fittings are two-part fastening systems very similar to those used on mass-produced knockdown furnishings. The cam fits into a 15-mm hole drilled into the horizontal member and the screw assembly is fitted into an 8-mm hole in the vertical member. The screw head is inserted into the cam, and a setscrew in the cam is tightened to twist the cam and draw the parts together. A decorative cap is then snapped over the cam opening.

Screw assembly

Cam

Blum brand barrel-type two-part fasteners are used mainly to attach shelves in cabinets. The threaded nylon barrel is fitted into a 25-mm hole in the cabinet side, then the collared screw is driven into the end of the shelf so the duple-type head projects out. The head fits into the barrel, which is tightened by turning a screw-activated metal gripping plate.

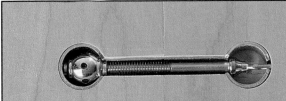

Tite-Joint brand fasteners are especially useful for joining two sheet goods panels end to end, as with countertops. The heads of the fastener are mortised into adjoining panels. The mortises are connected by a groove or a guide hole that houses a threaded shaft. The sphere (the left head above) contains grip-holes so it can be spun with a scratch awl or small allen wrench to tighten the joint.

Cross-dowel fasteners can be used to reinforce right-angle corners and to support shelving. The threaded steel dowel is screwed into a barrel cam that's mortised into the horizontal member. With cross-dowels, joints can be fastened and unfastened repeatedly without stripping the screw guide hole.

How to use a pocket-screw jig to reinforce joints

Depth stop collar

1 Clamp the workpiece that will contain the screw starter holes (usually the rails on a face frame, as shown above) into the pocket-screw jig. The center of the jig should align with the centerline of the workpiece. Mount the step drill bit that came with the jig into a portable drill, then drill through the guide bushings and into the workpiece until the depth stop makes contact with the mouth of the guide.

2 Clamp the workpiece containing the starter holes to the mating workpiece, then drive pocket screws through the starter holes and into the mating workpiece. Pocket screws are sold in packets at woodworking stores. They're thinner than regular wood screws to prevent the workpieces from splitting when they're driven. Most have square drive heads. Take care not to overdrive the screws.

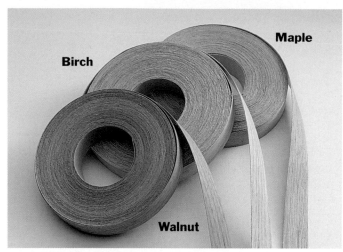

Iron-on edge banding is sold in common plywood face veneer species. It can be purchased in 8-ft. lengths or in rolls of 50 or 250 ft.

Veneer edge banding is applied to conceal the exposed edges of sheet goods panels so they more closely resemble solid lumber. You can purchase veneer edge banding to match the species of most common plywood face veneers. Throughout this book, we use iron-on edge banding that has heat-activated glue pre-applied to the back of the tape. You can also purchase edge banding without preapplied adhesives: this type is affixed with contact cement applied to the tape and to the edge of the workpiece.

For ¾-in.-thick plywood, use 13⁄16-in.-wide tape (the extra width allows you to trim the tape to fit exactly). When taping shelving, apply the tape before installing the shelving.

How to apply iron-on edge banding

1 Begin by cutting the edging for vertical surfaces to length with a utility knife. Cut the pieces slightly over-long.

2 Cover the foot of a household iron with foil to protect the iron from the glue. Set the iron to a low heat setting. With the veneer strip in position, press with the iron, moving away from one corner.

3 To guarantee a good glue bond, roll the edge banding with a wallpaper seam roller after each piece is applied. Try to work the roller in one direction only in case there are any trapped air bubbles.

4 Once the vertical pieces are applied, measure the horizontal pieces for the top, bottom and fixed shelves. Cut these pieces to exact length using a square to guide the cut.

5 When all the pieces are applied, trim the overhang. Work in the same direction as the grain. We used a special edge-banding trimmer, but you can also use a cabinet scraper or a sharp utility knife.

Choosing and applying your own wood veneer to your sheet goods project creates a host of new options in exotic wood species, distinctive grain figure and in grain pattern matching. Veneer can be applied to a flat substrate or to surfaces that are bent or shaped during the project construction.

The following photos illustrate how to apply non-adhesive-backed wood veneer. For many projects, you may prefer to use adhesive-backed veneer designed mostly for refacing cabinets. To apply adhesive-backed veneer, match the sheets as discussed in Step 1, below, then simply remove the backing, position the veneer and roll with a J-roller or wallpaper roller. Trim off the excess as in Step 4, below.

Exotic and distinctive veneer types include: (A) Zebrawood; (B) Birdseye maple; (C) African Padouk (vermillion); (D) Madrone burl; (E) Maple burl; (F) Purpleheart. All shown with oil finish.

How to apply sheet veneer to a panel

1 If joining multiple sheets of veneer, lay the sheets together edge to edge in your chosen pattern. Use short strips of tape to hold the joint tight. Then lay a strip of tape down the entire length of the seam. TIP: Use low-adhesive painter's masking tape or special, water-activated veneer tape.

2 Apply an even, light coat of glue to the face of the substrate (we used a glue roller). Because the glue sets up quickly, have the veneer and your veneer press close at hand. If you're working with veneer for the first time, you may want to use white glue, which has a longer open working time.

3 Clamp the veneer to the glued-up panel in a veneer press—we made one from clamps, particleboard "plates" and wood strips (called cauls). Allow a few minutes for the glue to squeeze out, then check to see if the clamps need tightening. Let the glue dry for at least four hours before you remove the veneered panel from the press.

4 Trim off the excess veneer with a router or a laminate trimmer and a piloted, flush-cutting bit. You can also use a sharp utility knife if you work very carefully.

1 Test-fit the carcase side, front and back panels by fitting and clamping them together. Adjust the parts as needed to achieve square corners and flush joints.

Cauls

2 Apply wood glue to the edges of the parts, then clamp the parts together to form the carcase. Wood cauls (straight strips of scrap wood) distribute the clamp pressure evenly.

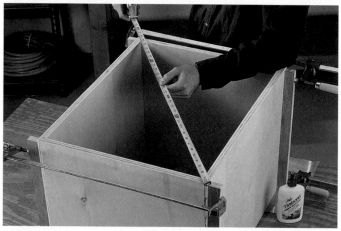

3 Test the carcase to see if it's square, using a framing square or by measuring diagonally from opposing corners—when the diagonal measurements are equal, the carcase is square and you can go ahead and reinforce the joints with wood screws.

TIP: Adjust the carcase by applying a bar clamp or pipe clamp along one of the diagonals. Tightening the clamp will cause the carcase to "rack" slightly in the direction of pressure. You can also push or pull on the clamp heads to make adjustments.

Making face frames

Traditional cabinetry projects are designed with a hardwood face frame that's mounted to the front opening of the cabinet. The face frame conceals the edges of the carcase, provides bearing surface for hinges and generally dresses up the cabinet (many contemporary cabinet styles do not employ face frames). Generally, the rails (horizontal members) and stiles (vertical members) of a face frame are butted together, not mitered. The stiles are allowed to run the entire height of the cabinet, with the ends of the rails butted against them. Glue and dowels, pocket screws and splines are normally used to reinforce the joints.

Face frames are built independently from the cabinet carcase so they can be squared up accurately before they're mounted.

Applying plastic laminate

Durable, inexpensive and available in many dozens of colors and styles, plastic laminate is a building product you should get to know. Used most frequently as a countertop or tabletop surface, it also can be applied to drawer fronts, cabinet doors, or even inside cabinets and drawers where a moisture-resistant, easy-to-clean surface is desirable.

Plastic laminate is sold in standard widths of 24, 36, 48 and 60 in. at building centers (or, simply look in your telephone book under the *Counter Tops* listing). You can order it in other sizes or even have it laminated onto a custom-sized substrate.

Particleboard and MDF are the two most common substrate for applying plastic laminate. Both have smooth surfaces that accept cement well. They are also very stable. But if your project will be exposed to constant moisture, use sanded, exterior-grade plywood for the substrate.

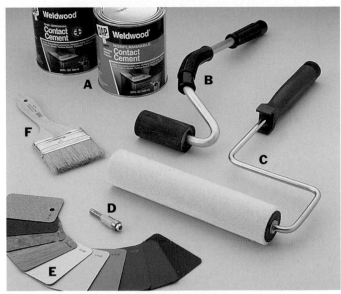

Tools and materials for working with plastic laminate include: **(A)** Contact cement to bond laminate to substrate (use nonflammable product if working indoors or in an enclosed area); **(B)** J-roller; **(C)** paint roller with short-nap adhesive sleeve; **(D)** Flush-cutting, piloted router bit; **(E)** Sample chips for making product selection; **(F)** Disposable paintbrush for applying cement in tight areas.

How to apply plastic laminate

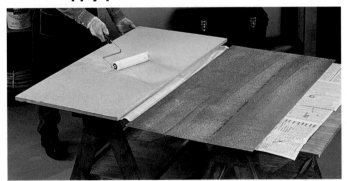

1 The laminate sheet should overhang the edges of the substrate by ½ to 1 in. on all sides. Working on a flat, smooth surface, use a paint roller with a short-nap adhesive sleeve to roll a thin, even coat of contact cement onto the top surface of the substrate and the back face of the laminate.

2 To prevent the two cemented surfaces from bonding together while you position the laminate sheet, insert thin wood spacers at 6-in. intervals between the laminate and the substrate. Once the laminate sheet is positioned correctly, remove the spacers one at a time, starting at one end and working in order to the other end.

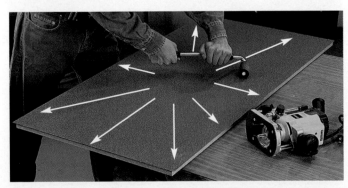

3 Use a J-roller to roll the laminate. Rolling creates a strong bond between the laminate and the substrate. Start in the middle of the workpiece and work toward the edges, rolling the J-roller in one direction only (this allows any trapped air bubbles to escape).

4 Trim off the excess laminate so the edge is flush with the substrate. For best results, use a router or laminate trimmer with a piloted, flush-cutting bit. Smooth out any roughness from the router using a fine file.

Many woodworking projects built from sheet goods contain shelving. Because the edges of most sheet goods products are not meant to be left exposed, some type of shelf edge treatment is desirable. There are a number of ways to neatly and simply conceal the edges of shelving (See photo, left). When choosing which method to use, consider the complexity, the cost and how well each

(A) Solid-wood shelf edge can be purchased ready-made in a variety of sizes, wood species and profiles. Or, you can cut your own by shaping the edge of a board and ripping it to width on your table saw (See sequence, below).

(B) Iron-on edge tape made from matching wood veneer is a convenient, economical and attractive product for treating shelf edges (See page 20).

(C) Exposed edge. For some types of projects made with higher-grade plywood (such as apple ply or Baltic birch), leaving the shelf edge untreated can be an effective design feature.

(D) Filled and painted. If you're planning to paint your woodworking project, you can simply fill any voids or imperfections in the shelf edge with wood putty or even joint compound, then sand the edge smooth before painting.

(E) Plastic T-slot shelf edge trim can be used to cover the exposed edges of shelving. Available at most woodworking or cabinet supply stores, it fits into a T-slot in the edge (the slot can be cut with a router or on your table saw). T-slot trim has definite commercial characteristics and the color selection is usually limited to white, black or brown.

How to make custom shelf edge

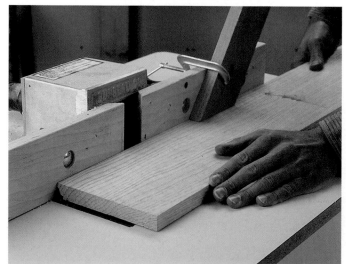

1 Choose a board that's the same thickness as the shelving material and the same species as the face veneer. Mount an edge-forming bit into your router table (a single or double Roman ogee bit is a good choice) and shape the edge of the board.

2 Rip-cut the board to width on your table saw. If your shelving is ¾ in. thick, rip the shelf edge so it's ¾ × ¾ in. To make more shelf edge, shape the freshly-cut edge, then rip to width again.

type will meet your design standards. Make this decision up front, since it can have an effect on the dimensions of your project (if you are using solid shelf edge, for example, you'll normally want to reduce the width of your shelving by ¾ in.).

The other shelving decision you'll need to make is choosing a method for supporting the shelves: particularly any adjustable shelves you may be building into the project design. A common practice when designing larger casework, like bookcases and entertainment centers, is to glue a fixed shelf (usually a middle shelf) into dadoes in the cabinet side, then install adjustable shelves above and below. The adjustable shelves typically employ pins or another type of shelf hardware. When designing your project, calculate your likely adjustable shelf heights so you can keep guide holes to a minimum.

Options for supporting shelves

Dado grooves cut to the thickness of the shelves (¾ in. wide, typically) can be cut up to halfway through the thickness of the cabinet side or shelf standard (⅜ in. for ¾-in stock). The dado provides a very sturdy bed for the shelf, especially when reinforced with glue and finish nails. But if the fit is too tight or the wood moves, bowing or breaking of the joint can occur. Often, a dado is used for the fixed shelf or shelves in a project only.

Shelf brackets recessed into grooves in the cabinet side or standard can be connected mechanically to shelf support tabs. This type of system provides strong support and plenty of shelf positioning options. The main drawback is their appearance: in most cases, the brackets will be visible when viewing your project from the front. Cutting the grooves also takes a little patience, and getting the slots in the brackets to line up can be tricky.

Shelf shown in cut-away

Shelf pins are made in many sizes, styles and materials. The brass pins with mating grommets shown above are on the higher end of the shelf-pin spectrum. The grommet prevents the weight of the shelf from causing the support pin to ream out the guide hole. Use a piece of perforated hardboard as a drilling guide for locating guide holes.

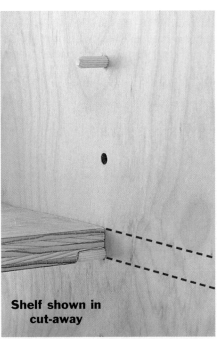

Shelf shown in cut-away

Dowel pins are very economical to use. The photo above shows fluted, ¼-in.-dia., dowel pins. You can make your own pins simply by cutting doweling to length (be sure to use hardwood doweling, however). If you rest the shelf directly on the dowel pins, it can roll, so cut dowel recesses in the shelf ends with a router and straight bit.

Shelf shown in cut-away

Plastic clips are inexpensive and reasonably sturdy. They're inserted into guide holes like those drilled for shelf pins, but the shape of the clips transmits part of the shelf load onto the cabinet sides.

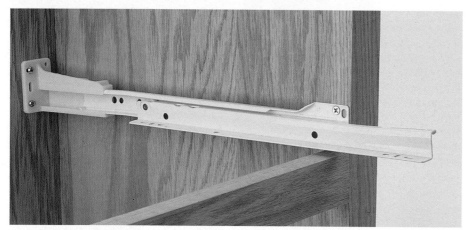

Side-mounted drawer glides are installed in cabinets and casework that do not have a face frame.

Mounting drawers and cabinet doors is one of the last steps in a woodworking project.

When it comes to hanging drawers, you can spend a lot of time building custom wood slides and glides, or you can purchase metal drawer slides that are sized to match the drawers and drawer openings in your project. By the same token, you can use a combination of traditional butt hinges and latches to hang doors on your cabinetry project; or you may prefer to try some of the contemporary and European self-closing hinges that most cabinetmakers have come to depend on. These newer products are usually easier to install and almost always easier to adjust, eliminating most of the headaches associated with hanging cabinet doors and drawers.

As a rule, decide which kind of hinges, slides and hangers you'll be using before you finalize your project design.

Rear/front-mounted drawer glides are installed in cabinets and casework that do have a face frame. The rear mounting bracket is sold as an accessory for most side-mounted glides.

How to hang a drawer using metal slides

1 Mount the inner half of each drawer glide assembly to a drawer side. Follow the manufacturer's instructions for spacing. With some hardware, you may need to trim the back end to fit.

2 Mount the outer half of the glide mechanism to the inside of the cabinet, according to the manufacturer's directions for spacing. Most drawer glides have adjustable screw holes so you can locate the glide precisely where you want, after testing the fit by inserting the drawer into the drawer opening.

Cabinet door types

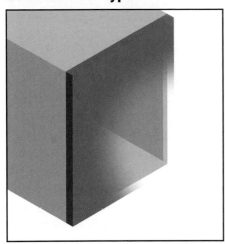

Full overlay door is flush with outer edges of face frame (or cabinet sides if no face frame is used).

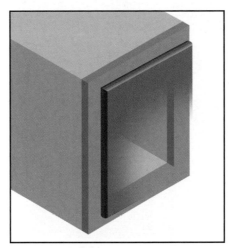

Half overlay door closes against the outer face of the face frame, but does not fully obscure the face frame when closed.

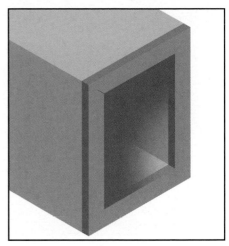

Flush-mounted door fits inside the face frame opening for a more contemporary appearance.

How to hang a wall-hung cabinet with French cleats

3-in. wood screws driven at wall stud locations

French cleats are made by bevel-ripping a board that's at least 4 in. wide, then fastening one half of the board to the wall and the other to the back of your cabinet. The cleats distribute the load of the cabinet over a broad area, reducing the strain on individual screws and the cabinet structure.

1 Bevel-rip a piece of ¾-in. plywood or 1-in. (nominal) dimension lumber at 45°. Attach one half to the back of your cabinet, with the bevel facing down. The back panel of the cabinet should be recessed into the sides to allow for the thickness of the cleat. Attach the other half of the cleat to the wall, using two 3-in. wood screws driven at each wall stud location spanned by the cleat.

1

2 Test the wall-mounted half of the cleat to make sure it's securely fastened to the wall, then lift the cabinet over the cleat and slide it down so the cabinet-mounted half fits over the wall-mounted half of the cleat. Check with a level and adjust, then drive a couple of screws through the back panel and into the wall to keep the cabinet from shifting or falling if it is bumped.

2

Fill nail and screw holes, voids in plywood edges, and other surface defects with paintable or stainable wood putty. Overfill the area slightly, then sand the putty so it's even with the surface of the adjoining wood once the putty has dried.

A lot of people are intimidated by the prospect of applying a finish to their carefully crafted woodworking project. But whether you're dealing with a plywood armoire or a solid walnut bandsaw box, the keys to getting a satisfactory finish are the same: do careful, thorough prep work; make a wise product choice; and follow the product manufacturer's directions closely when applying the product. When clear-finishing or staining a plywood project, condition the wood first (See photos, below).

Tips for sanding sheet goods

Use a random-orbit sander with dust extraction for most of your finish-sanding. this type of sander leaves minimal sanding marks. With sheet goods, it's seldom necessary to sand past 150 grit.

Avoid oversanding. Face veneer on most American and Canadian produced plywood is about ⅟₃₂ in. thick. Even when using medium or fine sandpaper, it doesn't take long to sand through the face veneer.

Wood surface preparation methods compared

Liquid stain applied over untreated pine veneer looks blotchy and dark and is hard to control.

Liquid stain applied over pine treated with a wash coat of commercial wood conditioner (can use diluted shellac instead) has even color penetration and is lighter in tone.

Gel stain applied over untreated pine also provides even color penetration since gel stains do not penetrate wood surfaces as deeply as liquid stains.

Visual reference chart: Common wood stain tones applied to plywood

PINE PLYWOOD	OAK PLYWOOD

Clear topcoat only

Clear topcoat only

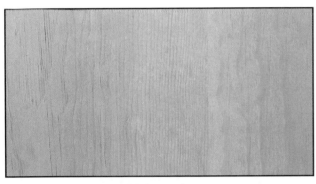

Light stain

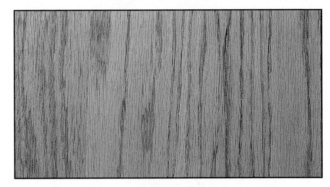

Light stain

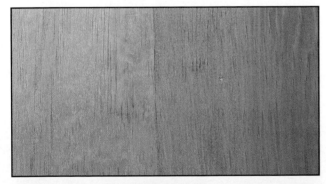

Medium stain

Medium stain

Dark stain

Dark stain

Furniture projects made with sheet goods are prime candidates for receiving painted finishes. The key, as with any finish, is to choose good finishing products and apply them carefully and correctly.

While latex-based paints are less toxic and easier to clean up than their oil-based counterparts, most furnituremakers and cabinetmakers still prefer oil-based products. Enamel oil-based paint dries to create a very hard protective surface. It's also easier to create a smooth finish with oil-based paints. Still, if you prefer working with latex paints, you can get reasonably good results as long as you use an enamel primer.

Supplies for painting furniture include: sandpaper; wood putty for filling voids, nail and screw holes, and wood defects; oil-based enamel paint; primer/sealer; a paint roller for broad surfaces; and sponge brushes for smooth paint application.

How to paint furniture

1 Fill nail holes or screw holes, knots and other surface defects with paintable wood filler putty. Apply the putty so its surface is slightly higher than the surrounding wood surface when dry.

2 Sand the filled areas so they're smooth and level with the surrounding wood. For most projects, use 100- or 150-grit sandpaper to remove the excess material, then sand with 180-grit sandpaper to remove rough spots and sanding marks. Wipe the surface thoroughly with a damp rag or a tack cloth.

3 Apply a thin coat of primer/sealer. Primer/sealer helps the paint bond more evenly, and forms a protective layer to prevent agents within the wood from seeping out and causing stains in the painted surface. It's not critical, but generally you should use oil-based primer with oil-based paint. NOTE: Instead of commercial primer/sealer, some woodworkers prefer to use a mixture of thinned orange shellac and boiled linseed oil for the primer coat.

4 Scuff the primed surface lightly with 180- or 220-grit sandpaper after the primer dries. This creates "tooth" on the surface so the paint will bond better. Be sure to wipe the primed surface with a tack cloth or damp rag before applying the first coat of paint.

5 Apply a thin, even coat of enamel oil-based paint to all surfaces. The most common mistake made when painting is to apply layers that are too thick. An overly heavy coat of paint can sag and dry unevenly. If you can't see the primer coat at all through the first coat of paint, you've probably applied too much paint.

6 Apply the next coat. As a rule, let the first coat dry overnight no matter what the paint can tells you: a chief cause of paint failure is moisture trapped between coats. Apply additional coats, scuff-sanding lightly between coats. Three to four thin coats should yield a fine painted finish.

Projects

Sheet Goods Cart (72)

Changing Table/Dresser (140)

Wall-hung Cabinet (44)

Plant Stand (54)

Play Table & Chairs (100)

Base Cabinet (34)

Sailboat Sandbox (62)

Projects

Entertainment Center (80)

Desktop Console (118)

Walnut Writing Desk (110)

Country Cupboard (150)

Corner Booth (126)

Hallway Bookcase (92)

Base Cabinet

The appeal of custom cabinetry can be yours at a fraction of the price by building this attractive cabinet base. Our simple design features a plastic laminate countertop with solid-oak edging, frame-and-panel doors, a white melamine interior, adjustable shelf and two drawers that ride on full-extension drawer slides. This base cabinet has finished veneer sides, so it could serve as a stand-alone unit for the kitchen, pantry, laundry room or even the workshop. But you could also modify the design and build as many units as you need to outfit a whole kitchen. If this sounds appealing, see pages 44 to 53 (and photo, below) for plans on building a matching oak wall-hung cabinet with glass doors.

See pages 44-53 to build a matching wall-hung cabinet.

Vital Statistics: Base Cabinet

TYPE: Base cabinet

OVERALL SIZE: 25D × 32W × 36H

MATERIAL: Melamine particleboard, red oak plywood, solid red oak, red oak veneer, plastic laminate, CDX plywood

JOINERY: Miter, biscuit, dado, dowel joints

CONSTRUCTION DETAILS:
· Durable plastic laminate countertop surface
· Frame-and-panel doors
· Cabinet sides laminated with adhesive-backed veneer
· Full-extension metal drawer slides

FINISH: Golden oak stain, two coats satin polyurethane varnish

Building time

PREPARING STOCK
3-4 hours

LAYOUT
2-3 hours

CUTTING PARTS
2-3 hours

ASSEMBLY
4-5 hours

FINISHING
1-2 hours

TOTAL: 12-17 hours

Tools you'll use

· Table saw
· Power miter saw (optional)
· Drill/driver
· Circular saw
· Biscuit joiner
· Iron
· Veneer edge trimmer
· J-roller
· Router table
· Router with flush-trimming bit, ¼-in. straight bit, chamfer bit
· Clamps
· Doweling jig

Shopping list

- [ ] (1) ¼ × 48 × 48 in. melamine
- [ ] (1) ½ × 24 × 48 in. melamine
- [ ] (1) ¾ in. × 4 ft. × 8 ft. melamine
- [ ] (1) ¾ × 6 in. × 3 ft. red oak
- [ ] (1) ¾ × 2 ft. × 4 ft. CDX plywood
- [ ] (1) ¼ × 24 × 24 in. oak plywood
- [ ] (1) 1/32 in. × 2 ft. × 3 ft. laminate
- [ ] (1) 1/32 in. × 2 ft. × 6 ft. adhesive-backed red oak veneer
- [ ] Red oak edge banding (15 ft.)
- [ ] PVC white edge banding (15 ft.)
- [ ] (4) 2 × 1½-in. ball-tip hinges
- [ ] (4) ¼-in.-dia. brass shelf pins
- [ ] (4) 1³⁄₁₆-in.-dia. brass knobs
- [ ] (4) 20-in. drawer slides
- [ ] (1) Magnetic door latch
- [ ] Biscuits, ⅜-in.-dia. dowel
- [ ] Contact cement

Base Cabinet

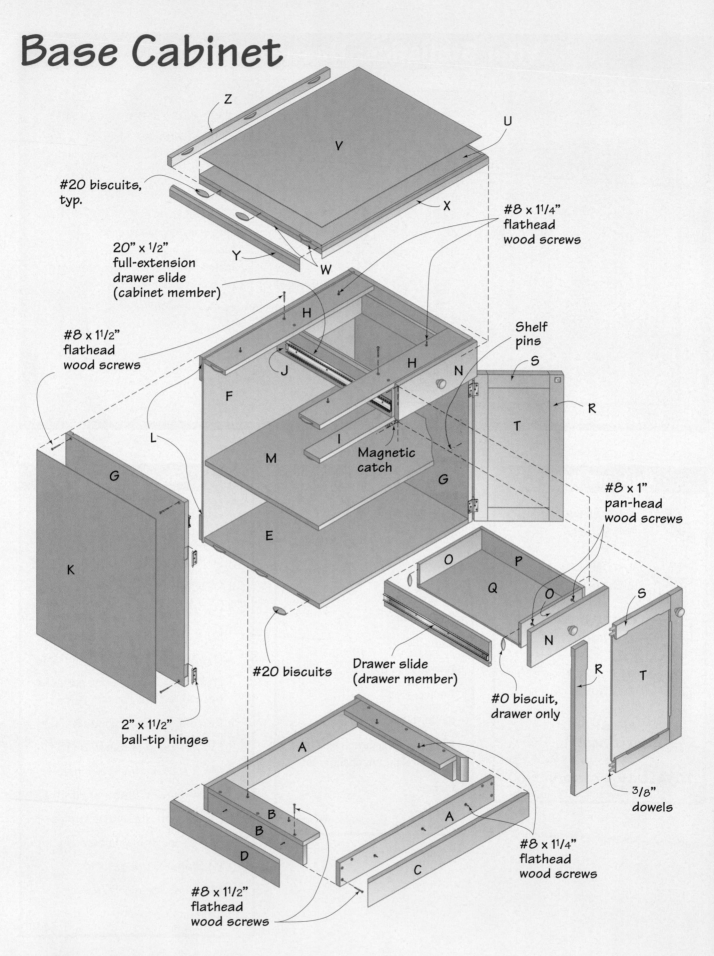

#20 biscuits, typ.

Z

V

U

X

#8 x 1¼" flathead wood screws

20" x ½" full-extension drawer slide (cabinet member)

Y

W

#8 x 1½" flathead wood screws

H

H

Shelf pins

S

N

R

J

F

T

L

I

Magnetic catch

G

G

M

#8 x 1" pan-head wood screws

K

E

O

P

Q

O

S

N

R

T

#0 biscuit, drawer only

#20 biscuits

Drawer slide (drawer member)

R

2" x 1½" ball-tip hinges

3/8" dowels

A

B

B

A

D

C

#8 x 1½" flathead wood screws

#8 x 1¼" flathead wood screws

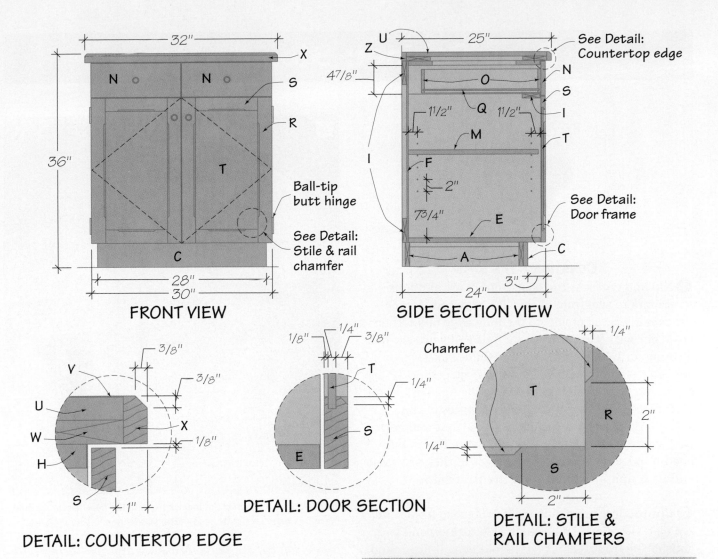

FRONT VIEW

SIDE SECTION VIEW

DETAIL: COUNTERTOP EDGE

DETAIL: DOOR SECTION

DETAIL: STILE & RAIL CHAMFERS

Cabinet Cutting List

Part		No.	Size	Material
A.	Base front/back	2	¾ × 4 × 26½ in.	CDX plywood
B.	Base stretcher	4	¾ × 3¼ × 18¼ in.	"
C.	Front toekick	1	¾ × 4 × 28 in.	Red oak
D.	Side toekick	2	¾ × 4 × 21 in.	"
E.	Bottom	1	¾ × 22¼ × 28½ in.	Melamine
F.	Back	1	¼ × 29 × 30½ in.	"
G.	Side	2	¾ × 23½ × 30½ in.	"
H.	Top stretcher	2	¾ × 4 × 28½ in.	"
I.	Drawer rail	1	¾ × 3 × 28½ in.	"
J.	Drawer divider	1	¾ × 4⅞ × 22¼ in.	"
K.	Veneer face	2	1⁄32 × 24 × 32 in.	Oak veneer
L.	Back blocking	2	¾ × 4 × 28½ in.	CDX plywood
M.	Shelf	1	¾ × 21¾ × 28¼ in.	Melamine

Drawers Cutting List

Part		No.	Size	Material
N.	Face	2	¾ × 5¹³⁄₁₆ × 14¹⁵⁄₁₆ in.	Red oak
O.	Front/back	4	½ × 4 × 11¹³⁄₁₆ in.	Melamine
P.	Side	4	½ × 4 × 20 in.	"
Q.	Bottom	2	¼ × 12⁵⁄₁₆ × 19½ in.	"

Doors Cutting List

Part		No.	Size	Material
R.	Stile	4	¾ × 2¼ × 24⁷⁄₁₆ in.	Red oak
S.	Rail	4	¾ × 2¼ × 10⁷⁄₁₆ in.	"
T.	Panel	2	¼ × 10¹⁵⁄₁₆ × 20¹¹⁄₁₆ in.	Oak plywood

Countertop Cutting List

Part		No.	Size	Material
U.	Core	1	¾ × 23½ × 30½ in.	Melamine
V.	Top	1	1⁄32 × 24 × 32 in.	Laminate
W.	Build-up	2	¾ × 4 × 15½ in.	Melamine
	Build-up	2	¾ × 4 × 30½ in.	"
X.	Front edge	1	¾ × 1½ × 32 in.	Red oak
Y.	Side edge	2	¾ × 1½ × 25 in.	"
Z.	Back edge	1	¾ × 1½ × 30½ in.	"

CONSTRUCT THE BASE

❶ Rip and crosscut the base front, back and four stretchers to size from ¾-in. CDX plywood. Attach the face of one stretcher to the long edge of another stretcher with glue and 1½-in. flathead wood screws, forming an L-shaped assembly. Build another L-shaped assembly with the other two stretchers. Place the assembled stretchers between the base front and back pieces, keeping the outside surfaces of the stretchers flush with the ends of the front and back. Drill countersunk pilot holes and drive 1½-in. flathead wood screws through the faces of the base front and back and into the ends of the stretchers.

❷ Cut the front and side toekicks to size from solid red oak. Bevel one end of each side toekick and both ends of the front toekick so the pieces will fit around the assembled base with no visible end grain. Make these miter cuts on a power miter saw or on the table saw with the blade tilted to 45°. Set the toekick parts in position and mark the back ends of the side toekicks so they'll extend ½ in. beyond the back of the base. Crosscut the side toekicks to length. Turn the entire base unit upside down and attach the toekick parts to the base with glue and countersunk 1¼-in. screws, driven from inside the base (**See Photo A**). Be sure the miters meet snugly at the corners and the top and bottom edges are flush all around.

BUILD THE CABINET CARCASE

❸ Cut the cabinet sides, top stretchers, bottom, drawer rail, drawer divider and adjustable shelf to size from ¾-in. white melamine-covered particleboard. NOTE: *Melamine is particularly prone to tearout or chipping. If you cut these parts on a table saw or with a circular saw, install a plywood blade, triple-chip blade or combination blade set low to minimize chipping the melamine. For added insurance, run a strip of masking tape along your cutting lines*

PHOTO A: Glue and screw the toekick parts to the base assembly. Hold the miters together tightly as you drive screws from inside the base.

before you cut the parts. Masking tape will help keep the melamine edges intact while you saw. Remove the tape once the parts are cut.

❹ Lay out and drill ¼-in.-dia. shelf pin holes in the sides, spaced vertically, 2 in. on-center and 1½ in. from each edge. We started the holes 8½ in. up from the bottom ends of the cabinet sides. The holes must align on both cabinet sides, or the shelves won't be level when the cabinet is assembled. To help align the holes, make a drilling template using pegboard, and clamp it in the same position when you lay out the holes on each cabinet side. Drill the shelf pin holes ⅜ in. deep (a depth stop installed on your drill bit will keep you from accidentally drilling through the cabinet sides).

❺ Cut a ¼-in.-wide, ⁵⁄₁₆-in.-deep dado, ¹³⁄₁₆ in. from the back inside edge of each cabinet side. The cabinet back will slide into these dadoes later. NOTE: *Since sheet material often does not match the nominal thickness precisely, measure the thickness of the panel you'll use for the cabinet back and adjust the width of*

PHOTO B: Assemble the cabinet carcase. Cut biscuit slots to align the parts, then glue and clamp the carcase and fasten the joints with screws. Drill countersunk pilots holes before driving the screws.

PHOTO C: After you apply adhesive-backed veneer to one cabinet side, trim off overhanging veneer with a router and piloted flush-trimming bit. Apply veneer to the other cabinet side using the same method.

the dadoes accordingly so your cabinet back will be sure to fit.

6 Lay out and cut slots for #20 biscuits in the cabinet sides, top stretchers, drawer rail, and bottom to help line up the parts during assembly. The cabinet sides overlap the ends of the bottom and stretchers. Lay out the cabinet parts so the back edges of the bottom and rear top stretcher are flush with the front edge of the cabinet back dadoes. The front edges of the front top stretcher and the cabinet bottom should be flush with the front edges of the cabinet sides. Glue biscuits into the ends of the top stretchers, drawer rail, and bottom, and wipe off excess glue with a damp cloth. Dry-fit the assembly and hold it together with clamps. Drill countersunk pilot holes for 1½-in. flathead wood screws through the cabinet sides and into the horizontal cabinet parts. Disassemble the cabinet and spread glue into the remaining biscuit slots and mating joint surfaces. Reassemble and clamp up the cabinet, checking to make sure it is square. Reinforce the joints with screws **(See Photo B)**. Measure and mark the drawer divider location, centering it on the cabinet width. Attach the divider with 1½-in. countersunk screws driven down through the top stretchers and up through the drawer rail.

7 Apply red oak iron-on veneer tape to the front edges of the cabinet sides, bottom, top front stretcher,

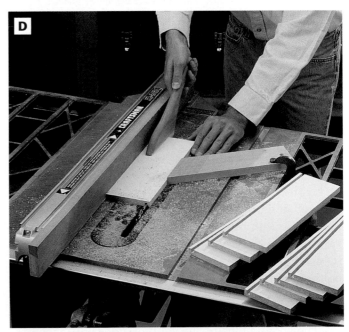

PHOTO D: Cut dadoes for the drawer bottoms in the drawer fronts, backs and sides. Adjust the dado width to match the thickness of the drawer bottom panels you buy—panel thickness may vary.

drawer rail, and the front end of the drawer divider. Trim off overhanging tape with a hand edging trimmer, or hold a sharp chisel flat against the panel and push it slowly along to slice away the excess.

8 Cut the cabinet back to size from ¼-in.-thick white melamine board. Slide the cabinet back into

PHOTO E: Dry-fit the drawer box parts, then glue and clamp up each drawer, with the drawer bottom inserted in its dado. Use #0 biscuits to align the joints. Wax paper protects your worksurface from excess glue. Check the drawers for square and adjust the clamps as needed.

PHOTO F: Use spring clamps to hold the drawer face in position on the drawer while you drill pilot holes and insert screws. Since the drawer front overhangs the bottom of the drawer by ½ in., shim the back of the drawer above the worksurface with ½-in. scrap plywood.

the dadoes on the cabinet sides so the melamine side faces into the cabinet. Check the cabinet for square by measuring diagonally from the cabinet bottom to the top in both directions. When the measurements match, the cabinet is square. Attach the back with countersunk 1¼-in. screws driven through the back and into the cabinet bottom and top rear stretcher.

9 Cut the two back blocking pieces to size. Glue and screw the blocking flush against the back edges of the cabinet sides, at the top and bottom of the carcase, using countersunk 1½-in. screws. Since the cabinet sides will be covered with veneer, attach the blocking by driving the screws through the cabinet sides behind the back panel dadoes and into the ends of the back blocking. The back blocking pieces serve as fastening cleats when you screw the cabinet to a wall. Fill the screw holes in the cabinet sides with wood putty and sand smooth.

ATTACH THE SHEET VENEER

10 Cover the cabinet sides with sheet veneer (we used adhesive-backed cabinet veneer). Cut the veneer to size according to the dimensions given in the *Cutting List*, page 37, using a scissors or a utility knife against a steel straightedge. The veneer sheets are oversized at this stage to allow some leeway in positioning them, since the adhesive grabs on contact.

11 Scuff the outer melamine faces of the cabinet sides with 80-grit sandpaper to degloss the melamine, which improves the bonding surface for the veneer adhesive. Lay the cabinet on its side on strips of scrap plywood. Place one of the veneer sheets on the cabinet side, adhesive side down, and center the veneer so there is an even overhang all around. Hold it in place by clamping a couple spring clamps along one edge. Peel back the backing paper a few inches from the opposite edge. Press this edge down firmly to bond the adhesive, then remove the spring clamps and begin to slowly pull the paper off while you press the veneer down flat with a J-roller or scrap of 2 × 4 wrapped in a towel. Smooth the veneer using overlapping strokes all the way across the sheet as you remove the paper. Try not to trap air bubbles. Proceed with this peeling and smoothing process until all the paper is removed and you have completely flattened the veneer. TIP: *If you do get an air bubble trapped beneath the veneer, push a stick pin through the veneer or make a tiny slit with a thin craft knife. This perforation should allow the air to escape so you can roll or press the veneer flat.*

12 Trim away the excess veneer. Use a router with a piloted flush-trimming bit to trim the overhanging veneer all around **(See Photo C)**. Turn the cabinet over and veneer the other cabinet side.

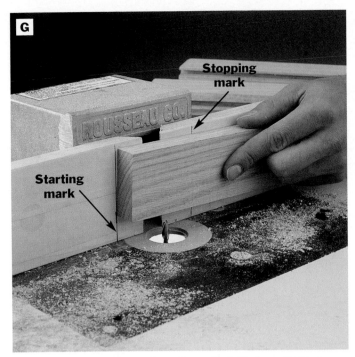

PHOTO G: Draw referencs marks on the router table fence that index the starting and stopping points for cutting the stopped dadoes in the door stiles. Start each stopped dado by aligning one end of a stile with the starting mark on the fence and lowering the workpiece onto the bit.

PHOTO H: Once the bit is buried in the workpiece at the starting mark, slide each door stile along the fence until the other end of the workpiece reaches the stop mark. Turn off the router and lift up the board to finish the cut.

MAKE THE DRAWERS

⓫ Prepare the drawer box parts. Cut the drawer fronts, backs and sides to size from ½-in. melamine particleboard. Cut the drawer bottoms from ¼-in. melamine. Use a table saw and dado-blade set to machine a ¼-in.-wide, ⁵⁄₁₆-in.-deep dado ¼ in. from one long edge into the drawer fronts, backs and sides **(See Photo D)**. The dadoes will house the drawer bottoms. Conceal the top edges of the drawer fronts, backs and sides with white iron-on edge tape, and trim the tape flush.

⓮ Build the drawer boxes. Lay out and cut centered #0 biscuit joints for assembling the drawers. Lay out the biscuit joints so the drawer front and back panels fit between the sides. Glue and clamp up the drawers with the drawer bottoms in place **(See Photo E)**.

⓯ Install the drawer faces. Cut the drawer faces to size from ¾-in. solid red oak. Attach them to the fronts of the drawers so that the faces overhang the bottom edges of the drawer box by ½ in. The inside end of each drawer front should overhang the drawer side by ½ in., and the outside end should be flush with the outside face of the cabinet side. Drill pilot holes through the insides of the drawers and into the backs of the drawer faces. TIP: *Enlarge the holes from side to side in the drawer fronts so that you can align*

the faces after the drawers are hung. Screw the drawer faces to the drawer fronts, using two 1-in. pan-head screws per drawer **(See Photo F)**.

BUILD & HANG THE DOORS

⓰ Cut the door stiles and rails to size from solid red oak stock and flatten the edges on a jointer or with a hand plane. The edges must be flat so the rails and stiles will fit together tightly where the parts meet in the corners. Cut the door panels from ¼-in. red oak plywood.

⓱ The door panels "float" in dadoes cut on the inside edges of the door stiles and rails. The dadoes in the stiles must stop 2 in. from the ends, so cut the dadoes on a router table with starting and stopping marks laid out on the fence to guide the cuts **(See Photo G)**. Install a ¼-in.-wide straight bit and raise the bit to ⁷⁄₁₆-in. above the table. Set the router fence ⅛ in. away from the bit. This way, the dadoes will be offset across the width of the door frame parts to allow for a ⅜-in. reveal between the door panel and the face of the door frame.

⓲ Cut the door stile dadoes. To make the stopped dadoes, start the router, align the stile with the starting mark on the router fence and lower it slowly down onto the bit **(See Photo H)**. Slide the stile

PHOTO I: Stain the door panels, then glue and clamp up the doors using ⅜-in.-dia. dowels to reinforce the rail and stile corner joints.

PHOTO J: Attach solid-oak edging pieces around the laminate counter-top, using biscuits and glue. The edging fits flush with the countertop.

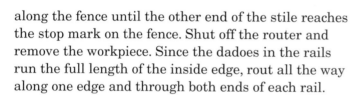

along the fence until the other end of the stile reaches the stop mark on the fence. Shut off the router and remove the workpiece. Since the dadoes in the rails run the full length of the inside edge, rout all the way along one edge and through both ends of each rail.

⑲ Rout a ¼ × ¼-in. chamfer along the inside front edge of each door stile and rail. Stop the chamfers 2 in. from the ends of the rails and 4¼ in. from the ends of the stiles. Use a chamfering bit in the router table, and mark starting and stopping points on the router fence to make these stopped cuts.

⑳ Drill ⅜-in.-dia. dowel joints with a doweling jig to join the rails to the stiles. Position the dowel holes on the mating surfaces of the rails and stiles, ½ in. and 1½ in. from the top and bottom edges of the door. Drill the holes ⅞ in. deep in all the parts.

㉑ If you plan to stain this project, stain the door panels before assembling the doors, since you'll still have full access to the door panels. We used golden oak stain.

㉒ Assemble the doors. Dry-assemble the rails, stiles and panels first to check the fit of the parts. Disassemble the doors and spread glue into the dowel holes

and mating surfaces of the joints. Insert 1½-in.-long dowels and clamp up both doors **(See Photo I)**. Check for square and clean up glue squeeze-out before the glue dries.

㉓ Lay out and cut mortises on the front edge of the cabinet sides and the back face of the stiles for ball-tip hinges.

MAKE THE COUNTERTOP
㉔ Cut the countertop core and four build-up pieces to size from ¾-in. melamine particleboard. Glue and screw the build-up to the underside of the core with 1¼-in. screws.

㉕ Cut the laminate to the oversized dimensions given in the *Cutting List*. Use a laminate scoring knife (score the laminate several times against a steel straightedge, then break it along the scored cut) or cut the laminate on the table saw using a laminate-cutting blade. Scuff the glossy melamine surface of the core with 80-grit sandpaper. Apply contact cement to both the laminate and the top core, using a paint roller with a foam sleeve. After the contact becomes tacky, set the laminate in place on the core. Be careful here. The cement bonds instantly on contact, making it extremely difficult to remove or

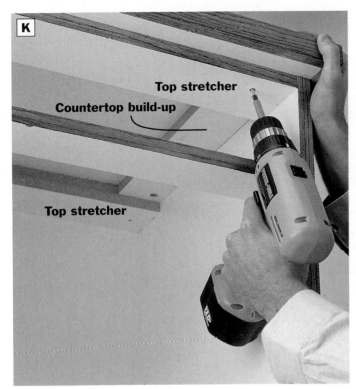

PHOTO K: Attach the countertop to the top stretchers with countersunk 1½-in. screws, driven from inside the cabinet, up through the stretchers and into the countertop build-up.

PHOTO L: Hang the doors and install door and drawer knobs. Loosen the drawer face screws a bit and adjust the drawer faces so they fit evenly above the doors and are flush with the cabinet sides. Tighten the screws.

reposition the laminate. To make this process more foolproof, lay several thin plywood strips across the width of the core, say every 6 in. or so. Lay the laminate on top of the strips and align the laminate over the core. Starting at one end, remove one stick at a time and press down the laminate with a J-roller. Once you've removed all the sticks, roll the laminate down firmly all over the surface with the J-roller to ensure a good bond. Trim the laminate to final size with a router and flush-trimming bit. (See page 23 for more information on applying laminate.)

26 Rip and crosscut the front, side and back countertop edging from solid red oak. Fit these edges around the core, mitering the front corners and butting the rear corners. Cut slots for #20 biscuits in the edging and core to help align the parts. Glue and clamp the edging to the core **(See Photo J)**. When the glue dries, remove the clamps and ease the edges and corners of the side and front edging by routing a ⅜-in. chamfer. Rout the chamfer on the front edging first, then rout the side edging (doing this will keep the bit from tearing out the corners).

FINISHING TOUCHES

27 Sand all the red oak surfaces and ease sharp edges with 150-grit sandpaper. Apply the finish of your choice. We finished our cabinet with golden oak stain to match the door panels and applied two coats of satin polyurethane varnish.

28 Attach the base to the cabinet with countersunk 1¼-in. screws driven up from under the base. Assemble the parts so the back of the base is flush with the back of the cabinet and the cabinet overhangs the base evenly on both sides.

29 Attach the countertop to the cabinet with countersunk 1½-in. screws driven through the top stretchers into the countertop build-up **(See Photo K)**. The countertop should be flush with the back of the cabinet and overhang the cabinet sides equally.

30 Attach the metal drawer slide hardware to the drawer boxes, drawer divider and inside cabinet faces according to the manufacturer's instructions. Hang the drawers. Insert the shelf pins into the holes and set the shelf in place. Attach the hinges to the doors and cabinet carcase, and hang the doors. Loosen the drawer face screws just enough to adjust the alignment of the drawer faces so they're centered over the doors, then tighten the screws. Install the knobs on the doors and drawers **(See Photo L)**.

Wall-hung Cabinet

Create attractive storage space for displaying glassware, china or collectibles with this oak wall-hung cabinet. The shelves are adjustable to accommodate items of varying sizes, and the cabinet mounts to a wall with hidden, interlocking French cleats. We've styled this cabinet with glass doors to function as a companion piece for the base cabinet project found on pages 34 to 43.

Vital Statistics: Wall-hung Cabinet

TYPE: Wall-hung cabinet

OVERALL SIZE: 15D × 32W × 31½H

MATERIAL: Red oak plywood, solid red oak, glass

JOINERY: Dowel, miter, biscuit, dado joints

CONSTRUCTION DETAILS:
- Solid-oak door frames
- Glass mounted in door rabbets and held in place with wooden glass stops
- Iron-on oak veneer edge tape
- Cabinet mounted with concealed French cleats
- Two adjustable shelves

FINISH: Golden oak stain; two coats satin polyurethane varnish

Building time

 PREPARING STOCK
4-5 hours

 LAYOUT
3-4 hours

 CUTTING PARTS
2-3 hours

 ASSEMBLY
6-8 hours

 FINISHING
1-2 hours

TOTAL: 16-22 hours

Tools you'll use

- Table saw
- Power miter saw (optional)
- Drill/driver
- Doweling jig
- Biscuit joiner
- Clamps
- Router with ⅜-in. rabbeting bit, piloted chamfer bit, ¼-in. roundover bit
- Chisel
- Marking knife
- Brad pusher
- Nailset

Shopping list

- ☐ (1) ¾ in. × 4 ft. × 8 ft. red oak plywood
- ☐ (1) ¼ in. × 4 ft. × 8 ft. red oak plywood
- ☐ (1) ¾ × 4 in. solid red oak (16 lineal ft.)
- ☐ (2) ⅛ × 10¹⁵⁄₁₆ × 26⅛ in. tempered glass
- ☐ (1) Red oak edge banding (20 ft.)
- ☐ (4) 2 × 1½-in. ball-tip hinges
- ☐ (8) ¼-in.-dia. shelf pins
- ☐ (2) Brass door knobs
- ☐ (2) Magnetic door catches
- ☐ #8 × 2-in. flathead wood screws. ¾-in. wire brads
- ☐ #20 biscuits, ⅜-in.-dia. dowel
- ☐ Wood glue
- ☐ Finishing materials

Wall-hung Cabinet

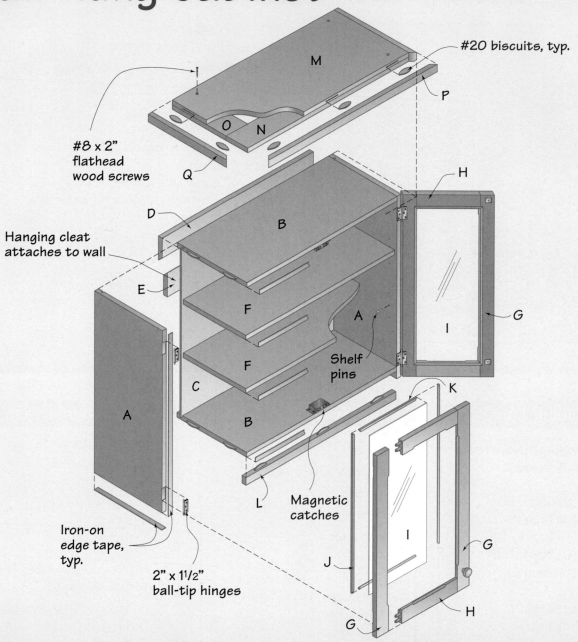

#20 biscuits, typ.

#8 x 2" flathead wood screws

Hanging cleat attaches to wall

Shelf pins

Magnetic catches

Iron-on edge tape, typ.

2" x 1½" ball-tip hinges

Wall-hung Cabinet Cutting List

Part		No.	Size	Material	Part		No.	Size	Material
A.	Side	2	¾ × 13⅛ × 30 in.	Red oak plywood	J.	Glass stop	4	¼ × ⅜ × 26⅞ in.	Red oak
B.	Top/bottom	2	¾ × 13⅛ × 28½ in.	"	K.	Glass stop	4	¼ × ⅜ × 10⁷⁄₁₆ in.	"
C.	Back	1	¼ × 29 × 28 in.	"	L.	Light valance	1	¾ × 1¼ × 28½ in.	"
D.	Cabinet cleat	1	¾ × 4 × 28½ in.	"	M.	Crown	1	¾ × 14¼ × 30½ in.	Red oak plywood
E.	Wall cleat	1	¾ × 4 × 26½ in.	"	N.	Build-up	1	¾ × 4 × 30½ in.	"
F.	Shelf	2	¾ × 11¾ × 28½ in.	"	O.	Build-up	2	¾ × 4 × 10¼ in.	"
G.	Door stile	4	¾ × 2¼ × 29⅞ in.	Red oak	P.	Front edge	1	¾ × 1½ × 32 in.	Red oak
H.	Door rail	4	¾ × 2¼ × 10⁷⁄₁₆ in.	"	Q.	Side edge	2	¾ × 1½ × 15 in.	"
I.	Glass panel	2	⅛ × 10¹⁵⁄₁₆ × 26⅛ in.	Tempered glass					

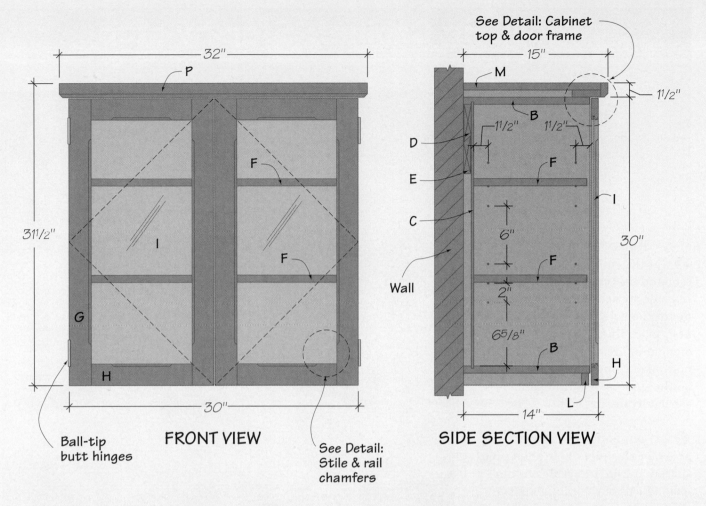

32"

P

31 1/2"

F

I

F

G

H

30"

Ball-tip
butt hinges

FRONT VIEW

See Detail: Stile & rail chamfers

See Detail: Cabinet top & door frame

15"

M

B

1 1/2"

D

1 1/2"

1 1/2"

E

F

C

I

6"

30"

F

2"

6 5/8"

B

Wall

H

14"

L

SIDE SECTION VIEW

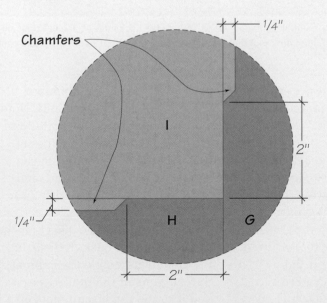

Chamfers

1/4"

I

2"

1/4"

H

G

2"

**DETAIL: STILE &
RAIL CHAMFERS**

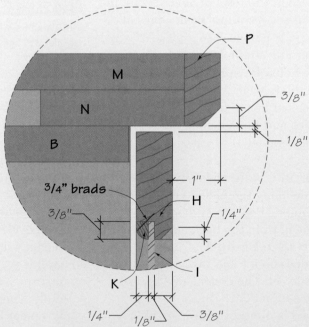

P

M

N

3/8"

1/8"

B

3/4" brads

1"

H

3/8"

1/4"

K

I

1/4"

1/8"

3/8"

**DETAIL: CABINET TOP &
DOOR FRAME**

BUILD THE CARCASE

1 Cut the cabinet sides, top, bottom and shelves to size from ¾-in. red oak plywood, according to the dimensions given in the *Cutting List,* page 46. Use a sharp plywood or combination table saw blade to minimize chipping out the veneer on the underside of the panels, especially during crosscutting.

2 Lay out and drill ¼-in.-dia. holes for the adjustable shelf pins, spaced at 2-in. intervals on the inside faces of the cabinet sides. Position the rows of holes 1½ in. in from the front and back edges of the side panels. Use a piece of pegboard as a template for drilling the holes. Be sure to set up the template exactly the same way on each cabinet side so the shelf pin holes will line up once the carcase is assembled.

3 Cut a ¼-in.-wide, ⁵⁄₁₆-in.-deep dado along the inside faces of the cabinet sides, top and bottom, ¹³⁄₁₆ in. from the back edge of each part **(See Photo A)**. Cut the dadoes on a table saw with a dado-blade set. The dadoes will house the cabinet back. Since ¼-in. plywood is almost never exactly ¼ in. thick, measure the thickness of the panel stock you'll use for the back before setting up the dado blade. This way you can be sure the back will fit the dadoes.

PHOTO A: Cut a ¼-in.-wide, ⁵⁄₁₆-in.-deep dado, ¹³⁄₁₆ in. in from the back edge of each of the cabinet sides, top and bottom. Adjust the exact dado width to match the actual thickness of the cabinet back panel.

4 Rip- and cross-cut the cabinet back to size from ¼-in. red oak plywood.

5 Fasten iron-on red oak veneer edge tape to the front edges of the cabinet sides, top, bottom and adjustable shelves (See page 20). Trim off overhanging tape with a hand edge-trimming tool or use a sharp chisel, holding it flat against the panel as you run it carefully along the edges. Then apply veneer tape to the bottom edges of the cabinet sides.

6 Lay out and cut slots for #20 biscuits in the ends of the cabinet top and bottom, and in the inside faces of the sides to help align these parts during assembly. Note that the cabinet bottom is located 1¼ in. from the bottom edges of the sides. Glue biscuits into the ends of the top and bottom, and wipe away excess glue with a rag.

7 Dry-fit the carcase parts (sides, top, bottom and back) to test the fit, then disassemble the cabinet. Spread glue on the mating parts and into the the biscuit slots on the cabinet sides, and reassemble the carcase. Clamp up the cabinet, making sure it is square and adjusting the clamps as necessary before the glue dries **(See Photo B)**. Clean up glue squeeze-out.

8 Cut the light valance strip to size from solid red oak. Cut slots for #20 biscuits in the top edge of the valance and in the underside of the cabinet bottom. Glue and clamp the valance in place.

9 Cut the cabinet cleat and the wall cleat to size, bevel-ripping one edge of each cleat at 45°. Glue and clamp the cabinet cleat in place, butting it up against the bottom edge of the cabinet top and flat against the back panel (See *Side Section View,* page 47). The beveled edge should face down and toward the cabinet back panel so it will interlock with the wall cleat when you hang the cabinet.

BUILD THE DOORS

10 Cut the door stiles and rails to size from solid red oak stock. It is important that the stile and rail stock be straight and flat, espe-

PHOTO B: Glue up the cabinet carcase with the back in place. Measure across the diagonals to make sure the assembly is square, and adjust the clamps as needed. Use scrap wood blocks to pad the clamps and protect the cabinet sides.

TIP

Milling flat stock from thicker lumber

Finding flat stock can be difficult when you are buying ¾-in.-thick boards planed smooth on two faces. This is because wood typically is not jointed flat before it is planed to final thickness at the mill, and any internal stresses in the wood cause it to warp again. If you can't find suitable surfaced lumber, you may need to joint and plane your ¾-in. stock from thicker ⁴⁄₄ boards (about 1 in. nominal thickness). First joint the faces of ⁴⁄₄ stock to flatten them. If the lumber was warped or twisted when you bought it, let it sit for a few days, then joint the board faces flat again. Once you've corrected for warp or twist by repeated passes over a jointer, plane the flattened stock down to ¾ in.

PHOTO C: Glue and clamp up the door frames with ⅜-in.-dia. dowel joints. Line your work area with wax paper to protect the benchtop from glue squeeze-out.

PHOTO D: Use a piloted rabbeting bit to rout a ⅜ × ⅜-in. rabbet around the inside back edge of each door frame for the glass panel. Rout the rabbets in two passes.

cially in cases when the door won't be stiffened with a wood center panel. Stock that isn't flat and straight will produce warped or twisted doors that won't sit flat against the cabinet and will be uneven. If your red oak stock is less than ideal, a better alternative might be to mill your door stock from thicker oak lumber (See *Tip,* page 49).

11 Use a doweling jig to drill ⅜-in.-dia., ⅞-in.-deep dowel holes in the ends of the rails and the edges of the stiles for assembling the door frames. Space the dowel holes ½ in. and 1¼ in. from both ends of each stile, then drill corresponding holes in the rails. Spread glue over the mating parts of the joints, insert 1½-in.-long, ⅜-in.-dia. dowels and clamp up the door frames **(See Photo C)**. Make sure the frames are square.

12 Mill a ⅜ × ⅜-in. rabbet inside the door frames to house the glass panels. Install a ⅜-in. piloted rabbeting bit in your router. To rout the rabbets, clamp the door frames to your worksurface, with the inside face up. Set the bit depth to about ¼ in. Rout a rabbet all around the inside edge of the frame. Then, set the bit to the full ⅜-in. depth and make a second pass to complete each rabbet **(See Photo D)**. Since the router will leave rounded corners in the door frames, square corners with a sharp chisel.

13 Turn the door frames over with their front faces up. Install a piloted chamfer bit in the router. Rout a ¼ × ¼-in. chamfer along the inner edges of the rails and stiles. Start and stop the chamfer on each rail and stile 2 in. from the inside frame corners, as shown in the *Detail: Stile & Rail Cham-*

fers drawing, page 47. Clamp temporary stop blocks to the door frames to index your router base when routing these chamfers.

14 Lay out and mark hinge mortises on the inside faces of the doors. Locate the hinges 2 in. in from the top and bottom door ends. For greatest accuracy, use a marking knife or sharp utility knife against a straightedge to lay out the mortises, instead of a pencil. Using one of these two marking tools scores the wood grain, making it easier and neater to pare right up to your layout lines with a chisel.

15 Remove the waste in the hinge mortise areas with a chisel (**See Photo E**). The metal hinge leaves should sit flush with each door face once the mortises are cut. To keep the chisel from diving too deeply into the wood as you pare the mortises, hold it with the blade bevel facing down and shear off thin shavings up to your layout lines. You could also cut these hinge mortises with a straight bit in the router set to a depth that matches the hinge leaf thickness. When routing hinge mortises, stop short of your layout lines and clean out the rest of the waste in the mortise area with a chisel.

16 Drill pilot holes for the screws and mount the hinges to the doors. Lay a door into position on each side of the cabinet, and support the doors from beneath with scrap wood blocks. Align the ends of the doors with the top and bottom of the cabinet, and trace around the hinge leaves to mark mortise locations on the front edges of the cabinet (**See Photo F**).

17 Cut hinge mortises in the cabinet with a chisel as before, then

PHOTO E: Lay out and cut mortises in the doors for the butt hinges (two per door). Work carefully, especially when chiseling next to your mortise layout lines.

PHOTO F: Support the doors next to the cabinet with scrap, and trace around the hinges to mark mortises on the cabinet sides. Cut these mortises with a chisel.

PHOTO G: Screw the front and side build-ups to the underside of the crown, with the edges flush all around. Center the screws across the width of the build-ups.

PHOTO H: Glue the solid oak front and side edging to the crown. Miter the front corners and install #20 biscuits to keep the edging aligned. Clamp up the assembly to hold the mitered corners tight while the glue dries.

drill pilot holes for the hinge screws and install the doors. Test the action of the doors and their relationship to one another when closed. You can make minor door adjustments by loosening the hinge screws and moving the hinges out or in slightly, or by shimming beneath the hinge leaves with strips of paper or masking tape. Remove the doors and hinges.

MILL THE GLASS STOPS

⓲ The glass panels are secured in the door rabbets with wooden stops and ¾-in. brads. To make the stops, start with a length of ¾-in.-thick red oak with one edge jointed flat and square. Rout a ¼-in. roundover along the top and bottom of this edge. Set the table saw rip fence ⅜ in. from the blade. Lay the board facedown on the saw table with the roundover edge against the rip fence, and rip a ⅜-in. strip off the board, using a pushstick to guide the narrow strip past the blade. Now set the saw fence ¼ in. from the blade. Lay the roundover strip flat on the saw table and rip a ¼-in.-wide piece. This ⅜ × ¼-in. stick, with one rounded edge, forms a length of glass stop. Flip the initial remaining strip around so the other rounded edge is against the saw fence and rip a second stop. Mill all eight stops similarly, then crosscut four glass stops per door and miter the ends so the stops fit tightly in the rabbets.

BUILD THE CABINET CROWN

⓳ Cut the cabinet crown to size and lay it upside down on the workbench. Cut the side and front build-ups to size and fasten them to the crown with 1¼-in. counter-sunk wood screws. Center the screws across the width of the build-up pieces (See Photo G).

20 Rip the front and side edges to width from ¾-in. solid red oak, leaving the pieces longer than necessary. Miter the front corners of the front and side edging to fit around the crown using a power miter saw or the table saw. Trim the back ends of the side edging square and flush with the back of the core.

21 Cut slots for #20 biscuits in the front and side edges and the crown to help align the parts. Glue and clamp the edging to the crown **(See Photo H)**.

22 Use a router with a piloted chamfer bit to rout a ¼-in. chamfer around the bottom edge of the crown. Rout the chamfer along the front edging piece first, then cut the chamfers along the sides. Cutting the chamfers in this order minimizes tearout on the ends of the front edging piece.

FINISHING TOUCHES

23 Sand all inside and outside cabinet surfaces with 120-grit sandpaper, then finish-sand with 150-grit.

24 Apply the finish of your choice. We used golden oak stain and topcoated with two coats of satin polyurethane varnish to match the base cabinet project, pages 34-43. Leave the top of the cabinet and the bottom of the crown free of wood finish.

25 Place the crown on the cabinet top and adjust it so the back of the crown is flush with the back edge of the top and the sides overhang evenly. Drill countersunk screw holes, counterbored for wood plugs, down through the crown (in the build-up area) and into the cabinet top. Fasten the crown to the cabinet with glue and 2-in.

PHOTO I: Secure the glass in the door recesses with wooden glass stops. Drive ¾-in. wire brads at a 45° angle through the stops and into the door frames. Use a brad pusher (foreground) to avoid hammering close to the glass. Then tap the brad heads flush with a nailset.

wood screws. Plug the holes and cut the plugs off flush. Sand the plugs smooth and touch up with stain and varnish.

26 Lay the glass panels in the door rabbets. NOTE: *We used tempered glass, a slightly more expensive alternative to standard window glass that does not shatter into splinters when it breaks.* Clamp the doors to the workbench. Set the glass stops in place and fasten with ¾-in. wire brads **(See Photo I)**. Insert each brad at a 45° angle, being careful to avoid hitting the glass. A brad pusher is helpful for inserting the brads. Use a nailset to carefully drive the brad heads flush with the glass stops. Protect the glass around the

work area with a piece of corrugated cardboard.

27 Drill guide holes then mount the knobs. Attach the hinges and hang the doors on the cabinet. If you wish, you can install an under-cabinet light behind the valance to illuminate a countertop area below the cabinet.

28 Level and attach the wall cleat to the wall with 2-in. screws, making sure to hit two wall studs with the screws. Mark the stud locations on the wall above. Hang the cabinet on the cleat, then drive 3-in. screws through the cabinet back and cabinet cleat and into the wall studs.

Plant Stand with Hidden Storage

If you are like most people, you'd rather look at lush greenery and a classical column than plastic CD or video cases. This striking plant stand with its hints of Grecian styling is really a clever storage cabinet that can hold 80 CDs or several dozen videos. We used dentil and embossed moldings to accentuate our plant stand, but you could use any moldings you prefer to add your own personal touch.

Vital Statistics: Plant Stand with Hidden Storage

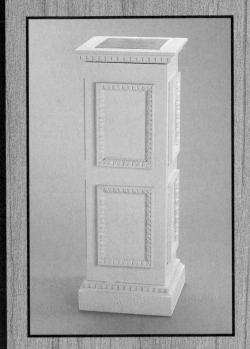

TYPE: Plant stand

OVERALL SIZE: 12W × 12D × 33¾H

MATERIAL: MDF, birch plywood, solid poplar, dentil & embossed trim molding

JOINERY: Biscuit, miter, edge-glued butt joints

CONSTRUCTION DETAILS:
· Tile set into recessed frame on cabinet top
· Adjustable shelves on flush-mounted metal standards in cabinet interior
· Dentil and embossed molding applied to the top, bottom and cabinet faces
· "Hidden" door opens with magnetic touch latch

FINISH: Primer & enamel paint

Building time

PREPARING STOCK
3-4 hours

LAYOUT
3-4 hours

CUTTING PARTS
2-3 hours

ASSEMBLY
3-4 hours

FINISHING
1-2 hours

TOTAL: 12-17 hours

Tools you'll use

· Table saw
· Drill/driver
· Power miter saw (optional)
· Biscuit joiner
· Clamps
· Router with ⅜-in. cove bit
· Drill press
· Tack hammer
· HVLP paint sprayer (optional)
· ¼-in. notched trowel

Shopping list

☐ (1) ¾ × 4 ft. × 4 ft. MDF
☐ ¾ × 12 × 12 in. scrap plywood
☐ ¾ × 6 in. × 4 ft. poplar
☐ (2) ¹³⁄₃₂ × ⅞ in. × 4 ft. dentil trim molding
☐ (7) ⁷⁄₁₆ × 1 in. × 4 ft. embossed trim molding
☐ (2) European-style full-overlay hinges
☐ (1) Magnetic touch latch
☐ (4) ³⁄₁₆ × ⅝ × 30 in. metal shelf standards & supports
☐ #20 biscuits
☐ #8 flathead wood screws (1-, 1¼-, 1½-in.)
☐ 1-in. brads
☐ (1) 8 × 8-in. floor tile
☐ Tile adhesive
☐ Grout or clear silicone caulk

Plant Stand with Hidden Storage

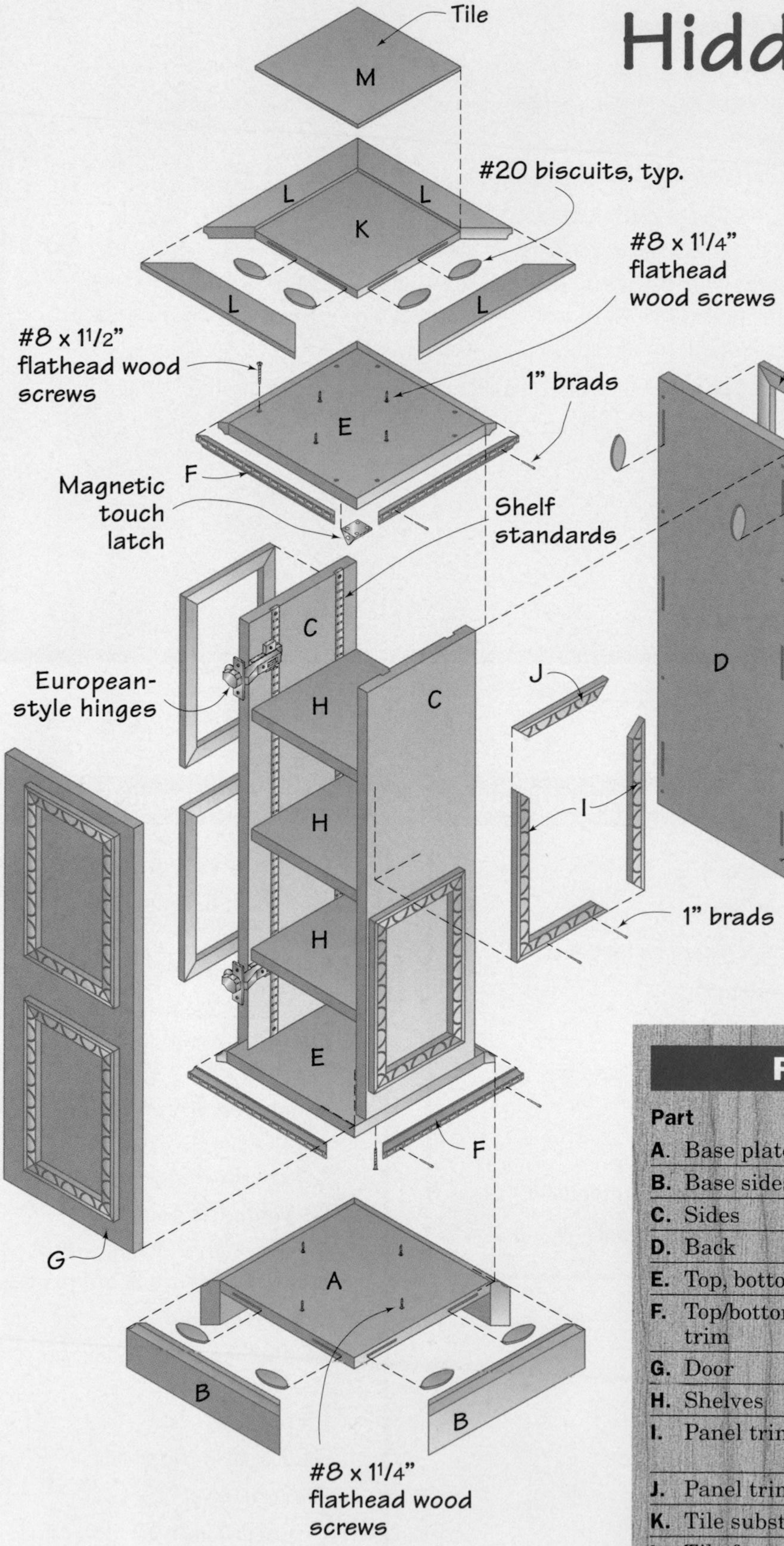

Tile

M

L L L

K

#20 biscuits, typ.

L L

#8 x 1¼"
flathead
wood screws

#8 x 1½"
flathead wood
screws

E

F

Magnetic
touch
latch

1" brads

Shelf
standards

J

I

European-
style hinges

C

C

H

H

J

D

H

I

E

#8 x 1½"
flathead wood
screws

G

F

1" brads

A

B

B

#8 x 1¼"
flathead wood
screws

Plant Stand Cutting List

Part	No.	Size	Material
A. Base plate	1	¾ × 10½ × 10½ in.	MDF
B. Base sides	4	¾ × 3 × 12 in.	Poplar
C. Sides	2	¾ × 8⁷⁄₁₆ × 28½ in.	MDF
D. Back	1	¾ × 10 × 28½ in.	"
E. Top, bottom	2	¾ × 10 × 10 in.	"
F. Top/bottom trim	8	1³⁄₃₂ × ⁷⁄₈ × 10¹³⁄₁₆ in.	Dentil molding
G. Door	1	¾ × 10 × 28⅜ in.	MDF
H. Shelves	3	¾ × 8⅜ × 8¼ in.	"
I. Panel trim	16	⁷⁄₁₆ × 1¹⁄₃₂ × 10¹⁵⁄₁₆ in.	Embossed molding
J. Panel trim	16	⁷⁄₁₆ × 1¹⁄₃₂ × 7 in.	"
K. Tile substrate	1	½ × 8 × 8 in.	Plywood
L. Tile frame	4	¾ × 2 × 12 in.	Poplar
M. Tile	1	¼ × 8 × 8 in.	Floor tile

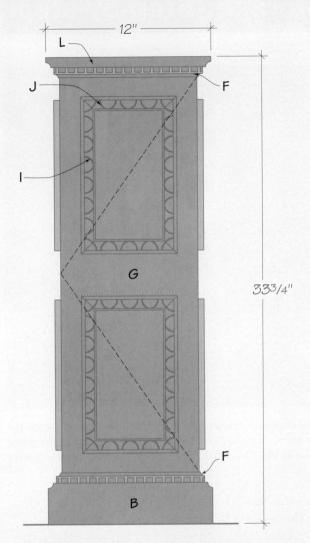

12"

L

J

F

I

G

F

B

33³/4"

FRONT VIEW - DOOR SIDE

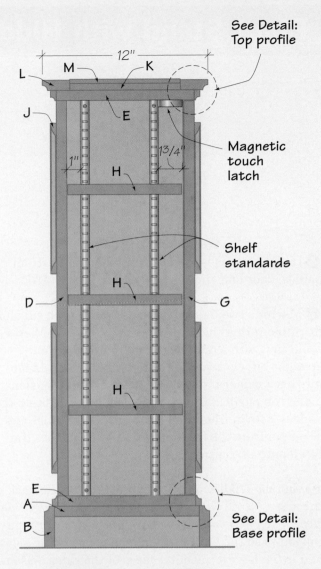

See Detail: Top profile

12"

L M K

J

E

1" 1³/4"

H

Magnetic touch latch

Shelf standards

D H G

H

E
A
B

See Detail: Base profile

SIDE SECTION VIEW

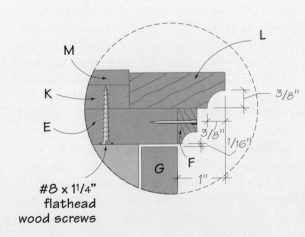

M

L

K

E

3/8"

3/8"
1/16"

G F

1"

#8 x 1¹/4" flathead wood screws

DETAIL: TOP PROFILE

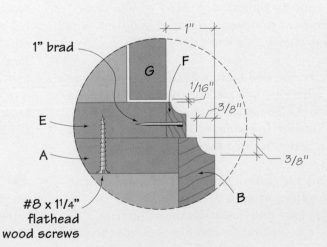

1"

1" brad

G

F

E

1/16"

3/8"

A

3/8"

B

#8 x 1¹/4" flathead wood screws

DETAIL: BASE PROFILE

BUILD THE CARCASE

1 Cut the base plate, sides, back, top and bottom panels, door and shelves to size from ¾-in. MDF.

2 Machine two dadoes into one face of each side for flush-mounting the shelf standards. Using either a table saw with a dado-blade set or a router and straight bit, cut two ⅝-in.-wide, 3⁄16-in.-deep dadoes into each side (establish the exact dado dimensions using the particular standards you buy). Position the dadoes 1 in. in from the back edges of the sides and 1¾ in. in from the front edges. Run the dadoes the full length of the sides.

3 Cut six #20 biscuit joints for attaching the back to the sides. NOTE: *Be sure to keep the dado orientation clear when assembling the back and sides.* Arrange the joints so the back overlaps the edges of the sides and is flush with the outer faces of the sides. Assemble the parts with glue and 1½-in. screws. Be sure to drill countersunk pilot holes for the screws first. Scrape away any glue squeeze-out when the glue reaches a rubbery consistency. (MDF swells some when it comes in contact with water, so do not wipe away excess glue with a wet rag.)

4 Attach the top and bottom to the ends of the back and sides with glue and countersunk 1½-in. screws **(See Photo A)**. The edges of the top and bottom should be flush with the faces of the sides and back but overhang the front edges of the sides by 13⁄16 in.

5 Bevel-cut the ends of the dentil trim molding at 45° to fit together around the top and bottom of the cabinet. Use glue and brads to attach the trim, drilling pilot holes first for the brads. Since the molding is ⅞ in. wide, trim ⅛ in. off of one edge of the molding pieces so they do not overhang the edges of the cabinet top and bottom.

PHOTO A: Attach the cabinet sides to the back, then glue and screw the top and bottom in place. The edges of the top and bottom pieces should be flush with the cabinet sides and back but overhang the door opening by 13⁄16 in.

6 Cut the embossed molding pieces to length and miter the corners to form decorative frames for the cabinet front, back and sides. Lay out the cuts so the embossed pattern will be symmetrical in the corners. The lengths of these parts will vary, depending on the molding pattern you buy. Draw layout lines on the faces of the sides, back and door to position the molding evenly. NOTE: *Remember to account for the fact that the door is ⅛ in. shorter than the cabinet sides. Place the door molding so it will align with the decorative molding on the sides and back once the door is hung.* Attach the trim frames to the cabinet sides, back and door with glue and brads **(See Photo B)**. Set the brad heads below the surface with a nailset.

MAKE THE BASE & THE TILED TOP

7 Cut the substrate for the tile top from ½-in. plywood. Use the actual (not nominal) size of the tile you'll be installing to size the substrate. (The substrate should be about ¼ in. larger than the tile in both directions to create a ⅛-in. grout or caulk gap on all sides.) Rip the tile frame pieces to width from ¾-in. solid poplar stock, and miter-cut the ends so

PHOTO B: Fasten the dentil molding aroung the cabinet top and bottom. Attach the embossed molding frames with glue and 1-in. brads. Miter-cut the molding so the patterns mirror one another on the frame corners. Drill pilot holes for the brads.

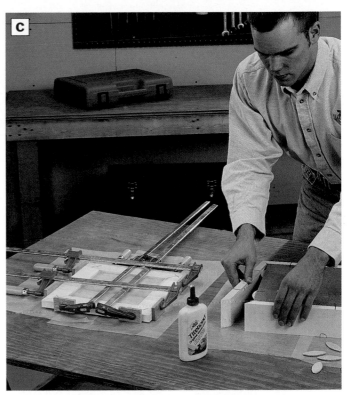

PHOTO C: Glue the four frame pieces to the tile substrate and attach the base sides to the base plate, using biscuits to align the joints. Clamp the frames to hold the miter joints closed.

that the frame pieces fit around the plywood substrate. Cut two #20 biscuit slots to join each frame piece to the substrate. The bottom face of the tile substrate should be flush with the bottom faces of the tile frame when assembled. This offset will create a ¼-in. recess to inset the tile.

❽ Cut the base plate to size from MDF, then rip and crosscut the four base pieces from poplar. Bevel the ends of the base pieces at 45° so the parts wrap around the base plate. Make these angled cuts with a power miter saw or on the table saw, against the miter gauge with the blade tilted to 45°. Cut #20 biscuit slots to attach the base members to the base plate. The base requires no biscuits along the beveled corners. Arrange the biscuit joints so the top face of the base plate is flush with the top edges of the beveled base members. Glue and clamp the base assembly (**See Photo C**) and clean away excess glue from the joints.

❾ Install a ⅜-in. piloted cove bit in your router and rout a cove around the top edge of the base and the bottom edge of the tile top (**See Photo D**). Rout the cuts in several passes to keep the bit from tearing out the corners by "hogging out" too much material in a

PHOTO D: Rout a cove into the bottom edge of the tile frame and the top edge of the base using a ⅜-in. piloted bit. This is a deep cut, so make it in at least two passes, lowering the bit for the second pass. We used a non-slip router mat to keep the parts from moving while routing the coves. You could also clamp the workpieces to the workbench with bench dogs.

PHOTO E: Use a large spring clamp to hold the base in position on the bottom of the cabinet carcase while you fasten the parts with 1¼-in. countersunk screws. Then, attach the tile top to the cabinet top with 1¼-in. flathead wood screws.

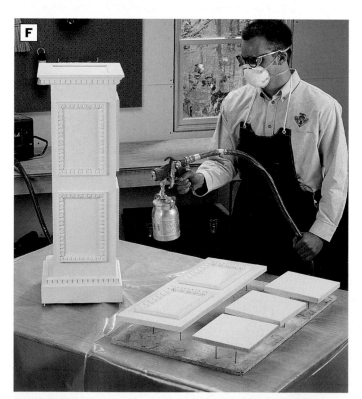

PHOTO F: Prime and paint the cabinet, door and shelves. We used an HVLP sprayer (See tint box, right), but you could also apply the finish with a brush or painting pad. If you opt for HVLP spraying, spray with even back-and-forth strokes, holding the gun at about 90° to, and a constant distance from, the part you are spraying. A good way to paint both sides of a flat part without waiting for one side to fully dry is to flip the part over and set it on the points of four sharp wallboard screws driven up through some scrap plywood.

single pass. You can make these cuts safely by setting the parts on a non-slip pad or by clamping between a bench dog and workbench vise. Either way, immobilize the workpieces in some fashion before cutting the coves freehand with the router.

❿ Attach the base to the cabinet. Turn the carcase upside down and center the base on the underside of the cabinet bottom. Use a large spring clamp to hold the base in place while you attach it with 1¼-in. countersunk screws driven through the base plate and into the cabinet bottom (**See Photo E**). Next, turn the cabinet right side up and center the tiled top on the carcase top. Attach the tile top assembly to the cabinet with 1¼-in. countersunk flathead wood screws driven up through the cabinet top and into the tile substrate.

HANG THE CABINET DOOR

⓫ Bore holes into the door back for European door hinges. We installed our hinges so the cabinet door would hinge on the left side, but the door could be

TIP

HVLP sprayers

HVLP (high-volume low-pressure) paint sprayers deliver 80% to 90% of the paint or finish, at low pressure, for a softer, easier-to-control spray than can be had from other compressor-driven paint sprayers. That means you use less of your expensive paint or stain, and have much less of a mess (the overspray) to deal with. HVLP spray systems don't use compressed air, relying instead on a steady supply of air at about 3- to 6-PSI delivered from a special turbine. You get tight control of the spray pattern, adjusting it from a narrow pinpoint pattern to as wide as 12 in. HVLP systems can be used with acrylics, stains, lacquers, oil and latex paints, enamels and varnishes. They're compact and portable. For the typical home workshop, you'll probably want a single-stage turbine with a 7-amp or higher motor. HVLP spray guns are connected to the turbine with an air hose. Excess air usually escapes from bleed holes in the gun when it's not being used.

hung to swing either direction. Place the hinges at equal distances from the top and bottom of the door. Use a 35-mm Forstner bit in a drill press to drill the hinge cup holes. Install the hinge hardware on the inside face of the cabinet in front of the front shelf standards. Hang the door and test the action of the hinges. Install the latch hardware, then remove the hinges to prepare the cabinet and door for finishing.

FINISHING TOUCHES

⑫ Make sure all brad and screw heads are sunk below the wood surfaces. Fill the brad and screw holes with wood putty. Sand all cabinet surfaces with 120-grit sandpaper and clean off sanding dust with a tack cloth. Wear a particle mask to protect yourself from fine MDF dust particles.

⑬ Prime and paint the cabinet, door and shelves. We used an HVLP sprayer to make painting corners and molding details easier and neater (**See Photo F**). Thin your primer and paint according to the instructions that come with the sprayer to keep from clogging the spray gun. HVLP guns produce considerably less overspray than conventional compressor-driven spray gun systems, but they still shoot a powerful mist of paint, so wear an organic vapor respirator mask (either a disposable mask or a plastic one with replaceable cartridges). Protect surfaces you do not want painted with drop cloths or plastic sheeting. Practice spraying on scrap first to get the feel of using the gun. Adjust the spray to produce a full, wet coat but not so heavy that the paint drips and runs. Spray in horizontal overlapping swaths back and forth. Two light coats of primer and paint should provide adequate coverage.

⑭ Install the tile. Spread an even coat of tile adhesive on the back of the tile with a ¼-in. notched trowel. Lay the tile carefully into place in the top recess (**See Photo G**). After the adhesive has set, fill the gaps between the tile and the tile frame with grout or clear silicone caulk.

⑮ Cut the metal shelf standards to fit the cabinet dadoes using a hacksaw or a metal-cutting blade in your jig saw. Make the cuts on the same ends of the four standards so the slots will line up when you install the standards. Drill pilot holes and screw the standards into their dadoes (**See Photo H**). Reinstall the hinges, hang the door and install a magnetic touch latch. Clip the shelf supports into the standards and set the shelves in place.

PHOTO G: Apply an even coat of tile adhesive to the back of the tile with a ¼-in. notched trowel, and lay the tile into the framed top to glue it down. Wear gloves to protect your hands.

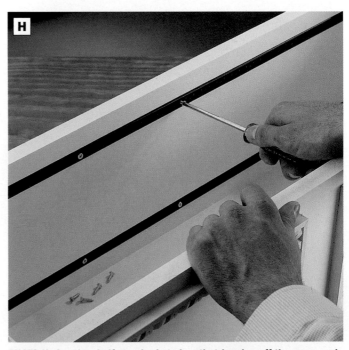

PHOTO H: Cut the shelf standards to length, trimming off the same end of each shelf standard. Screw them into the dadoes in the sides of the carcase with short screws, to keep the screws from piercing through.

Sailboat Sandbox

We'll bet a little "skipper" you know would love to cast off for hours of fun in this sailboat-inspired sandbox. You'll have a good time building it, too, kerf-bending the curved plywood hull and topping the project off with a spirited paint scheme. Our sailboat features a removable seat to make room for more crew members. The lid keeps sand protected from weather, pests or neighborhood cats, and it lifts off in five sections for easy handling.

Vital Statistics: Sailboat Sandbox

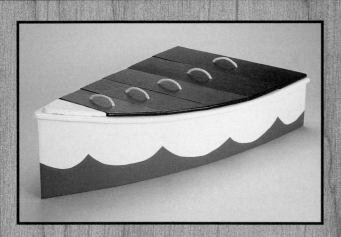

TYPE: Sailboat sandbox

OVERALL SIZE: $37\frac{1}{2}$W $\times$ $61\frac{5}{16}$L $\times$ 16H

MATERIAL: BC treated plywood, 2×2 treated lumber

JOINERY: Dowels, screws

CONSTRUCTION DETAILS:

· Kerf-bent plywood boat sides

· Removable bench seat
· Segmented cover with hidden cleats keeps sand dry and protected from pets or pests
· Side and transom caps fit over boat sides and transom with dadoes

FINISH: Exterior latex enamel paint

Building time

PREPARING STOCK
4-5 hours

LAYOUT
3-4 hours

CUTTING PARTS
4-5 hours

ASSEMBLY
6-8 hours

FINISHING
2-4 hours

TOTAL: 19-26 hours

Tools you'll use

· Combination square
· Jig saw
· Circular saw
· Router table with $\frac{1}{2}$-in. straight bit & $\frac{3}{8}$-in.-radius roundover bit
· Belt sander
· Clamps
· Drill/driver
· File or chisel

HANDYMAN Shopping list

☐ (2) $\frac{3}{4}$ in. $\times$ 4 ft. $\times$ 8 ft. exterior plywood

☐ $1\frac{1}{2} \times 1\frac{1}{2} \times 24$ in. treated lumber

☐ (5) 2-ft. lengths of nylon rope

☐ #8 galvanized wood screws ($1\frac{1}{4}$-, $1\frac{1}{2}$-in.)

☐ $\frac{3}{8}$-in.-dia. hardwood dowel

☐ Finish nails

☐ Moisture-resistant wood glue

☐ Finishing materials

Sailboat Sandbox

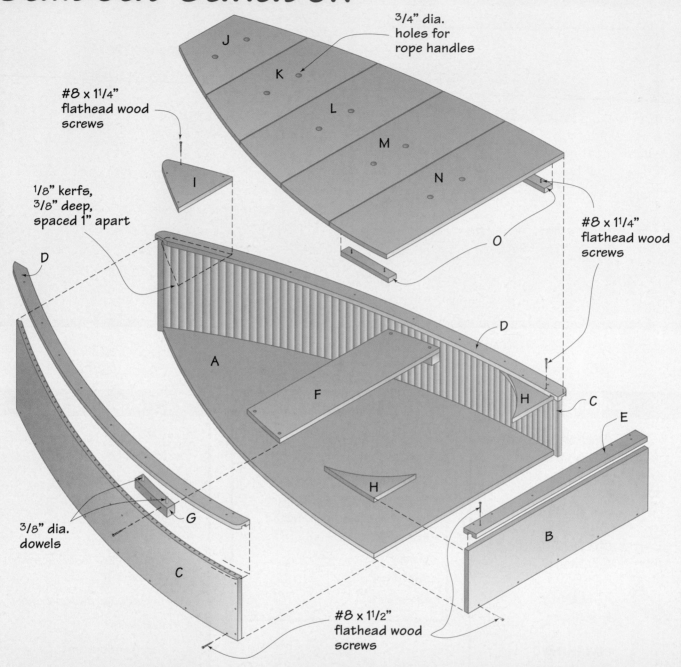

3/4" dia. holes for rope handles

#8 x 1¹⁄₄" flathead wood screws

1/8" kerfs, 3/8" deep, spaced 1" apart

#8 x 1¹⁄₄" flathead wood screws

3/8" dia. dowels

#8 x 1¹⁄₂" flathead wood screws

Sailboat Sandbox Cutting List

Part	No.	Size	Material	Part	No.	Size	Material
A. Bottom	1	¾ × 34½ × 57⅞ in.	Exterior plywood	I. Deck	1	¾ × 10 × 12* in.	Exterior plywood
B. Transom	1	¾ × 10⅜ × 34½ in.	"	J. Lid piece	1	¾ × 9⅞ × 21* in.	"
C. Sides	2	¾ × 15⅜ × 64* in.	"	K. Lid piece	1	¾ × 9⅞ × 28* in.	"
D. Side caps	2	¾ × 2¼ × 63* in.	"	L. Lid piece	1	¾ × 9⅞ × 32* in.	"
E. Transom cap	1	¾ × 2¼ × 33 in.	"	M. Lid piece	1	¾ × 9⅞ × 35* in.	"
F. Seat	1	¾ × 8 × 30½ in.	"	N. Lid piece	1	¾ × 9⅞ × 36* in.	"
G. Seat supports	2	1½ × 1½ × 8 in.	Treated lumber	O. Lid cleats	10	¾ × 2 × 8 in.	"
H. Knees	2	¾ × 8 × 10 in.	Exterior plywood	* Indicates oversized or curved workpieces			

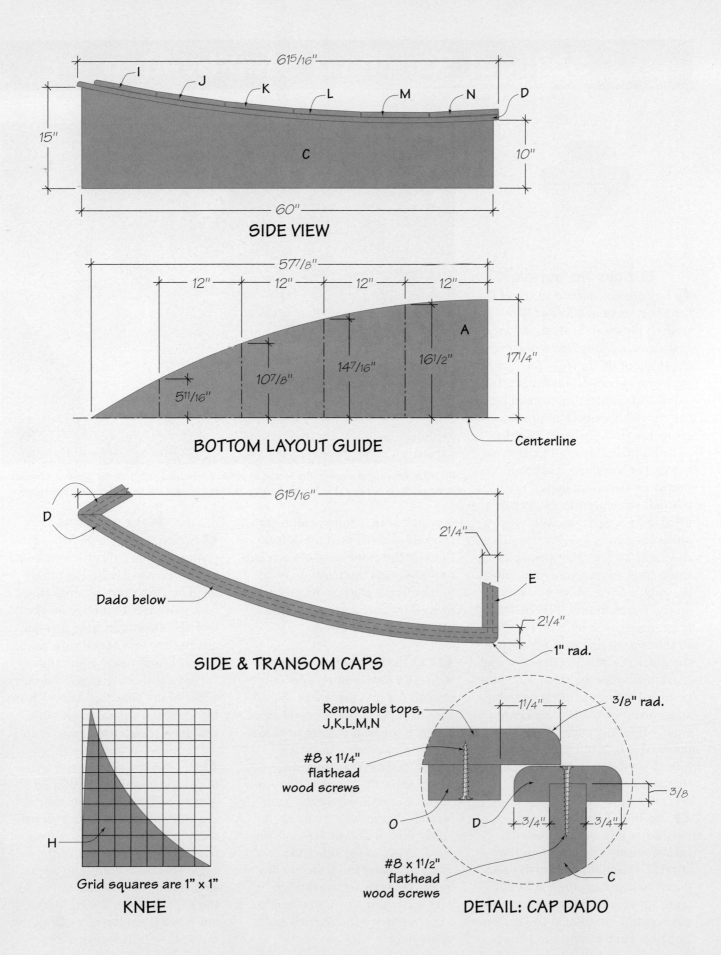

SIDE VIEW

61⁵/₁₆"

I J K L M N D

15"

C

10"

60"

BOTTOM LAYOUT GUIDE

57⁷/₈"

12" 12" 12" 12"

17¹/₄"

16¹/₂"

14⁷/₁₆"

10⁷/₈"

5¹¹/₁₆"

A

Centerline

SIDE & TRANSOM CAPS

61⁵/₁₆"

D

Dado below

2¹/₄"

E

2¹/₄"

1" rad.

KNEE

H

Grid squares are 1" x 1"

DETAIL: CAP DADO

Removable tops, J,K,L,M,N

3/8" rad.

1¹/₄"

#8 x 1¹/₄"
flathead
wood screws

O

D

3/8

3/4" 3/4"

#8 x 1¹/₂"
flathead
wood screws

C

CUT OUT THE BOTTOM

1 Lay out the curved shape of the boat bottom on a sheet of ¾-in. treated plywood. Starting at one end, draw a centerline along the sheet about 66 in. long. You'll measure and mark perpendicular lines across this centerline to establish the curved boat-bottom profile. Draw the first perpendicular line parallel to and about 3 in. in from the end of the sheet. This line marks the transom end of the boat bottom. Draw four more perpendicular lines at 12-in. intervals along the centerline, starting from the transom line. Plot points along these lines to give you your symmetrical curves. Make two marks on the transom line, 17¼ in. from the centerline in both directions, so the overall distance between the marks is 34½ in. Measure and mark points on the other four perpendicular lines using the dimensions given in the *Bottom Layout Guide* drawing, page 00. Make a mark 57⅞ in. from the transom line to establish the front tip of the boat bottom.

2 Use thin, flexible wooden battens to join the boat bottom layout marks and complete the curves. Drive pairs of finish nails partway into the plywood at both transom layout marks and at the boat bottom tip to hold the battens in place. Then gently bend the bat-

PHOTO A: Lay out the shape of the bottom by plotting measured points on the plywood. Connect these points by bending thin, flexible battens so they intersect the points to create the curves.

tens and tack a single nail near the rest of the layout mark locations so the outer edge of each batten intersects the plotted layout marks. Trace the curved profiles formed by the battens onto the plywood **(See Photo A)**.

3 Cut the boat bottom to shape with a jig saw, making one long, smooth cut for each curve. Be sure to support the plywood sheet beneath the boat bottom area and the larger surrounding sheet. Start the cuts from the transom. NOTE: *Make the jig saw cuts carefully. Once you remove the boat bottom, the cutout area on the larger plywood sheet becomes the inside edges of the side caps.* Then cut along the transom line on the boat bottom workpiece with a circular saw and straightedge to remove the narrow end wastepiece.

MAKE THE CAPS

4 Scribe the two side caps to shape. Set the rule of a combination square to 2¼ in. Rest the head of the square against the boat bottom cutout edge on the plywood sheet and hold a pencil against the end of the rule. Slide the rule and pencil along the curved cut lines to mark the outer edges of the side caps **(See Photo B)**. The caps should meet where you drew the centerline in Step 1.

5 Cut out the side caps. First make a straight cut with a jig saw along the centerline where the side caps meet. Doing so will create a miter joint at the front of the boat when you install the side caps. Then saw along the waste side of the curved lines to cut out the caps. Smooth the cut edges, but leave the mitered ends as they are so they'll fit together tightly.

6 Cut the transom cap to size from ¾-in. plywood. The cap ends should be square, and the width should match the side caps.

7 Rout a ¾-in.-wide, ⅜-in.-deep dado in the bottom faces of the side and transom caps so they'll fit over the top edges of the sides and the transom. Install a ½-in. straight bit in your router table. Raise the router bit ⅜ in. and set the fence ¾ in. away from the bit. Mount a featherboard to the fence, about ⅝ in. above the bit, to keep the caps held firmly against the router table. Rout a ½-in.-wide dado into both side caps, keeping the curved outer edges tight against the center of the fence as you make the cuts **(See Photo C)**. Cut a dado along one face of the transom cap and into a length of plywood scrap stock as well. Since the dadoes need to be ¾ in. wide to match the thickness of the sides and transom, readjust the router fence so it is 1 in. away from the router bit. Test this second fence setting by cutting the scrap piece first. Rout the second cuts on the three caps to complete the dadoes.

PHOTO B: Use a combination square set to 2¼ in. to draw the outlines of the side caps parallel to the cutout left after removing the boat bottom.

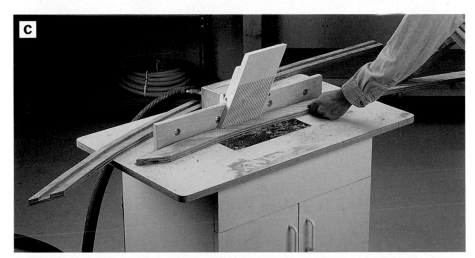

PHOTO C: Rout a dado in the side caps and transom caps. Use a featherboard as a hold-down to keep the parts tight against the router table where they pass over the bit.

Kerf-bending plywood

Cut ⅜-in.-deep parallel kerfs across both side panels to make the plywood bendable. A shop-built circular saw jig makes it easy to locate consecutive kerfs at regular measured marks down the panels. Construct a circular saw cutting jig to help align the saw blade with the kerf cut lines and to ensure accurate, parallel cuts. To build the jig, fasten a narrow (2- to 3-in.-wide) strip of ¾-in. plywood to a length of ¼-in. plywood about 12 to 14 in. wide. Assemble the parts so the ¼-in. plywood projects beneath the ¾-in. "fence" a distance greater than the width from the outer edge of your circular saw

base to the blade on the wide side of the saw base. The jig parts should be several inches longer than the width of the two boat sides clamped together. To prepare the jig for use, run the saw along the jig with the edge of its base against the ¾-in. strip, trimming the ¼-in. plywood to match your saw's exact width of cut. This way, you can use the edge of the ¼-in. plywood as a reference line for indexing the saw blade. Screw blocks to the ends of the jig so it seats tightly against the edges of your clamped-up side assembly.

PHOTO E: After attaching the transom to the bottom, glue and screw one side panel to the transom and to the bottom, placing countersunk screws every 6 to 8 in.

PHOTO F: Trim the first side you attach so the bow end matches the bottom curve angle. When you attach the second side, overlap the bow ends, and fasten the sides together with 1¼-in. galvanized screws.

MAKE THE SIDES

Exterior ¾-in. plywood is too stiff to bend and conform to the boat bottom curves. To accomplish this feat, we used a technique called *kerf bending* (See tint box, page 67). By cutting a series of parallel saw kerfs partway through each side piece, you can make the plywood bendable. The kerfs must be cut straight and at regular intervals in order for the plywood to bend in a smooth arc.

8 Cut rectangular blanks for the boat sides out of ¾-in. plywood, according to the dimensions given in the *Cutting List*, page 64.

9 To set up for the kerf cuts, clamp the two side blanks edge-to-edge with their ends flush. This way, you can mark and gang-cut the kerfs into both sides at once. Space the cuts 1 in. apart, marking kerf locations on the clamped-up workpieces. Align the circular saw jig with the first two kerf marks on the side assembly and clamp the jig in place. Set the saw's depth of cut to ⅝ in. and slide the saw along the jig to cut the first ⅜-in.-deep kerf. Shift the jig to the next set of kerf marks and cut the second kerf. Repeat this procedure across the length of the sides until all kerfs are cut **(See Photo D)**.

10 Cut the top edge profiles in the sides. Clamp the two sides together so the unkerfed faces point out-

ward. At the boat bow (front), make a pencil mark 15⅜ in. up from the bottom edge. Mark the stern (back) edge 10⅜ in. up from the bottom. Make a third layout mark 10¾ in. from the bottom, halfway along the length of the side. Tack nails temporarily at the layout marks, and connect these three layout marks with a flexible wood batten to form the curved top edge profile. Draw the profile on the top side piece. Gang-cut the curve along both sides with a jig saw, and smooth the cuts with a file or sanding block. Unclamp the sides.

ATTACH THE TRANSOM & SIDES TO THE BOTTOM

11 Cut the transom to size from ¾-in. plywood. Fasten the transom to the stern edge of the boat bottom using moisture-resistant wood glue and countersunk 1½-in. galvanized deck screws. Attach the transom so it overlaps the end of the boat bottom but sits flush with the bottom of the boat.

12 Attach one of the sides, starting at the stern of the boat. Apply moisture-resistant wood glue along the edges of both the transom and the bottom. Set the back edge of the side into position against the transom and bottom, overlapping both parts. Drive several countersunk 1½-in. screws through the side into the bottom and the transom. Keep the back edge of the side flush with the outer face of the transom. Work your way forward along the curved edge of the

PHOTO G: Attach the transom cap. Lay out and cut short, stopped dadoes on each side cap at right angles to the existing ones to allow them to seat over the transom at the ends of the transom cap. Cut one side cap to length and attach it to the side with glue and screws.

PHOTO H: Clamp the second side cap in place and use a combination square to scribe the cutoff length so the cap will be flush with the back edge of the transom cap. Trim the cap and fasten it in place.

boat bottom, attaching the side with screws placed every 6 to 8 in. **(See Photo E)**. When you reach the bow of the boat, the side should extend past the tip of the boat bottom.

13 Trim the front end of the side you just fastened at an angle that matches the curve of the opposite long edge of the boat bottom. Doing this will allow you to overlap the second side over the first side at the bow and create a solid joint. To lay out the cut, butt the head of your combination square against the end of the attached side near the boat bottom, and extend the rule until it touches the boat bottom edge. Draw a line along the inside face of the side, holding a pencil against the end of the rule and sliding the square along the front edge of the side from bottom to top. Draw a line across the width of the side panel at the top that matches the boat bottom angle, then extend a line down the outside face of the side to complete your bow-edge cutting line. Set your jig saw base to match the angle formed by the layout lines on the side panel, and trim the side panel flush with the tip of the boat bottom, starting at the top edge. Clean up the edge with a file or sander. Attach the other side panel with glue and screws, working from stern to bow as you did for the first side. When you arrive at the bow, overlap the first side. Mark and trim the second side flush with the outside face of the first side. Spread glue along the end of the first side and rein-

force the miter joint formed at the bow with galvanized 1¼-in. deck screws **(See Photo F)**. Ease and smooth the front edge with a sander.

INSTALL THE CAPS

14 Set the side caps in place first for reference, then fit the transom cap over the transom edge and between the two side caps. Fasten the transom cap to the transom with moisture-resistant wood glue and countersunk 1½-in. galvanized screws.

15 Install the side caps. Mark and trim one side cap to length so it fits flush with the back edge of the transom cap. Both side caps will need a short dado cut 90° to the long dado so the caps can fit over the ends of the transom. Clamp the side caps in place with their angled tips tight together, and mark the undersides where the short transom dadoes need to be cut. Rout these stopped dadoes, ¾ in. wide by ⅜ in. deep in the side caps. Clamp the side cap you trimmed to length and fasten it to the side panel with moisture-resistant glue and countersunk 1½-in. galvanized screws **(See Photo G)**. Clamp the other side cap in position so the miter at the bow end of the boat fits tightly. Mark the side cap where it should be trimmed to length at the stern **(See Photo H)**. Trim it to length and attach the cap with glue and screws. Use a belt sander to round the three outside corners of the caps to about a 1-in. radius. Ease the inside

PHOTO I: Clamp the seat to the seat supports with the seat supports screwed in place in the boat. Remove the seat assembly (the seat supports and the seat) and drill two ⅜-in.-dia. dowel holes in each end for mounting the seat to the supports.

PHOTO J: Set the lid sections in position, with ⅛-in. spacers between them, and trace the inside profiles of the side caps onto the bottom of each lid piece. You'll need these reference lines for aligning the lid cleats later.

and outside edges of the caps with a ⅜-in.-radius roundover bit.

INSTALL THE SEAT & KNEES

16 Cut the seat and two seat supports to size. Mark the location of the seat supports on the inside faces of the boat sides. The back edge of the seat should be 20 in. from the inside face of the transom and the top of the seat should be 8 in. above the bottom of the boat. Drill pilot holes (three screws per seat support) through the sides and into the seat supports. Fasten the seat supports temporarily to the sides with countersunk 1½-in. galvanized deck screws from the outside. Now fit the seat to the boat. Measure the distance across the width of the boat at the front and back of the seat supports and transfer these dimensions to your seat. Draw layout lines and make the angled cuts on the seat ends with a jig saw. Cut the seat slightly undersized so it fits loosely between the boat sides. It is designed to be removed if you want to create more playing space in the sandbox.

17 Clamp the seat to the seat supports and remove the seat assembly (both seat supports and seat) from the boat. Drill ⅜-in.-dia. dowel holes (2 in each end) through the seat and into the seat supports (**See Photo I**). Widen the dowel holes in the seat by rocking the drill bit from side to side. This way, the dowels won't swell up in the seat holes and lock it in place if they get wet. Remove the clamps and glue the dowels into the holes in the seat supports. Round over all exposed edges of the seat supports and the seat with a router and a ⅜-in.-radius roundover bit. Reattach the seat supports, this time using both glue and screws. Make sure the seat fits cleanly onto the seat supports.

18 Cut the two knee braces from ¾-in. plywood using the *Grid Drawing* on page 65 as a guide. Round over the curved edges of each knee brace with a router and a ⅜-in.-dia. roundover bit. Attach the knees in the corners of the stern beneath the transom and side caps with glue and 1¼-in. countersunk screws.

BUILD THE DECK & LID

19 Cut blanks for the deck and five lid pieces from ¾-in. plywood. Set the longest lid piece across the boat's width and over the side and back caps, keeping its back edge flush with the outside edge of the transom cap. Clamp the lid section in place. Reach inside the boat and trace the outline of the inside cap edges on this lid piece. Set successive smaller lid sections in place, inserting ⅛-in. spacers between each section. Trace the outline of the inside edges of the caps onto all lid parts **(See Photo J)**. Remove the lid pieces and lay them upside down on a flat surface, in the same order they were laid out on the boat. Draw a second set of reference lines on each lid piece 1¼ in. closer to the ends. The inside layout lines determine the location of the lid cleats, while the outside lines establish the final length of each lid section. Cut along the outside layout lines using a jig saw, and clean up the ends with a belt sander. Round over the curved outside top edges with a ⅜-in. roundover bit in a router.

㉔ Cut and install the deck. Place the lid pieces back on the boat with ⅛-in. spacers between them, and set the deck blank into position over the caps at the bow. Clamp the deck in position, and use the ends of the closest lid piece as references for keeping the deck overlap consistent with the rest of the lid sections. Outline the triangular deck board shape and cut it out with a jig saw. Round the sharp bow tip on the deck to a 1-in. radius. Ease the top edges of the deck with a ⅜-in. roundover bit. Attach the deck to the side caps with glue and 1½-in. countersunk galvanized screws, fastening the screws down through the deck board and into the side caps.

㉑ Cut lid cleats from ¾-in. scrap plywood. Glue and screw them to the undersides of the lid pieces, about ¼ in. inside the side cap reference lines. Use countersunk 1¼-in. screws **(See Photo K)**.

㉒ Drill pairs of ¾-in. guide holes, about 10 in. apart, through the lid sections for rope handles. Drill ¾-in.-dia. holes, spaced about 1 ft. apart, through the boat bottom to serve as weep holes for water drainage, if the sand should get wet.

FINISHING TOUCHES

㉓ Fill exposed fastener holes with auto body filler or exterior-grade wood putty. Sand all surfaces smooth and splinter-free. Prime and paint the sandbox and lid sections inside and out with two coats of exterior enamel paint. We chose a fairly complex painting scheme—you can paint the whole project one color if you prefer.

㉔ Feed a 2-ft. length of ½- or ¾-in.-dia. nylon rope through each pair of holes in the lid sections and knot the ends to form handles for the lids.

PHOTO K: Trim the curved ends of the lid sections. Glue and screw cleats to the inside faces. Place the cleats about ¼ in. inside the traced outlines of the side caps, so the cleats will fit between the side caps when the lid sections are set in place.

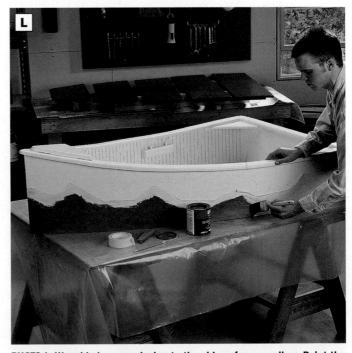

PHOTO L: We added a wave design to the sides of our sandbox. Paint the base color first, then use tape to mark the wave contours. Trim the tape with a utility knife. Remove the tape below the cut lines to form a clean edge above the waves. Paint the waves and remove the tape.

Sheet Goods Cart

Every shop can benefit by increasing storage and reducing clutter. If wall space is at a premium in your shop, our sheet goods cart is a clever alternative to permanent shelving. Made of inexpensive CDX plywood, the cart occupies only 12 square ft. of floor space, yet it provides ample storage for full-sized sheet stock, center shelves for longer boards and five bins of various widths for shorter cutoffs and scrap. The top shelf is perfect for storing containers of hardware or smaller tools, and one end of the cart sports notched holders for pipe or bar clamps. Casters allow you to roll the cart right where it's needed or out of the way entirely.

Vital Statistics: Sheet Goods Cart

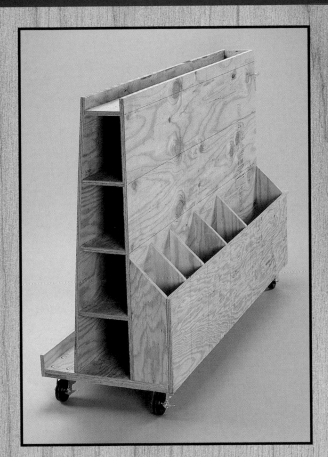

TYPE: Rolling storage cart

OVERALL SIZE: 53H x 72L x 24W at base

MATERIAL: CDX plywood

JOINERY: Dadoes, screwed butt joints

CONSTRUCTION DETAILS:

- Cart side that stores full sheets angled back 5° to keep sheets from tipping over
- Shelves between tall sides secured with dadoes and screws
- Storage bins separated by angled dividers
- Cart bottom reinforced with blocking to provide solid base for mounting casters
- Built-in clamp rack constructed from scrap CDX

FINISH: None

Building time

PREPARING STOCK
2 hours

LAYOUT
2-3 hours

CUTTING PARTS
3-4 hours

ASSEMBLY
2-3 hours

FINISHING
None

TOTAL: 9-12 hours

Tools you'll use

- Table saw
- Circular saw
- Drill/driver
- Sliding power miter saw (optional)
- Router and ¾-in. straight bit
- Jig saw
- Clamps
- Sockets

Shopping list

- ☐ (4) ¾ in. x 4 ft. x 8 ft. CDX plywood
- ☐ (16) ⅜ x 2-in. carriage bolts, nuts & washers
- ☐ (2) 4-in. straight casters
- ☐ (2) 4-in. swiveling casters with brakes
- ☐ #8 flathead wood screws (1¼-, 1½-, 2¼-in.)
- ☐ Wood glue

Sheet Goods Cart

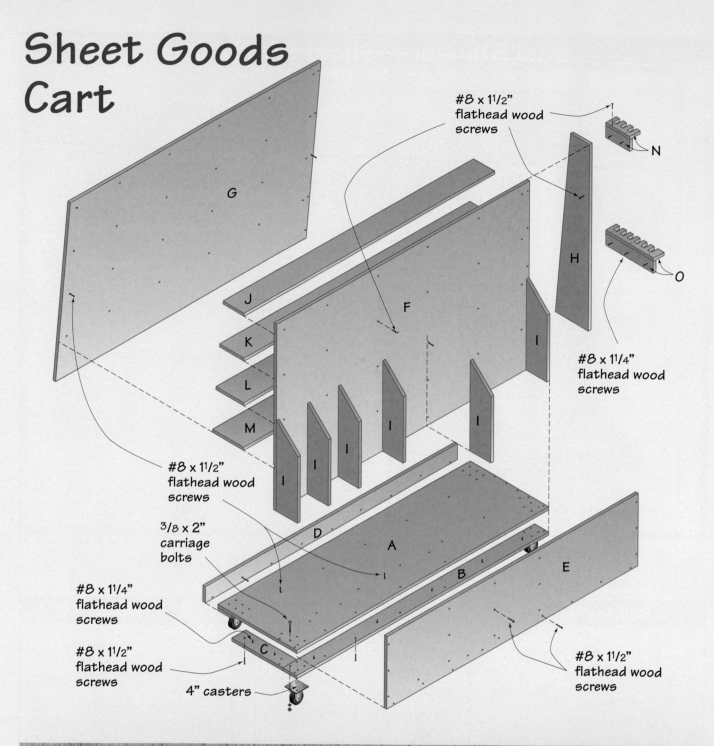

#8 x 1¹/₂"
flathead wood
screws

N

O

#8 x 1¹/₄"
flathead wood
screws

#8 x 1¹/₂"
flathead wood
screws

³/₈ x 2"
carriage
bolts

#8 x 1¹/₄"
flathead wood
screws

#8 x 1¹/₂"
flathead wood
screws

4" casters

#8 x 1¹/₂"
flathead wood
screws

Sheet Goods Cart Cutting List

Part	No.	Size	Material
A. Base	1	¾ × 22½ × 72 in.	CDX plywood
B. Blocking (long)	2	¾ × 4 × 72 in.	"
C. Blocking (short)	2	¾ × 4 × 14½ in.	"
D. Short edge	1	¾ × 4 × 72 in.	"
E. Tall edge	1	¾ × 18 × 72 in.	"
F. Vertical side	1	¾ × 46½ × 72 in.	"
G. Angled side	1	¾ × 46¾ × 72 in.	"
H. End	1	¾ × 9¾ × 46½ in.	

Part	No.	Size	Material
I. Divider	6	¾ × 6 × 22½ in.	CDX plywood
J. Top shelf	1	¾ × 6³⁄₁₆ × 71¼ in.	"
K. Shelf	1	¾ × 7³⁄₁₆ × 71¼ in.	"
L. Shelf	1	¾ × 8⅛ × 71¼ in.	"
M. Shelf	1	¾ × 9⅛ × 71¼ in.	"
N. Clamp holder	2	¾ × 3 × 7 in.	"
O. Clamp holder	2	¾ × 3 × 13¾ in.	"

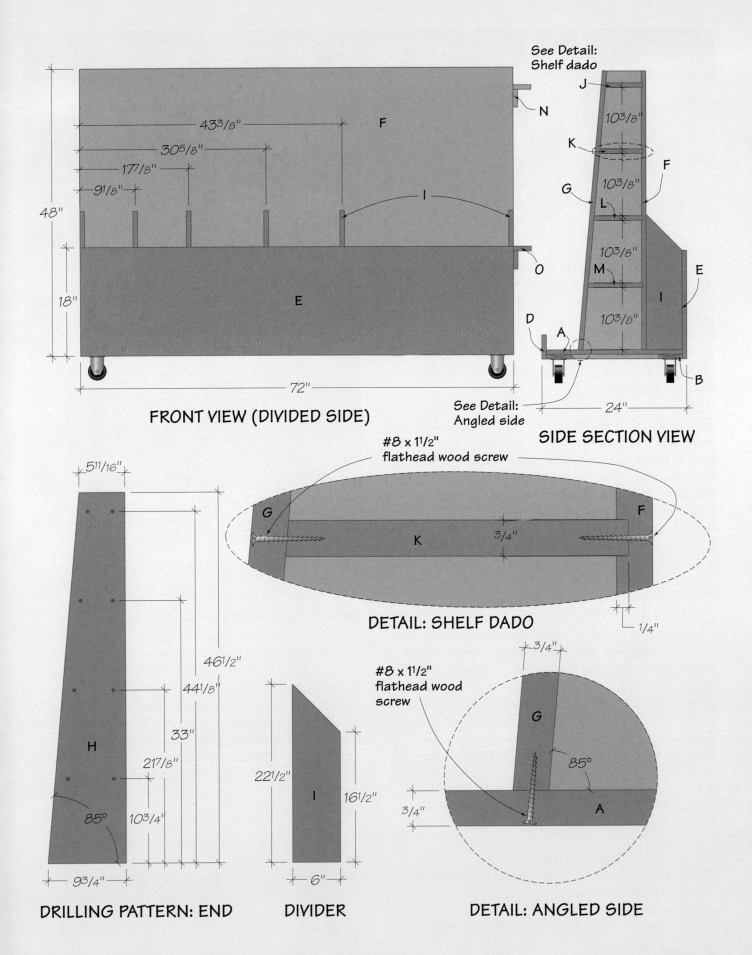

See Detail:
Shelf dado

43³/₈"

30⁵/₈"

17⁷/₈"

9¹/₈"

48"

18"

72"

F

I

E

N

O

FRONT VIEW (DIVIDED SIDE)

J

10³/₈"

K

10³/₈"

G

L

10³/₈"

M

10³/₈"

D

A

B

F

E

I

See Detail:
Angled side

24"

SIDE SECTION VIEW

#8 x 1¹/₂"
flathead wood screw

G

F

K

3/4"

1/4"

DETAIL: SHELF DADO

5¹¹/₁₆"

46¹/₂"

44¹/₈"

33"

21⁷/₈"

H

85°

10³/₄"

9³/₄"

DRILLING PATTERN: END

22¹/₂"

I

16¹/₂"

6"

DIVIDER

#8 x 1¹/₂"
flathead wood
screw

3/4"

G

85°

3/4"

A

DETAIL: ANGLED SIDE

BUILD THE BASE

1 Cut to size the base, bottom blocking and short and tall edge pieces from ¾-in. plywood. Use a circular saw and a straightedge guide for making the initial cuts to reduce full sheets to a more manageable size. (Remember to account for the offset between the blade and the saw foot as you line up the straightedge guide for your cuts.)

2 Lay the base on a flat worksurface and attach the short and long blocking to it. The ends of the short blocking pieces fit in between the longer blocking. Use glue and 1¼-in. flathead wood screws to fasten the parts **(See Photo A)**. Mark two reference lines along the length of the base on the blocking side to serve as centerlines for attaching the tall side pieces later. Draw a line for the angled side 5⅝ in. from one edge, and draw another line for the vertical side 6⅜ in. from the other edge.

3 Attach the short and tall edges to the base assembly using glue and 1½-in. flathead wood screws. Flip the base assembly over before attaching the edge pieces so the blocking faces down. Align the ends of the parts and make sure the bottoms of the edge pieces are flush with the bottoms of the blocking. Drill pilot holes first, spacing the screws about every 8 in. Alternate the screws between the base and blocking to increase the joint strength. Mark centerlines on the outside of the tall edge for fastening the dividers. See *Front View (Divided Side),* page 75, for locating the dividers. Position the outermost divider lines ⅜ in. from the ends of the tall edge.

INSTALL THE DIVIDERS

4 Cut the six dividers to size. Follow the measurements given on the *Divider* diagram, page 75, to mark the angled ends. We used a power miter saw to cut the dividers **(See Photo B)**, but you could also

PHOTO A: Attach the long and short blocking pieces to the bottom panel, flush around the perimeter, with glue and 1¼-in. flathead wood screws. Drill pilot holes for the screws first.

use a circular saw, table saw or hand saw to make these cuts.

5 Attach the dividers to the tall edge piece. The outer dividers are attached to the tall edge using glue and 1½-in. screws. Keep the outside faces of the outer dividers flush with the ends of the tall edge. Cut two scrap-plywood spacers, 8 and 12 in. wide, and insert a spacer between each pair of dividers as you attach the dividers with glue and screws **(See Photo C)**. Use the centerlines you drew on the outside of the tall edge for lining up the screws. Then, extend the divider centerlines down around the bottom blocking, and drive two 2¼-in. screws up through the cart base and into the bottom of each divider.

ASSEMBLE THE CENTER SECTION

6 Rip and crosscut the angled side and the four shelves to size. For each of these parts, tilt the saw blade 5° to create a bevel along one long edge. Mark the beveled edges on the parts to keep the orientation clear later.

PHOTO B: Cut the angled ends of the dividers. A power miter saw makes this task quick and easy, once you've established the cutting angle. You can also make these cuts with a jig saw, table saw or circular saw.

PHOTO C: Glue and screw the dividers to the tall edge with 1½-in. wood screws. Use scrap-wood spacers inserted between the dividers to establish divider spacing.

7 Cut the vertical side to size and rout the shelf dadoes into one face. The dadoes are ¾ in. wide and ¼ in. deep. Mark a set of long reference lines for each of the four dadoes using the *Side Section View*, page 75, to place the dadoes. Then, extend dado centerlines to the other face of the vertical side to serve as screw guide lines. Cut the dadoes with a router and a ¾-in. straight bit **(See Photo D)**. Clamp a straightedge on the vertical side to guide the router. To line up the guide, measure the distance from the edge of the router bit to the outer edge of the router base. This is the distance the straightedge must be offset from the closest marked dado line of each cut. Reset the straightedge for cutting each dado.

8 Attach the vertical side. Spread glue onto the edges of the dividers and clamp the vertical side in place so the dadoes face away from the dividers. Drive 1½-in. flathead wood screws through the vertical side into pilot holes in the two end dividers. Then, using your 8- and 12-in. spacers between the dividers as alignment aids, screw the vertical side to the inside dividers. Tip the cart assembly onto the face of the tall edge and drive 1½-in. screws along the vertical side reference line to attach the vertical side to the base.

PHOTO D: Cut shelf dadoes in the vertical side with a router and straightedge guide. Pull the router toward you as you make each cut, being careful to hold the router base tight against the straightedge as you work.

PHOTO E: Fasten the shelves to the vertical side with glue and screws. Support the shelves with scrap-wood spacers. Insert the square edge of the shelves into the dadoes, and keep the beveled edges facing up.

PHOTO F: Draw centerlines for the shelves on the angled side, then fasten the angled side to the shelves with glue and screws. Screw up through the bottom to attach the angled side from below.

9 Attach the shelves to the vertical side (**See Photo E**). Cut eight 10⅜-in.-long scrap spacers to support the ends of the shelves during assembly. Spread glue in the bottom dado and insert the square edge of the bottom shelf into the dado. With the divider side of the cart facing you, keep the end of the shelf flush with the left end of the vertical side. The dado joint for this bottom shelf will be fastened with glue only. Install this shelf so the beveled edge faces up (See *Detail: Shelf dado,* page 75) and clamp the shelf. Then, install the rest of the shelves into the dadoes with 1½-in. wood screws and glue. Arrange each shelf so the beveled edge faces up, and support the shelves with spacers. Make sure the left shelf ends are flush with the end of the vertical side.

10 Set the angled side against the shelves and clamp it in place temporarily. Draw shelf centerlines across the face of the angled side, then remove the shelf spacers. Glue and fasten the angled side to the shelves with 1½-in. screws (**See Photo F**). Screw the cart base to the angled side, following the angled side reference line you drew in Step 2.

11 Lay out and cut the end piece to size, using the measurements given in *Drilling Pattern: End,* page

75. Mark the screw locations on the end piece. Set the end piece into position on the end of the cart where the shelves are set back from the ends of the side panels. Attach the end piece to the ends of the shelves with glue and 1½-in. wood screws. Fasten the end piece with 2¼-in. screws driven up through the base and blocking.

INSTALL THE CASTERS

12 Tip the cart on its side and install the four casters. Lay the base of each caster in place on the blocking pieces and use the caster base holes to mark locations for carriage bolts. Position the casters so that all four corners of each caster rest firmly on the bottom blocking. Also, be sure the caster holes will not interfere with screws attaching the bottom blocking or dividers. Drill ⅜-in. pilot holes for each caster. Install the two straight casters on one end and swiveling casters on the other end, with the washers and nuts facing the caster wheels (**See Photo G**).

FINISHING TOUCHES

Expand the storage possibilities of your cart by adding clamp holders to one end. We made ours out of scrap CDX left over from the project. The holder configuration you choose will depend on the number,

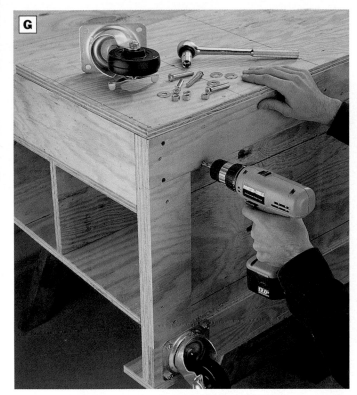

PHOTO G: Attach the casters. Mark bolt hole locations on the corners of the cart bottom, positioning the casters so they sit squarely on the bottom blocking. Drill the holes and bolt the casters in place, with the washers and nuts facing the cart bottom.

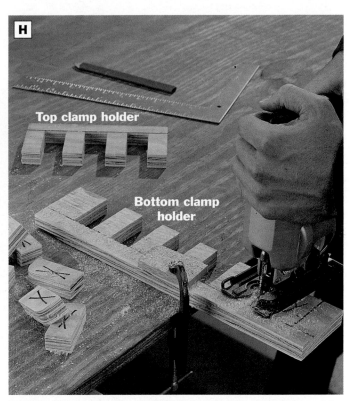

PHOTO H: Lay out the clamp holders and cut them to size. Notches 1 in. wide and 2 in. deep are a good size for holding standard pipe clamps. The bottom clamp holder can be made longer than the top, spanning across the end piece and the end divider.

style and length of clamps you have. We've designed the storage cart tall enough to hang several 4-ft.-long pipe or bar clamps without the clamps dragging on the floor. The bottom holder has additional cutouts for shorter clamps.

⑬ Make the clamp holders. Each clamp holder is composed of two parts that form an "L" when the parts are assembled. Mark cutouts on the top member of each holder and cut them out with a jig saw (**See Photo H**). For standard pipe clamps, 1-in.-wide cutouts 2 in. deep will hold each clamp securely. Assemble the holders with glue and 1½-in. screws. Then attach the holders to the closed end of the cart using glue and 1½-in. screws (**See Photo I**). Make sure to keep the top and bottom clamp holders aligned when fastening them to the cart so long clamps will hang straight.

⑭ Break all exposed sharp edges with sandpaper to minimize splinters. We chose not to apply any finish to our sheet goods cart, but you may prefer to dress yours up with a couple coats of enamel paint. If you plan to store veneered plywood sheets with finished faces on your cart, you may want to add strips of carpet to the face of the angled side to protect the veneer from scratches.

PHOTO I: Fasten the clamp holders to scrap blocking, and screw the blocking to the end of the cart with 1½-in. wood screws. Keep the slots aligned between the holders so the clamps will hang straight.

Entertainment Center

An entertainment center frequently is the focal point of a family room or rec room, so it's worth investing some time and money to build an interesting, attractive and efficient unit that's in proportion to your equipment and your room. Made mostly from cherry plywood, this armoire-style entertainment center combines an efficient footprint with elegant styling and rich wood tones.

Vital Statistics: Entertainment Center

TYPE: Television and stereo cabinet with storage

OVERALL SIZE: 56H × 44W × 24D

MATERIAL: Cherry plywood and solid cherry

JOINERY: Biscuit, dowel, miter, butt, screw, pocket screw

CONSTRUCTION DETAILS:

· Space for TV and four stereo components
· Drawers hold CDs, cassettes, videos
· Bifold doors permit complete access without protruding far into room
· Front and side face frames joined at corners to create thick upright members
· Lower side rails and back legs thickened with added plywood build-up

FINISH: Clear tung oil

Building time

PREPARING STOCK
2-4 hours

LAYOUT
2-4 hours

CUTTING
4-6 hours

ASSEMBLY
6-8 hours

FINISHING
2-4 hours

TOTAL: 16-26 hours

Tools you'll use

· Table saw
· Drill/driver
· Biscuit joiner
· Router and router table
· ³⁄₁₆-in. slot-cutting router bit
· Top-bearing flush-trim bit
· Chamfer bit
· ¼-in. straight bit
· Straightedge
· Pocket-screw drilling jig
· Jig saw
· Band saw
· Belt sander
· Drum sander
· Bar or pipe clamps
· Clamps
· Jointer
· Planer
· Dowel drilling jig
· Vix bit
· Screwdrivers

Shopping list

CHERRY PLYWOOD

☐ (1) ¼ in. × 4 ft. × 4 ft.
☐ (1) ¼ in. × 4 ft. × 8 ft.
☐ (1) ½ in. × 4 ft. × 4 ft.
☐ (1) ¾ in. × 4 ft. × 4 ft.
☐ (2) ¾ in. × 4 ft. × 8 ft.

☐ ⁴⁄₄ × 5 × 56 in. cherry
☐ (1) Cherry edge banding (50 ft.)
☐ (1) Cherry veneer (1½ in. × 8 ft.)
☐ (6) Non-mortising partial wrap hinges
☐ (6) Butt hinges
☐ (2) 1⅝-in. × 1½-in. cherry knobs
☐ (8) 20-in. drawer slides
☐ #8 × 1¼-in. flathead wood screws
☐ (1) ½-in. × 1⅝-in. × 1¾-in. magnetic catch
☐ #8 flathead wood screws (1-, 1¼-, 1½-in.)
☐ ⅜-in. dowels
☐ Biscuits (#0, #10, #20)
☐ Wood glue
☐ Finishing materials

Entertainment Center

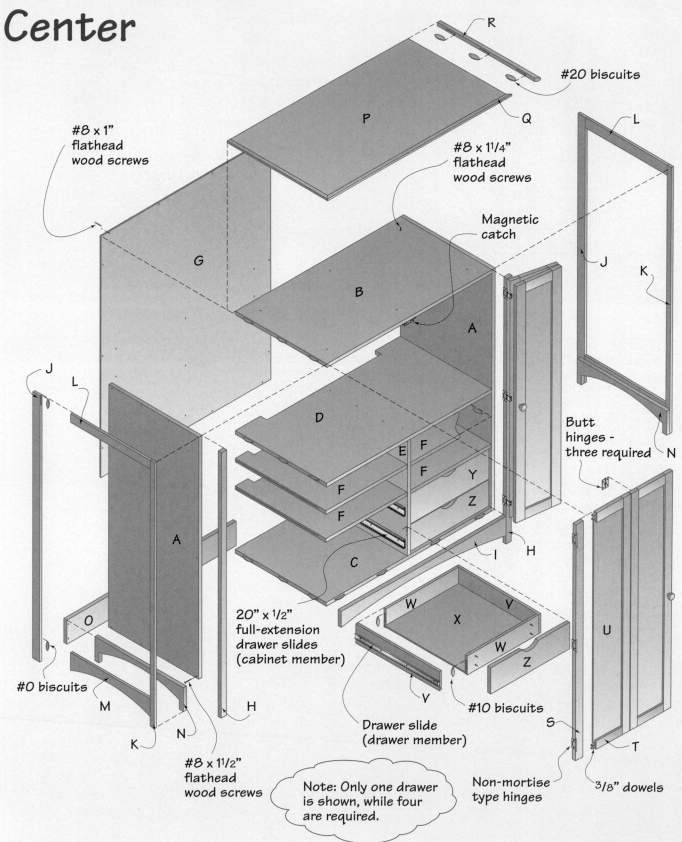

#8 x 1"
flathead
wood screws

#20 biscuits

#8 x 1¼"
flathead
wood screws

Magnetic
catch

R

Q

P

L

J

K

G

B

A

D

E F F

F

Y

F

Z

N

A

O

Butt
hinges -
three required

H

I

H

C

U

20" x ½"
full-extension
drawer slides
(cabinet member)

W V

X

W

Z

#10 biscuits

S

T

M

K N

#0 biscuits

#8 x 1½"
flathead
wood screws

Note: Only one drawer
is shown, while four
are required.

Drawer slide
(drawer member)

V

Non-mortise
type hinges

3/8" dowels

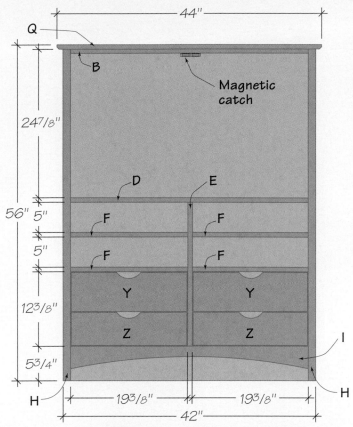

FRONT VIEW - DOORS REMOVED

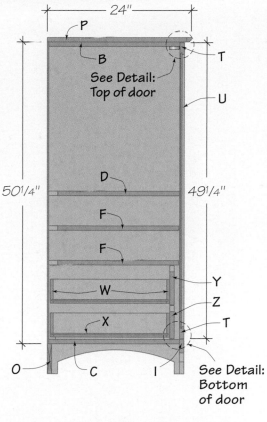

SIDE SECTION VIEW

Cabinet Cutting List

Part	No.	Size	Material
A. Sides	2	¾ × 21⅞ × 50¼ in.	Cherry ply
B. Top	1	¾ × 21⅞ × 39½ in.	"
C. Bottom	1	¾ × 21⅞ × 39½ in.	"
D. TV shelf	1	¾ × 21⅞ × 39½ in.	"
E. Vert. divider	1	¾ × 21⅞ × 23⅞ in.	"
F. Shelves	4	¾ × 21¾ × 19⅜ in.	"
G. Back	1	¼ × 41 × 50¼ in.	"
H. Front edge	2	⅞ × 1¼ × 55¼ in.	Solid cherry
I. Bottom rail	1	⅞ × 3¾ × 39½ in.	"
J. Back stile	2	½ × 1¾ × 55¼ in.	"
K. Front stile	2	½ × ⅞ × 55¼ in.	"
L. Top rail	2	½ × 2⅛ × 19½ in.	"
M. Bottom rail	2	½ × 3¾ × 19½ in.	"
N. Inner rail	2	¾ × 21⅜ × 5 in.	Cherry ply
O. Stretcher	1	¾ × 5 × 41 in.	"
P. Top core	1	¾ × 23¼ × 42½ in.	"
Q. Top trim	1	¾ × ¾ × 44 in.	Solid cherry
R. Side trim	2	¾ × ¾ × 24 in.	"

Doors Cutting List

Part	No.	Size	Material
S. Stile	8	¾ × 2 × 49¼ in.	Solid cherry
T. Rail	8	¾ × 2 × 5¾ in.	"
U. Panel	4	¼ × 6¼ × 45¾ in.	Cherry ply

Drawers Cutting List

Part	No.	Size	Material
V. Side	8	½ × 4 × 20 in.	Cherry ply
W. Front/back	8	½ × 4 × 17⁵⁄₁₆ in.	"
X. Bottom	4	¼ × 19½ × 17¹³⁄₁₆ in.	"
Y. Upper face	2	¾ × 6½ × 19⅛ in.	"
Z. Lower face	2	¾ × 5½ × 19⅛ in.	"

Grid squares are 1" x 1"

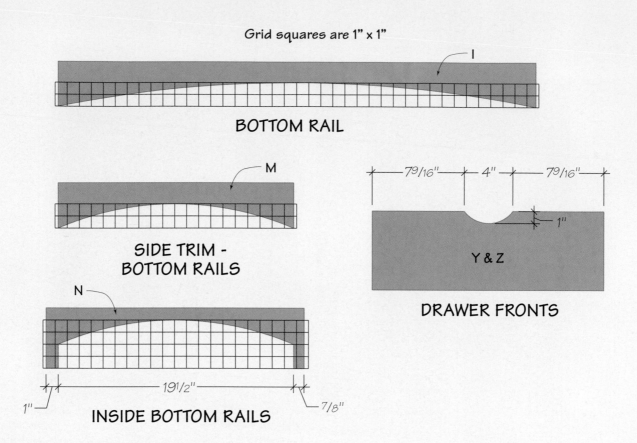

I

BOTTOM RAIL

M

**SIDE TRIM -
BOTTOM RAILS**

N

1"   19 1/2"   7/8"

INSIDE BOTTOM RAILS

7 9/16"   4"   7 9/16"

1"

Y & Z

DRAWER FRONTS

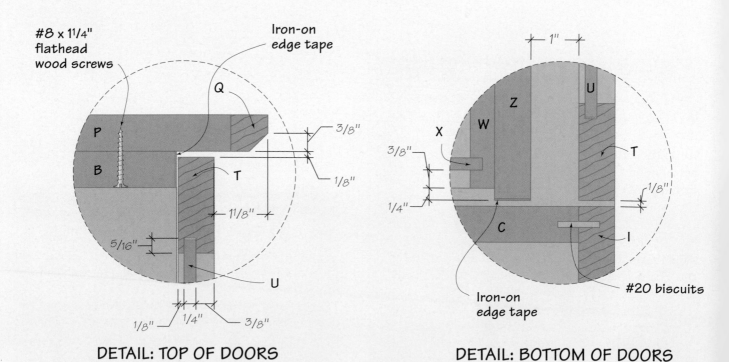

#8 x 1 1/4"
flathead
wood screws

Iron-on
edge tape

Q

P

B

T

3/8"

1/8"

1 1/8"

5/16"

U

1/8"   1/4"   3/8"

DETAIL: TOP OF DOORS

1"

U

Z

X

W

T

3/8"

1/4"

C

1/8"

I

Iron-on
edge tape

#20 biscuits

DETAIL: BOTTOM OF DOORS

NOTE: *The entertainment center described here was designed to accommodate common home electronic devices at the time of the publication of this book. Since the type and sizes of these devices changes regularly, it's always a good idea to measure the components you plan to keep in the entertainment center and make any needed adjustments to the shelf layout. As shown, the entertainment center will accept most television sets with a diagonal screen size of up to 27 in.*

BUILD THE CARCASE

❶ Cut the sides, top, bottom, TV shelf, vertical divider and component shelves to size from ¾-in. cherry plywood. On the inside face of each side, measure up 24⅝ in. from the bottom edge and mark reference points for the bottom edge of the TV shelf. With a straightedge, connect the points to create layout lines across the sides. Also measure and mark lines on the sides for the bottom edges of the component shelves, 13⅛ in. and 18⅞ in. up from the bottom. Then, mark corresponding lines on the vertical divider, 12⅜ in. and 18⅛ in. from the bottom. Mark a line on the top face of the bottom and the bottom face of the TV shelf, 19⅜ in. from the left end of each, for positioning the vertical divider.

❷ Cut slots for #20 biscuits in the faces of the sides, vertical divider, TV shelf and bottom; and in the edges of the TV shelf, component shelves and vertical divider **(See Photo A)**. Cut three slots per joint. Clamp a scrap plywood guide along the lines on the faces of the parts to register the base of the biscuit joiner against. Cut the mating slots in the edges of the parts. Using a pocket screw drilling guide (See page 19), drill a pocket screw hole in each end of each component shelf, for attaching the shelves to the vertical divider and the sides.

PHOTO A: Cut biscuit joints in the sides, top, bottom, TV shelf, vertical divider and component shelves. Clamp a strip of plywood along marked joint lines, as shown, to serve as a fence for cutting the joints.

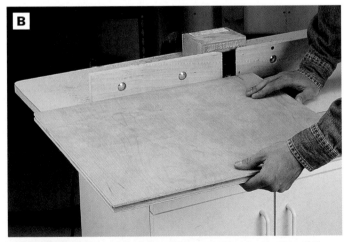

PHOTO B: Cut one long, continuous biscuit slot into each edge of the component shelves. Let the slot run clear through at the back edge, but stop it before the front edge so it doesn't show.

❸ For ease of assembly, connect the biscuit slots in each end of the component shelves into one long "sliding" slot. This will allow you to slide the shelves into position after the carcase is assembled. Install a 3⁄16-in. piloted slotting cutter in the router table. Set a component shelf on the router table and adjust the height of the cutters so they align with the centers of the biscuit slots already cut into the edges. Cut the slot 3⁄16-in. deep (this will be slightly shallower than the biscuit slot). Extend the biscuit slots—they can run out the back but not the front **(See Photo B)**.

4 Apply iron-on cherry veneer edge tape tothe front edges of the top, TV shelf, vertical divider, and component shelves (See page 20 for information on applying veneer edge tape). Use a sharp chisel or a hand trimmer to trim the overhanging tape flush with the faces and ends of the parts.

5 Make square-edged cutouts along the back edges of the TV shelf and the computer shelves for ventilation and for the electrical cords and cables to pass through. Make all cutouts 1½ in. deep. Center the TV shelf cutout so it's 6 in. from each end. The component shelf cutouts should run to 3 in. from each end. Make the cuts with a jig saw, then smooth the edges with sandpaper or a file.

PHOTO C: After all parts have been dry-fit, assemble the carcase with glue in the non-component shelf biscuit joints. Biscuits are already glued in place for the component shelves, but do not apply glue in the sliding slots on the shelves themselves.

6 To simplify assembly, glue #20 biscuits into the face slots of each joint now and clean up squeeze-out with a damp cloth. Before inserting the biscuits, use a belt sander or a stationary disc sander to trim about ⅛ in. off both edges of the component shelf biscuits. This way, the biscuits will fit into the shallower sliding slots in these shelves.

7 Before final assembly, dry-fit the carcase together so screw guide holes may be drilled in the correct positions. Before dry-fitting, mark a few reference lines for locating screw guide holes: Start by marking a reference line across the outside face of each side, at the centerpoint of the TV shelf, to serve as a screw placement guide. Also mark centerlines for the top and bottom, ⅜ in. from each end of both sides. Using a combination square, mark short vertical lines intersecting the centerpoint lines for the TV shelf. They should be located 1½ in.

PHOTO D: Complete the assembly by sliding the component shelves into place (but do not glue them). Drive in pocket screws to secure them.

from the back edge and ⅞ in. from the front edge, and will represent the boundaries of the area that you can place screws so the screw heads will be covered by the side trim stiles. The screws for the top and bottom can be placed all the way across, between the biscuits, since they will be covered by the side top and bottom rails. Drill countersunk screw pilot holes in your "safe" zones for the top, TV shelf and bottom.

❽ Mark screw centerlines on the TV shelf and bottom, and drill countersunk pilot holes for the vertical divider. On the TV shelf, position the first hole in far enough from the front edge so it will be covered by the TV. Locate the screw holes so they'll miss the biscuits.

❾ Cut the back panel out of ¼-in. cherry plywood, then dry-assemble the cabinet carcase. Assemble the TV shelf, vertical divider and bottom first. Fasten the parts together with 1½-in. screws. Then, add the sides and top and fasten them with screws driven through the guide holes. Make sure the front edges of all parts are flush with each other. Put the back into place against the rear edges of the parts. Use the back to square up the cabinet by flushing it up all around. Secure the back with 1-in. countersunk screws.

❿ With a pencil, trace the location of the vertical divider onto the inside face of the back panel. Slide the two upper component shelves into place along the preinstalled biscuits until the shelves strike the back (they should be inset ⅛ in. from the front edges of the sides and the vertical divider). Trace the shelf locations on the inside of the back, then remove

PHOTO E: Glue up the side trim frames with #0 biscuits in the joints. Pad the clamp jaws to protect the wood.

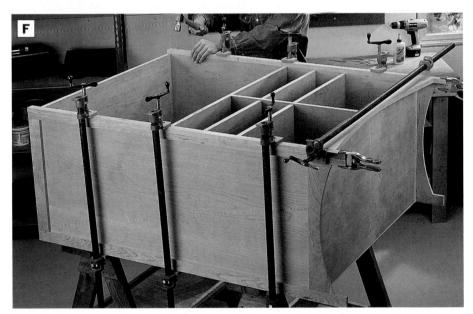

PHOTO F: Attach the front face frame parts (front edges and bottom rail) to the cabinet with glue and #20 biscuits. Clamp the parts and drive in finish nails.

the upper shelves and repeat with the two lower component shelves. Don't bother installing the pocket screws until final assembly. Make any adjustments necessary so all parts fit correctly, then disassemble the entire carcase.

⓫ Drill countersunk screw pilot holes at the marked locations in the back for attaching the vertical divider and component shelves. Finish-sand the interior faces of all parts up to 220-grit sandpaper and ease all sharp edges. Then, reassemble the carcase (See

Photo C) with glue in most joints. Apply glue sparingly so there will be little, if any, squeeze-out to clean off. Do not glue the component shelves: you'll find it much easier to remove them for finishing later than to try and apply finish in the small cubbies created by the shelves. Secure the component shelves temporarily with 1¼-in. pocket screws (**See Photo D**).

MAKE & ATTACH THE FACE FRAME & THE SIDE TRIM

⓬ Rip and crosscut to size the side trim back stiles, front stiles,

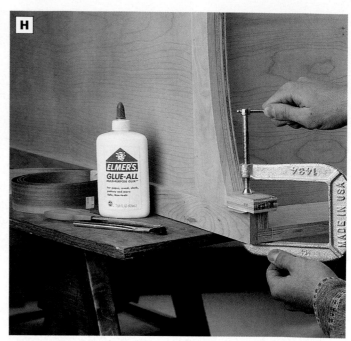

PHOTO G: Glue the inside bottom rails and clamp them to the side trim parts with spring clamps. Then, glue and screw the back stretcher to the ends of the inside bottom rails.

PHOTO H: To give a finished look to the back legs, veneer their inside faces with cherry veneer strips. Use white or yellow glue and a scrap block as a caul.

top rails and bottom rails from ¾-in.-thick solid cherry. Lay out an arc on one of the bottom rails, using the grid pattern on page 84 as a guide. You can achieve this by enlarging the diagram, or by marking the centerpoint of the arc 1¾ in. down from the top edge and springing a thin wood strip to a smooth curve intersecting the bottom corners and this centerpoint. Cut out the arc on your band saw or with a jig saw and smooth the edge with a drum sander attachment mounted in your drill press. Use this part as a pattern for laying out and cutting the other bottom rail.

⓭ Lay out and cut slots for #0 biscuits that will join the two side trim frames. Glue and clamp up the two frames (See Photo E). Clean excess glue from the joints with a damp cloth.

⓮ Finish-sand the outer faces of the carcase sides and the outer faces and inner edges of the side trim frames. Then attach the frames to the sides of the cabinet with glue and finish nails. Align the front edges of the frames with the front plywood edges of the carcase. The tops of the frames and the carcase should also be flush. Set the nails below the wood surface with a nailset.

⓯ Rip the front edges and bottom rail to width from ⅞-in. solid cherry, and crosscut to length. Lay out an arc on the bottom rail as you did with the side bottom rails. Cut it out on a band saw and smooth out the

saw marks with a drum sander. Lay out and cut slots for #20 biscuits for attaching the front edges to the front of the cabinet. The inside edges should be flush with the inside faces of the cabinet sides. Also, lay out and cut #20 biscuit slots for attaching the bottom rail—its top edge should be flush with the top face of the cabinet bottom.

⓰ Glue the parts to the cabinet with bar or pipe clamps (See Photo F). Use a spring clamp or small quick-action clamp to squeeze the parts together at the bottom "legs." Drive in finish nails and set them below the surface with a nailset. Clean off any glue squeeze-out.

⓱ Cut the inside bottom rails and back stretcher to size from ¾-in. cherry plywood. Position the inside bottom rails in place, up against the inside faces of the side trim bottom rails, with their front ends butted against the inside face of the front bottom rail. Trace the outline of the arc and legs onto each of the inside bottom rails. Cut close to the lines with a band saw or jig saw. Then glue the parts in place, securing them temporarily with spring clamps. Glue the L-joints at the back ends of the side bottom rails and put the back stretcher in position. Fasten it into the ends of the inside bottom rails with countersunk screws (See Photo G). After the glue has dried, use a router with a top-bearing flush-trim bit to trim the overhanging edges of the inside bottom rails to match the solid wood shapes (See *Tip,* page 131). Now you've created thick back "legs," but some plywood edges will be exposed. To give them a seamless, one-piece look, glue lengths of 1½-in-wide cherry veneer over the exposed edges, using a block of scrap wood as a caul **(See Photo H)**. When the glue is dry, trim the overhanging veneer with a sharp chisel or a hand edge trimmer.

MAKE & ATTACH THE TOP

18 Cut the top core to size from ¾-in. cherry plywood. Rip the front edge and side edges to width from solid cherry, leaving them a little long. Miter-cut the edges to fit around the top core. Cut slots for #20 biscuits to keep the parts aligned during glue-up. Glue the joints and the miters, and clamp the edges to the core with padded bar or pipe clamps. Wipe off glue squeeze-out.

19 Cut a ⅜-in. chamfer on the undersides of the front and side edges with a router and a chamfer bit. Finish-sand the top surface and the perimeter of the bottom surface (where it will overhang) up to 220-grit sandpaper. Center the top on the cabinet, keeping the back edge of the top flush with the back surface of the cabinet. Attach the top with screws driven up through the inside surface of the carcase top **(See Photo I)**.

BUILD & HANG THE DOORS

20 In order for the doors to fit properly, they must not be cupped or twisted. Therefore, it is imperative that the stiles and rails are flat. Since premilled lumber is hardly ever flat, you should really mill your own ¾-in. wood from 4/4 or 5/4 rough cherry (See *Tip,* page 49). Once you have reduced the stock to ¾ in. thick, rip and cross-

PHOTO I: After the top has been edged with solid wood and chamfered, attach it to the carcase with screws driven up from inside the cabinet.

PHOTO J: Cut dadoes for the door panels into the inside edges of the door stiles and rails. Use a fence and a ¼-in. straight bit. The dadoes in the stiles must be stopped at the dowel joint.

cut the door stiles and rails to size. *TIP: For a decorative touch, see if you can cut pairs of rails and stiles that butt against each other out of the same board so the grain matches.*

21 Use a dowel drilling jig as a guide for boring holes for two ⅜-in.-dia. dowels per joint, in all the door frame parts. Then install a ¼-in. straight bit in your router table and, using a fence as a guide,

PHOTO K: With each pair of doors clamped together, mount three butt hinges to each pair along the middle joint. Drill screw pilot holes through the guide holes in the hinge plate, using a Vix bit.

PHOTO L: Attach the bi-fold door pairs to the cabinet with non-mortise wrap hinges. Use three per door, positioned on the doors at the same heights as the middle joint hinges.

PHOTO M: Assemble the drawers with glue and #10 biscuits. Use padded bar clamps or long quick-action clamps. Adjust the clamps as necessary to square up the drawers.

cut a ¼-in.-dia. × ⁵⁄16-in.-deep dado in the inside edge of each rail and stile to create recesses for the door panels (See Photo J). Position the dado on the edge as shown in the Detail diagram on page 84. The dadoes can run through the rails, but must be stopped no more than 1⅝ in. from the ends of the stiles. Glue ⅜ × 1½-in. dowels into the ends of the rails and clean off any glue squeeze-out.

㉒ Cut the door panels to size from ¼-in. cherry plywood. Dry-assemble each door to make sure the parts fit together properly. Finish-sand the door panels and the inside edges of the stiles and rails (except the ends of the stiles where the joints are). Glue the joints and clamp up the doors on a flat surface, using pipe clamps or quick-action clamps. Make sure the door assemblies are flat and square. After the glue has dried, finish-sand the outer surfaces of the door frames.

㉓ In order to install the middle bi-fold hinges, clamp the left pair of doors together, side by side with ⅛-in. spacers between them; and do the same for the right pair. Their inside faces should be facing up. Face-mount three butt hinges to each pair of doors along the middle joint, following the hinge manufacturer's instructions (See Photo K). Install the top and bottom hinges 2 in. from each end. The center hinges should be positioned 24½ in. up from the bottoms of the doors.

㉔ Attach the door pairs to the sides of the cabinet with non-mortising wrap hinges (See Photo L). Install three hinges per door at the same heights as the middle hinges. Position the doors on the cabinet, allowing a consistent ⅛-in. gap at the top and bottom of each door. Mount the knobs and touch latches and test the operation of the doors, making adjustments as necessary.

BUILD & HANG THE DRAWERS
㉕ Cut the drawer sides, fronts and backs from ½-in. plywood (we used birch because it's cheaper than cherry, but you can use just about any hardwood veneer plywood). Cut the drawer bottoms to size. Cut a ¼-in.-wide × ⁵⁄16-in.-deep dado in the sides, fronts and backs, ⅜ in. up from their bottom edges, to create recesses for the drawer bottoms. Cut the dado on your table saw or on your router table using a ¼-in. straight bit. Don't worry that the through-dadoes will show on the assembled drawers. They will be covered by the applied drawer fronts. Cut slots for #10

biscuits for attaching the sides to the fronts and backs. The sides overlay the fronts and backs, as shown in the drawing on page 84. Apply iron-on cherry edge tape to the top edges of the fronts, backs and sides. Trim the tape with a chisel or an edge trimmer.

26 Glue biscuits into the ends of the fronts and backs and clean off excess glue. Finish-sand the interior surfaces of the drawer parts. Assemble the drawers with glue and clamps **(See Photo M)**. Check for squareness and adjust the clamps as necessary. Wipe out any excess glue. When dry, remove the clamps and sand the outside surfaces and top edges.

27 Mount the drawer slides to the drawers, ⅜ in. up from the bottom edges of the drawers. Mark and drill screw guide holes, and attach the slides with the screws provided, according to the manufacturer's instructions. Mount the mating parts of the slides to the interior of the cabinet. Locate the lower slides ⅜ in. up from the cabinet bottom, and the upper slides 5¾ in. from the cabinet bottom. *Tip: If you only install screws in the slotted slide holes first, you can adjust the drawers in the cabinet a bit before installing the rest of the screws permanently.* Slide the drawers into place.

28 Cut the upper and lower drawer fronts from ¾-in. cherry plywood. Lay out centered, scalloped cutouts along the top edge of each drawer front to serve as drawer pulls. Make each shallow arc 4 in. wide by 1 in. deep. Make the cuts with a band saw and clean up the edges with a drum sander. Apply iron-on edge tape to all edges of the drawer fronts and trim off excess. Finish-sand the drawer fronts to 220-grit.

29 Mount the drawer fronts to the drawers with 1-in. pan-head screws, driven from inside the drawer box **(See Photo N)**. Mount them temporarily with double-stick tape and align them with an even ⅛-in. gap all around. When the drawers are positioned correctly, drill screw pilot holes through the drawers and into the drawer fronts. Then, remove the fronts and enlarge the holes in the drawer boxes so they are a bit oversized. This will permit some adjustment of the

PHOTO N: After the drawers have been installed in the cabinet, attach the drawer fronts with 1-in. pan-head screws. The drawers should be aligned so the gaps around the drawer fronts are even.

fronts once they are mounted before fully tightening the screws.

FINISHING TOUCHES

30 Inspect the project for unsanded areas, scratches and glue; and touch these spots up as necessary. Remove hardware and slide out the component shelves. Apply the finish (we used three coats of clear tung-oil).

31 Reinsert the shelves; reattach the hardware. To keep CDs, cassettes and video tapes from banging around when the drawers are opened or shut, we installed plastic organizer inserts in the drawers. You can find these inserts at most woodworking stores and in woodworking catalogs.

32 Install the television and components in their compartments. You will need to drill a hole or two through the back of the cabinet with a hole saw for the electrical and speaker wires to exit.

Hallway Bookcase

Straightforward to build and a practical solution for adding hallway storage space, this contemporary bookcase may be just the impetus you need for organizing those photo albums, encyclopedias and book collections. Our painted MDF bookcase provides nearly 3 ft. of display space per shelf, but its angled front profile and slender 10-in. depth allow it to nestle conveniently along the wall of even a narrow hallway. The shelves tip back slightly to keep items from toppling off if they should get brushed by passersby. We've customized the bookcase design with knockdown hardware so it can be easily disassembled for storage.

Vital Statistics: Hallway Bookcase

TYPE: Bookcase

OVERALL SIZE: 60H x 36W x 10D

MATERIAL: MDF, solid poplar

JOINERY: Rabbet and butt joints

CONSTRUCTION DETAILS:

· Unit is easily assembled and disassembled with "knockdown" mechanical fasteners
· MDF panels are paint-ready and require no edge banding
· Solid-wood shelf stiffeners prevent the shelves from sagging
· Angled front profile adds a contemporary look

FINISH: Primer and enamel paint

Building time

PREPARING STOCK
1 hour

LAYOUT
1-2 hours

CUTTING PARTS
2-3 hours

ASSEMBLY
2-3 hours

FINISHING
1-2 hours

TOTAL: 7-11 hours

Tools you'll use

· Table saw
· Circular saw with straightedge guide
· Combination square
· Drill press
· Router
· ½-in.-rad. piloted roundover bit
· ½-in. piloted rabbeting bit or straight bit & router edge guide
· Dado-blade set (optional)
· Biscuit joiner (optional)
· Drill/driver
· Pocket-screw jig

Shopping list

☐ (1) ¾ in. × 4 ft. × 8 ft. MDF
☐ ½ × 35½ in. × 5 ft. MDF
☐ (1) ¾ × 1½ in. × 16 ft. poplar
☐ (20) mechanical fasteners
☐ #8 × 1¼-in. flathead wood screws
☐ #20 biscuits (optional)
☐ 1¼-in. pocket screws
☐ Wood glue
☐ Finishing materials

Hallway Bookcase

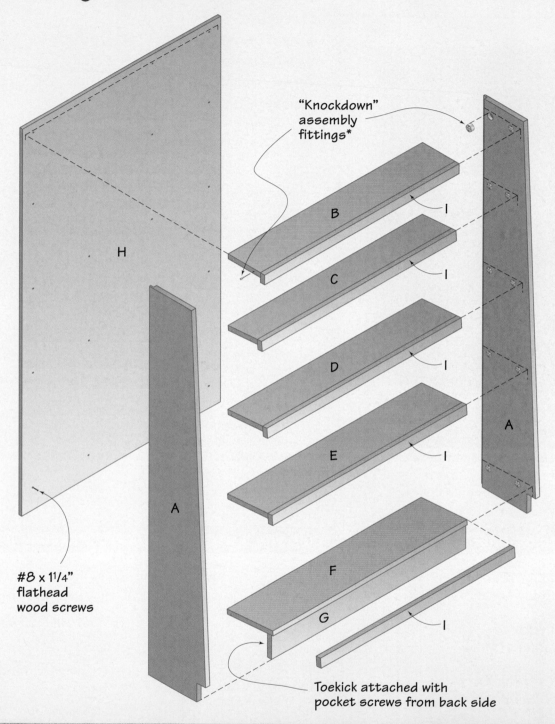

"Knockdown" assembly fittings*

B

C

D

E

F

G

I

I

I

I

I

H

A

A

#8 x 1¹/₄"
flathead
wood screws

Toekick attached with
pocket screws from back side

Hallway Bookcase Cutting List

Part	No.	Size	Material	Part	No.	Size	Material
A. Sides	2	¾ × 10 × 60 in.	MDF	**F.** Bottom	1	¾ × 8¼ × 34½ in.	MDF
B. Top	1	¾ × 5¾ × 34½ in.	"	**G.** Toekick	1	¾ × 3¾ × 34½ in.	"
C. Shelf	1	¾ × 5¼ × 34½ in.	"	**H.** Back	1	½ × 35½ × 59¾ in.	"
D. Shelf	1	¾ × 6¼ × 34½ in.	"	**I.** Shelf stiffeners	5	¾ × 1½ × 34½ in.	Poplar
E. Shelf	1	¾ × 7¼ × 34½ in.	"	* Blum-brand barrel-type fasteners			

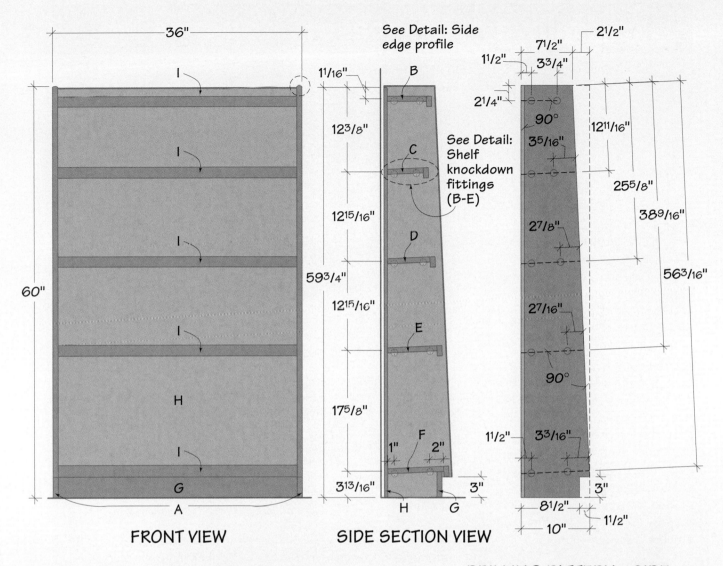

36"

I

60"

I

I

I

H

I

G

A

FRONT VIEW

See Detail: Side edge profile

1 1/16"

B

12 3/8"

C

See Detail: Shelf knockdown fittings (B-E)

12 15/16"

D

59 3/4"

12 15/16"

E

17 5/8"

F

1"   2"

3 13/16"

3"

H   G

SIDE SECTION VIEW

2 1/2"

7 1/2"

1 1/2"

3 3/4"

2 1/4"

90°

12 11/16"

3 5/16"

25 5/8"

38 9/16"

2 7/8"

2 7/16"

56 3/16"

90°

1 1/2"

3 3/16"

3"

8 1/2"

1 1/2"

10"

DRILLING PATTERN - SIDE

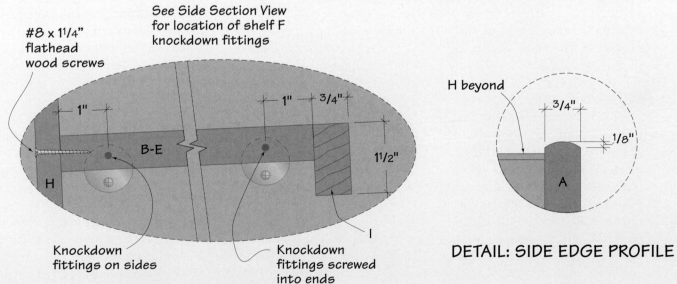

#8 x 1 1/4" flathead wood screws

See Side Section View for location of shelf F knockdown fittings

1"

1"   3/4"

B-E

1 1/2"

H

I

Knockdown fittings on sides

Knockdown fittings screwed into ends

H beyond

3/4"

1/8"

A

DETAIL: SIDE EDGE PROFILE

DETAIL: SHELF KNOCKDOWN FITTINGS DRILLING PATTERN (B-E)

CONSTRUCT THE SIDES

1 Cut the sides to size from ¾-in. MDF. A carbide-tipped plywood or panel-cutting blade works best for cutting MDF. Use the *Drilling Pattern-Side* drawing, page 95, as a guide for laying out the angled profile along the front edge of each side. The top edge of each side is 7½ in. wide. Use a straightedge to draw a line connecting this point with the lower front corner on one side piece. Now clamp the two sides together with the marked side facing out. Gang-cut the angled front profiles using a circular saw and a straightedge guide. Unclamp the side panels.

2 Lay out the toekick notches in the bottom front corner of each side using the measurements in the drawing. The notch is 3 in. high and 1½ in. deep.

3 Mark locations for the barrel-shaped knockdown housings that will be inset into the sides to support the top, shelves and bottom. The top is perpendicular to the *back* edge of the sides, so measure 2¼ in. down along the back edge and draw a line across the width of each side panel with a combination square. Use the *Drilling Pattern-Side* drawing, page 95, as a guide for laying out knockdown hardware positions for the shelves and bottom. Measure down from

PHOTO A: Mark centerlines for locating the mechanical fasteners in the side panels. Use a combination square to draw lines perpendicular to the front edges of the sides for the shelves and bottom.

the top front corner of each side and make a reference mark for each shelf and the bottom. The three shelves and bottom are perpendicular to the *front* edge, so use a combination square registered against this edge to extend the centerlines across the width of each side **(See Photo A)**.

4 Locate centerpoints for drilling holes for the knockdown housings along the layout lines you drew in Step 3. The rear fittings are 1½ in. in from the back edge of each side for the top and shelves and 1 in. for the bottom. To establish the front hole for the top, measure over 3¾ in. from the rear hole centermark. Measure from the front edge of the sides to determine front hole drilling locations for the

shelves and bottom. The shelf hole placement varies.

5 Drill the knockdown housing holes on a drill press. The Blum-brand fasteners we used require a 25-mm Forstner bit, set to drill ½-in.-deep holes. Test the drilling setup on a piece of ¾-in. scrap first. Drill all the holes in both sides **(See Photo B)**. Clamp each side panel to the drill press when drilling these holes. NOTE: *If you don't own a drill press, you could also drill these holes with a right-angle drilling guide and a portable drill. Be sure to mark the bit depth with a strip of masking tape so you don't inadvertently drill too far.*

6 Cut out the toekick notch at the base of each side with a jig saw

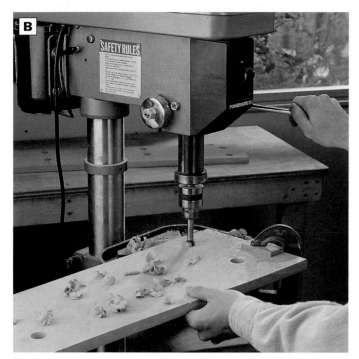

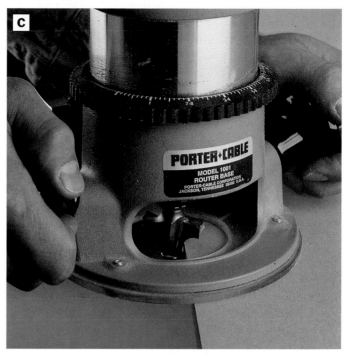

PHOTO B: Drill 25-mm holes for the mechanical fasteners, ½ in. deep into the side panels, using a Forstner bit in the drill press. Clamp each side panel to the drill press table to steady the parts as you drill.

PHOTO C: Ease the top and front edges of the side panels using a router with a piloted ½-in. roundover bit. Center the bit's bearing across the thickness of the panel to form a ⅛-in. "thumbnail" roundover.

and a fine-tooth blade to avoid chipping the cut edges. Sand the edges smooth.

7 Ease the top and front edges of the sides. To accomplish this, install a ½-in. piloted roundover bit in your router. Set the bit depth so the bearing rides along the stock about halfway across its thickness. This bit setting should produce a roughly ⅛-in.-rad. "thumbnail" roundover profile. Test the setup on a piece of ¾-in. scrap MDF to determine the appropriate bit setting. Rout this profile along the top and front edges of both sides (**See Photo C**). Smooth the profiles with sandpaper.

8 Cut rabbets along the inside back edges of the sides to house the bookcase back panel. Cut these rabbets with a piloted ½-in. rabbeting bit or a straight bit and edge guide. You could also cut these rabbets on the table saw with a dado-blade set. The rabbets extend the full length of the sides.

PREPARE THE TOP, BOTTOM & SHELVES

9 Cut the top, bottom and shelves to size. Drill holes for the knockdown connector pins in the ends of these parts. One way to ensure that your holes are straight and square is to drill these holes on a drill press with the table turned vertically and the part clamped flat against it (**See Photo D**). Tilt the drill press table and adjust it for plumb with a level. Use a 3⁄16-in. drill bit and a depth stop to drill two 1⅛-in.-deep holes in the end of each part, centered on the thickness of the boards. Locate the rear holes 1 in. from the back edge of each workpiece. On all parts but the bottom, the front holes should also be placed 1 in. from the front edges. Drill the front holes in the bottom 2 in. from the front edge.

10 Rip and crosscut five shelf stiffeners from ¾-in.-thick poplar. Clamp the stiffeners to the top, bottom and shelf panels, making

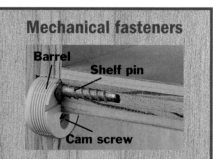

Mechanical fasteners

Barrel

Shelf pin

Cam screw

The top, bottom and shelves of this bookcase are attached to the sides with knockdown (KD) mechanical fasteners, often called RTA (ready-to-assemble) fittings. The hardware consists of a barrel-shaped plastic housing with a cam-style screw that fits into a 25-mm hole drilled into the vertical member of the joint. A coarse-threaded pin, fastened into the edge or end of the horizontal joint member, slides into a hole above the cam screw in the knockdown housing. By turning the cam screw clockwise, it intersects with the shelf pin, locking the joint parts together. To unlock the joint, simply turn the cam screw counterclockwise to release the pin. Knockdown hardware is a good solution for furniture that may need to be disassembled from time to time. Driving and removing ordinary screws would quickly strip screw threads in the wood, especially in materials like MDF or particleboard.

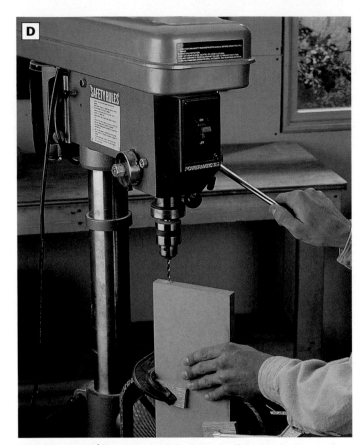

PHOTO D: Bore 1⅛-in.-deep holes in the ends of the top, bottom and shelf parts for the knockdown connector pins. Drill two ³⁄₁₆-in.-dia. holes in each end. We swiveled our drill press table vertically and clamped the parts to it to ensure square, straight holes.

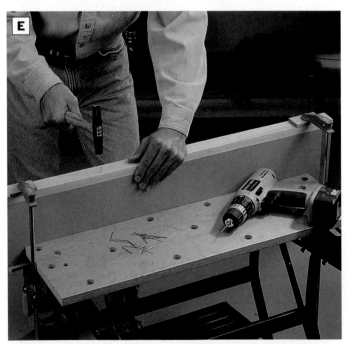

PHOTO E: Attach the shelf stiffeners to the front edges of the top, bottom and shelves. Clamp the stiffeners into place, aligning the top edge of the stiffeners with the top face of the MDF panels. Fasten the stiffeners with glue and 6d finish nails. For easier alignment, you could also cut #20 biscuit slots between the parts.

sure the top edge of each stiffener is flush with the top face of each shelf and the ends of the stiffeners line up with the shelf ends. Fasten the stiffeners in place with glue and 6d finish nails (**See Photo E**). Drill pilot holes for the nails to keep from splitting the poplar and the MDF. OPTION: *You could also cut #20 biscuit joints before installing the stiffeners to help align the parts.* Clean up excess glue with a chisel or scraper before it hardens.

CUT THE REMAINING CARCASE PARTS & DRY-ASSEMBLE THE BOOKCASE

⓫ Cut the back panel to size from ½-in. MDF and cut the toekick from ¾-in. MDF. Ease the top edges of the back using the same router technique you used for rounding over the top and front edges of the bookcase sides. You'll have to adjust the bit depth so the bearing rides along the center of the back panel thickness. Test on ½-in.-thick scrap first. Smooth the roundovers with sandpaper.

⓬ Dry-assemble the bookcase to check the fit of the parts. Be sure the top, bottom, shelves and toekick fit snugly between the side panels with the back panel set into place in the side-panel rabbets. Then disassemble the bookcase.

⓭ Prime and paint the faces, edges and ends of all the parts. You can prime and paint at this stage because all the fasteners used to assemble the bookcase will be hidden from view, so there is no need for covering nail or screw holes before finishing. Finishing the parts now is also an advantage because you have full access to all part surfaces.

INSTALL THE MECHANICAL FASTENERS

⓮ Press the barrel knockdown housings into the 25-mm holes in the side panels. Orient the straight groove in each plastic housing so it runs perpendicular to the front edge of the side panels, with the cam screw facing down toward the bottom of the bookcase. This way, you'll be able to set the top, bottom and shelves into place in the bookcase and tighten the knockdown fittings from just underneath the shelves. Tap the housings to seat them fully into their holes so the barrels sit flush with the inside faces of the sides.

⓯ Insert the knockdown connector pins into the ends of the top, bottom and shelves (**See Photo F**). Use a #2 Phillips screwdriver or a Phillips bit in a drill/driver to twist the connector pins into the holes until the collars on the pins seat against the workpieces.

PHOTO F: Tap the barrel-shaped knockdown housings into the side panels with a rubber mallet. Then screw the pin connectors into the ends of the top, bottom and shelves. Do not overdrive the pins.

PHOTO G: Assemble the bookcase by inserting the top, bottom and shelves into one side panel and tightening the cam screws. Then lay the assembly on its face and install the other side. Attach the toekick.

If your drill/driver has an adjustable clutch, dial it to a low setting to keep from overdriving the pins and stripping the holes in the parts.

ASSEMBLE THE BOOKCASE

16 Attach the top, fixed shelves and bottom to one side panel. Be sure to install the parts so the shelf stiffeners face the front edge of the bookcase. When assembling these parts, insert the pin connectors into the knockdown housings and tighten the joints by turning the cam screws clockwise (**See Photo G**). Lay the assembly on its face and attach the other side panel. Clamp the toekick in place and fasten it with pocket screws, drilling from the back side of the toekick into the side panels. Drive one pocket screw through the toekick and into the bottom of the bottom panel as well.

17 Measure and mark centerlines for the top, bottom and shelves onto the back edges of the sides to serve as reference marks for fastening the back panel. Set the back into the side panel rabbets and align the bottom edges of the back and sides. Draw screw reference lines across the back panel, connecting the marks you drew on the back edges of the sides. Drill countersunk pilot holes through the back and into the horizontal members of the bookcase with 1¼-in. flathead wood screws (**See Photo H**).

PHOTO H: Drill pilot holes through the back panel and into the top, bottom and shelves, and attach the back to the bookcase with 1¼-in. flathead wood screws.

Play Table & Chairs

Present this whimsical chair and table set to that special child in your life, and you can be sure that smiles and hugs will come your way. Made from a single sheet of paint-grade maple plywood and a little solid poplar, the project is as affordable as it is fun to build. We show two chairs built here, but you'll have enough plywood left over to build two more chairs if you like. We've chosen a mouse-and-cheese theme for this project, but you could modify the basic table and chair design to suit any theme you like.

Vital Statistics: Play Table & Chairs

TYPE: Play table and chairs

OVERALL SIZE: Table, 22-in.-dia × 20H; Chair, 12W × 10D × 22H

MATERIAL: "C-3" maple plywood, solid poplar

JOINERY: Half-lap joint, butt joints reinforced with screws, dowels, tee nuts and hanger bolts

CONSTRUCTION DETAILS:

· Entire project can be made from one 4 × 8 panel, with enough material left over for two extra chairs

· ¾-in. dowels join chair seats to backs

· Chair legs join to seats with hanger bolts and tee nuts

· Project parts profiled and detailed to create mouse-and-cheese theme

· Half-lap style table base

FINISH: Child-safe enamel primer and paint

Building time

 PREPARING STOCK
2 hours

 LAYOUT
3-4 hours

 CUTTING PARTS
3-4 hours

 ASSEMBLY
2-3 hours

 FINISHING
2-3

TOTAL: 12-16 hours

Tools you'll use

· Table saw
· Compound miter saw
· Router
· ½-in. single-fluted straight bit or up-twist spiral router bit
· Circle-cutting router jig
· Jig saw
· Band saw
· Drill/driver
· Right-angle drilling guide
· Drill press
· ¾-in.-dia. Forstner bit
· Drum sander
· Clamps
· Rubber mallet
· Files

Shopping list

☐ (1) ¾ in. × 4 ft. × 8 ft. C-3 maple plywood

☐ 1½ × 1½ in. × 8 ft. poplar

☐ Transfer or carbon paper

☐ (1) ¾-in.-dia. hardwood dowel

☐ (8) ⁵⁄₁₆-in. tee nuts

☐ (8) ⁵⁄₁₆ × 2-in. hanger bolts

☐ #8 flathead wood screws (1¼-, 1½-in.)

☐ (2) 1¼-in. wood drawer pulls

☐ Wood glue

☐ Finishing materials

Play Table & Chairs

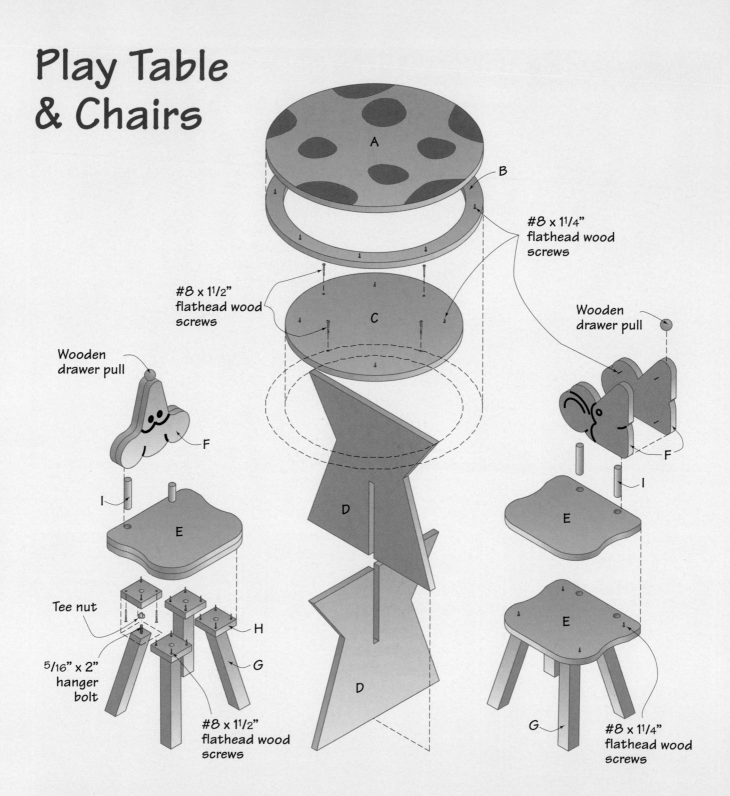

A

B

#8 x 1¹/₄"
flathead wood
screws

#8 x 1¹/₂"
flathead wood
screws

Wooden
drawer pull

C

Wooden
drawer pull

F

F

I

E

I

E

Tee nut

E

⁵/₁₆" x 2"
hanger
bolt

D

H

G

D

#8 x 1¹/₂"
flathead wood
screws

G

#8 x 1¹/₄"
flathead wood
screws

Play Table & Chairs Cutting List

Part	No.	Size	Material	Part	No.	Size	Material
A. Tabletop	1	³/₄ × 22 × 22 in.	C-3 maple plywood	**F.** Backs	4	³/₄ × 10 × 9 in.	C-3 maple plywood
B. Build-up	1	³/₄ × 22 × 22 in.	"	**G.** Chair legs	8	1¹/₂ × 1¹/₂ × 11 in.	Poplar
C. Subtop	1	³/₄ × 18 × 18 in.	"	**H.** Leg blocking	8	³/₄ × 3 × 3 in.	C-3 maple plywood
D. Table base	2	³/₄ × 18 × 18¹/₂ in.	"	**I.** Dowel	4	³/₄ dia.× 3¹/₂ in.	Hardwood dowel
E. Seats	4	³/₄ × 10 × 12 in.	"				

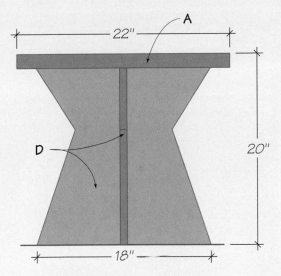

22"

A

20"

D

18"

FRONT VIEW - TABLE

Wooden ball

F

E

I

22"

H

12"

G

77.5°

SIDE VIEW - CHAIR

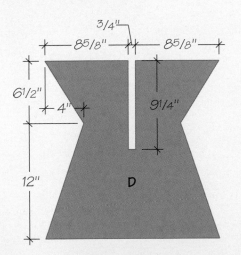

3/4"

8⁵/₈"   8⁵/₈"

6¹/₂"

4"

9¹/₄"

12"

D

TABLE BASE

Grid squares are 1" X 1"

E

1¹/₄"

Leg blocking (H) below seat

1¹/₄"

1¹/₄"

SEAT

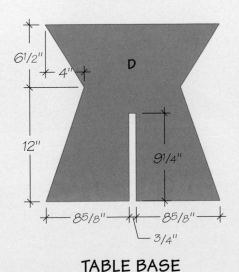

6¹/₂"

4"

D

12"

9¹/₄"

8⁵/₈"   8⁵/₈"

3/4"

TABLE BASE

F

6¹/₂"

CHAIR BACK

Dowel (I) locations

F

5¹/₂"

CHAIR BACK

For this project, we're using C-3 maple plywood. Although you wouldn't normally think of painting over maple plywood, C-3 maple plywood is paint-grade, which means the maple veneer is smooth and void-free but contains blemishes or other slight imperfections that would make it less desirable for clear or stain finishes.

MAKE THE TABLETOP

❶ Cut squares of C-3 maple plywood for the tabletop and build-up. The subtop will actually come from the same workpiece as the build-up ring. Use a straight-edge to draw diagonal lines across the faces of both blanks of plywood to establish centerpoints. Draw a 22-in.-dia. circle on each blank with trammel points or a piece of string and a pencil. Use a router circle-cutting jig to cut out these circles. Install a ½-in. sin-gle-fluted straight bit or an up-twist spiral bit in the router and adjust the jig for an 11-in. radius. Set the router bit depth to ¼ in., and tap the jig's trammel point spur firmly into the centerpoint of your layout. Plunge the bit down into the plywood (drill a starter hole if you don't own a plunge router) and pivot the router counterclockwise to cut a circular groove. Reset the router bit to a depth of ½ in. and deepen the groove by making another pass. Then, set the bit to just over ¾ in. to cut completely through the plywood. Clamp scrap spacers beneath the workpiece before routing the final pass to protect the worksurface underneath from the router bit. Cut the other ply-wood blank into a circle using the same procedure and jig settings.

❷ Reset the compass jig for a 9-in. radius and cut the 18-in.-dia. subtop circle out of the center of the build-up ring, routing the cut in three passes of increasing depth. Tack the subtop portion and the build-up ring to the spacers before you begin to rout

PHOTO A: Cut the 22-in.-dia. outer circles of the tabletop and the build-up with a router and a circle-cutting jig. Then cut the 18-in.-dia. subtop out of the build-up ring. Clamp the workpieces to scrap spacers before you make the final pass to protect the workbench.

PHOTO B: Cut the table base half-lap slots on the table saw with the blade raised to full height. Stop your cuts just shy of the layout marks at the bottom of each slot. Remove the slot wastepieces with a jig saw and square the slot corners with a file.

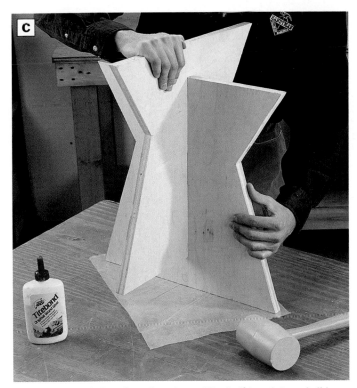

PHOTO C: Spread glue along the edges of the half-lap slots and slide the base pieces together to lock the joint. Tap the parts with a rubber mallet until the ends are flush.

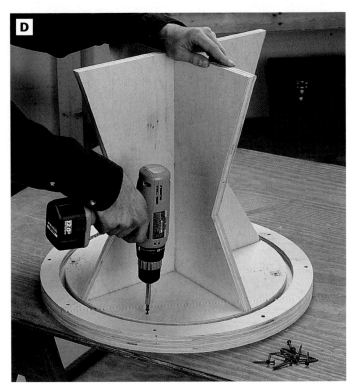

PHOTO D: Screw the subtop to the underside of the tabletop with glue and 1¼-in. screws. Make sure the gap between the subtop and the build-up is even all around so the legs are centered under the table.

the two workpieces apart. The screws will immobilize the parts once they separate (**See Photo A**).

MAKE THE BASE & ASSEMBLE THE TABLE

3 Lay out the table base pieces according to the dimensions given in the *Table Base* drawings, page 103. Note that the slots in the base pieces will be on the upper half of one base part and the lower half of the other so that the base pieces will fit together and interlock, forming a half-lap joint. Lay out the angled cuts. Make marks 12 in. up from the bottom ends of the base pieces along both edges. Use your combination square to square the marks, 4 in. from the edges, and mark these points. Draw straight lines from these points to the top and bottom corners to outline the angled side cuts on the base pieces.

4 Cut the long half-lap slots on the table saw with the blade raised up to its maximum height (**See Photo B**). NOTE: *The reason why you raise the blade to full height is to produce the steepest, and consequently squarest, cut possible where the cuts terminate in the base pieces.* Since the circular table saw blade will cut deeper into the bottom face of each panel than on top, stop the slot cuts just short of the 9¼-in. layout marks. Cut away the wastepieces from each slot with a jig saw or scroll saw, and square the

corners at the base of the slots with a file. Slide one base piece into the other to check the fit of the half-lap joint. If the fit is too tight, widen the slots slightly on the table saw so the base pieces fit snugly but do not bind. The ends of the base pieces should be flush with one another when the parts are fully interlocked. If they don't align, deepen the slots. Disassemble the base pieces and cut the angled sides with a jig saw. Sand the cut edges smooth.

5 Spread glue on the inside edges of the slots and slide the parts together to assemble the table base (**See Photo C**).

6 Lay the build-up ring on the tabletop and fasten the parts together with glue and 1¼-in. countersunk wood screws. Keep the outside edges flush.

7 Attach the subtop to the legs with glue and 1½-in. screws driven down through the subtop into the legs. Lay the subtop on the table base so the diagonal layout lines you drew in Step 1 face up, and center the diagonal lines on each base part. The subtop diameter should match the width of the base at the top, so align the edges before attaching the parts together. Drive screws along the diagonal layout lines.

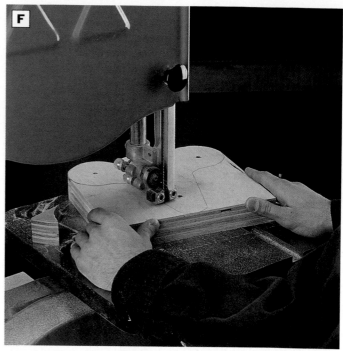

PHOTO E: Use transfer paper or carbon paper to trace the patterns for the two backs and the seat to the plywood blanks. Lay the pigment side of the paper facedown on the plywood when you outline the patterns.

PHOTO F: The chair seats and backs are composed of two pieces of ¾-in. plywood. Face-glue and screw them together to create thick blanks, then cut out the pattern shapes on a band saw.

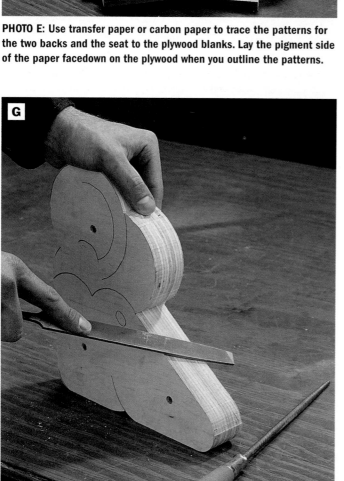

PHOTO G: Smooth the rough band-sawn edges of the backs with a drum sander or by hand. Use files to clean up corners.

8 Fasten the base to the tabletop. Turn the base assembly over and set it into the recess on the underside of the tabletop. Align the parts so there is an even gap between the subtop and the top build-up all around, then screw the subtop to the top with slightly countersunk 1¼-in. screws **(See Photo D)**.

MAKE THE CHAIR SEATS & BACKS

9 Cut the chair seat and back blanks to size. You'll need a total of four blanks for the chair seats and four for the chair backs.

10 On one face of the two seat blanks use a combination square to mark out the locations of the leg blocking. See the *Seat* grid drawing, page 103, to position the blocking correctly.

11 Create full-size patterns for the seat and two chair back styles. Trace each back shape onto a workpiece using transfer paper or carbon paper beneath each pattern. Transfer the seat pattern to the two blanks you marked for leg blocking **(See Photo E)**.

12 Use glue and countersunk 1¼-in. screws to attach the unmarked blanks to the underside of each patterned blank, creating two double-thick chair backs and two seats. Keep the screws within, but clear of the pattern outlines and leg blocking locations. Keep

PHOTO H: Clamp the chair backs upside down in a vise and set the seats in place over the backs. Drill pairs of ¾-in.-dia. holes through the seats and into the chair backs for dowels. A right-angle drilling guide ensures straight holes.

PHOTO I: Spread glue on the mating surfaces of the chair and seat backs and in the dowel holes. Tap dowels into the holes with a rubber mallet. If you use polyurethane glue, wear latex gloves to protect your hands, and clean up glue squeeze-out with denatured alcohol.

screws away from spots where the dowels will be used to attach the seats and chair backs. Cut out the seats and chair backs on a band saw (**See Photo F**).

⓭ Clean up the sawn edges of the seats and backs on a drum sander or with a sanding block. File the tight corners on the back shapes smooth (**See Photo G**).

ATTACH THE BACKS TO THE SEATS

⓮ The backs are joined to the seats with glue and ¾-in.-dia. hardwood dowels. Cut four dowels to length. Mark the dowel hole locations on the undersides of the chair backs using the *Chair Back* grid drawings, page 103, as guides. Note that the dowels are spaced differently on each back pattern, but center the dowels across the thickness of both chair backs. Pair a chair back with a seat and make drilling reference marks on the seat bottoms that correspond with the dowel reference marks you just drew on the chair backs. Mark the spots for drilling dowel holes on the same face as you drew the leg blocking locations. When aligning the parts to mark for drilling, the back face of each chair back should be flush with the long, flat back edge of the seats.

⓯ Drill the dowel holes to join the seats and backs. Clamp each chair back in a portable workbench or a bench vise. Orient the chair backs so the bottom

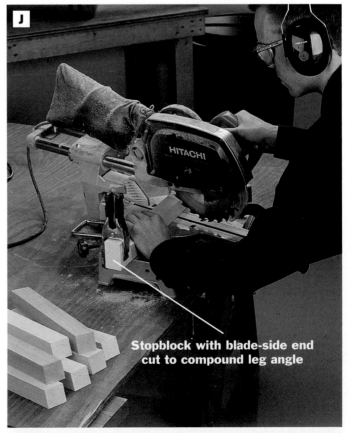

Stopblock with blade-side end cut to compound leg angle

PHOTO J: Cut compound 12.5° angles on the ends of the chair legs with a compound miter saw. Both ends of each leg should be parallel. Clamp a stopblock 10 in. from the blade to ensure that the legs will be cut the same length.

PHOTO K: Install tee nuts into counterbored holes in the leg blocking. The tee nuts should sit flush with or slightly below the faces of the blocking. Fasten the tee nuts with screws.

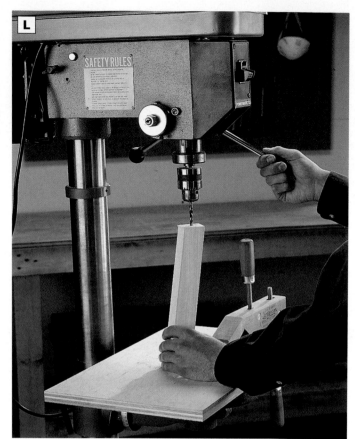

PHOTO L: Drill a ¼-in. pilot hole 1⅛ in. deep in the top of each leg for the hanger bolt. Screw the leg temporarily to a piece of scrap and clamp it to the drill press table to hold the leg steady while you drill.

edges are flush with the benchtop. Clamp the seats in place over the backs, making sure the back edges of both parts are flush and that the back is centered on the seat from side to side. Use a drill and a ¾-in. Forstner bit in a right-angle drilling guide to drill dowel holes through each seat and 2 in. into the chair backs. Set the depth stop on your right-angle drilling guide so that you don't drill too far (**See Photo H**).

🔟 Attach the backs to the seats. You can glue the parts together while they are still clamped up in the drilling setup. Simply unclamp and lift up the seat, spread glue on the mating surfaces of the seat and back, and replace the seat. Then spread glue into the dowel holes and tap the dowels into place (**See Photo I**). NOTE: *Some dowels are manufactured with diameters slightly smaller than holes drilled by standard drill bits. If this is the case for your project, remedy the loose dowel fit by using polyurethane glue to fasten the dowels. Polyurethane glue expands as it cures and fills gaps.* Drive the dowels into place with a rubber mallet, leaving just a trace protruding. Remove the chair assembly from the drilling setup and clamp the seat to the back. Once the glue dries,

trim off the protruding ends of the dowels flush with the seat bottom.

BUILD & ATTACH THE CHAIR LEGS

🔟 Cut the eight legs to length from 1½ × 1½-in. hardwood (we used poplar). The legs angle outward from the chair seats in two directions: sideways and front to back, forming 77.5° compound angles. Though the legs are angled, the ends must be cut parallel. The easiest way to make these cuts is with a compound miter saw (**See Photo J**). Tilt the blade 12.5° from vertical and swivel the blade 12.5° on the saw's protractor scale. Cut a scrap stopblock to these angle settings and clamp it to the saw fence, 10 in. from the blade. Cut the end of your leg stock to set the first leg angle, then slide it along the saw fence to rest against the stopblock and cut the first leg to length. Use the stopblock to index the cuts for the rest of the legs.

🔟 Install the leg blocking. Cut the leg blocking from ¾-in. plywood. Draw diagonal lines from corner to corner to mark the center of each piece. Drill a hole into the center of each blocking piece the diameter of

PHOTO M: Screw the leg hanger bolts into the tee nuts to attach the legs to the chairs. Adjust the legs so they are snug against the blocking and splay evenly out from the seat.

PHOTO N: Prime and paint all surfaces of the table and chairs. Apply base colors first to the large areas and let the paint dry. Then follow with the cheese and mouse face details.

the tee nuts you'll use to attach the legs (ours were 1¼ in.). The depth should be slightly deeper than the thickness of the flange of the tee nut. Then drill a hole through the center of each block the diameter of the threaded portion of the tee nut (ours were ⁵⁄₁₆). Attach four leg blocking pieces to the seat bottoms at the layout locations with glue and 1½-in. screws (if the threaded portion of the tee nut protrudes through the bottom of the blocking, extend the center tee nut hole slightly into the seat). Drop the tee nuts into their holes and screw them to the blocking pieces with the screws provided **(See Photo K)**.

❶❾ Attach the legs to the seats. Install hanger bolts in the tops of the legs so they can be screwed into the tee nuts in the leg blocking. To drill pilot holes for the lag ends of the hanger bolts, mark the centerpoint on one end of each leg. Screw the other end to a scrap piece of wood to anchor the leg in position when you drill the hanger bolt holes. Clamp the scrap piece to the drill press table and drill a ¼-in.-dia., 1⅛-in.-deep pilot hole in each leg **(See Photo L)**. Thread two nuts together onto the machine-threaded end of each hanger bolt and tighten them against one another

with two wrenches. Use an open-end or socket wrench to screw the lag end of each hanger bolt into the legs. Remove the two nuts from the hanger bolts and thread the hanger bolts into the tee nuts to attach the legs to the seats **(See Photo M)**.

FINISHING TOUCHES

❷⓿ Seal all exposed plywood edges with putty or wood filler. Fill exposed fastener holes with wood putty and sand flush. Break all sharp edges with sandpaper. Apply primer and two coats of child-safe enamel paint **(See Photo N)**. Paint the cheese holes on the tabletop and the mouse face details on the seat backs with contrasting colors. For the mice, paint the large face and ear areas first, leaving the eye, mouth and ear details for last.

❷❶ Attach and paint decorative "nose" balls to the mouse face chair backs. We used wooden drawer pulls. Fasten the balls securely with dowels and glue or with a screw driven through the ball into the seat back. Whichever method you choose, be sure the balls are fastened securely so they can't be accidentally removed by a child and pose a choking hazard.

Walnut Writing Desk

Create a dedicated space for keeping up on your correspondence when you build this Shaker-inspired writing desk. It's an attractive furnishing for the library, den or any other room in your home. The table's clean, understated styling and rich walnut wood tones give it the look and feel of solid hardwood construction—but here's the secret: Our table is built almost entirely of veneered plywood and MDF at a considerable savings over building with solid walnut. The table's legs taper on two faces and can be removed from the table, should the table need to be moved or stored.

Add more storage space to this desk project by building the matching desktop console (See pages 118-125).

Vital Statistics: Walnut Writing Desk

TYPE: Writing desk with drawer

OVERALL SIZE: 30W x 48L x 30H

MATERIAL: Walnut-veneer plywood, walnut veneer, solid walnut, birch plywood, MDF

JOINERY: Biscuit joints, face-glued laminated joints, tongue-&-groove corner joints, miter joints

CONSTRUCTION DETAILS:

· Legs are face-glued MDF, tapered and veneered
· Metal corner brackets attach legs to aprons
· Walnut plywood is cut so that grain matches across front aprons & drawer front
· Iron-on veneer edging tape
· Plywood drawer fitted with flush-fitting drawer front; tongue-and-groove construction

FINISH: Two coats of satin polyurethane varnish

Building time

 PREPARING STOCK
2 hours

 LAYOUT
2-4 hours

 CUTTING PARTS
2-4 hours

 ASSEMBLY
2-3 hours

 FINISHING
2-3 hours

TOTAL: 10-16 hours

Tools you'll use

· Table saw
· Tapering jig
· Clamps
· Band saw
· Jointer
· Biscuit joiner
· Drill/driver
· Right-angle drilling guide or drill press
· Pocket-screw jig
· Router with ⅜-in. roundover bit

HANDYMAN Shopping list

☐ (1) ¾ × 48 × 48 in. walnut plywood
☐ (1) ¾ × 48 × 48 in. MDF
☐ ½ × 18 × 48 in. birch plywood
☐ ¼ × 24 × 24 in. birch plywood
☐ 1/64 × 10 × 48 in. walnut veneer
☐ (4) ¾ × 1½ in. × 4 ft. walnut
☐ (1) 13/16 in. × 8 ft. walnut veneer edge banding
☐ (4) metal leg corner brackets
☐ (8) ¼ × 2-in. hanger bolts, washers & wing nuts
☐ (2) 20-in. full-extension drawer slides
☐ (8) 1-in. brass L-braces
☐ #20 biscuits
☐ #8 × 1¼-in. flathead wood screws

Walnut Writing Desk

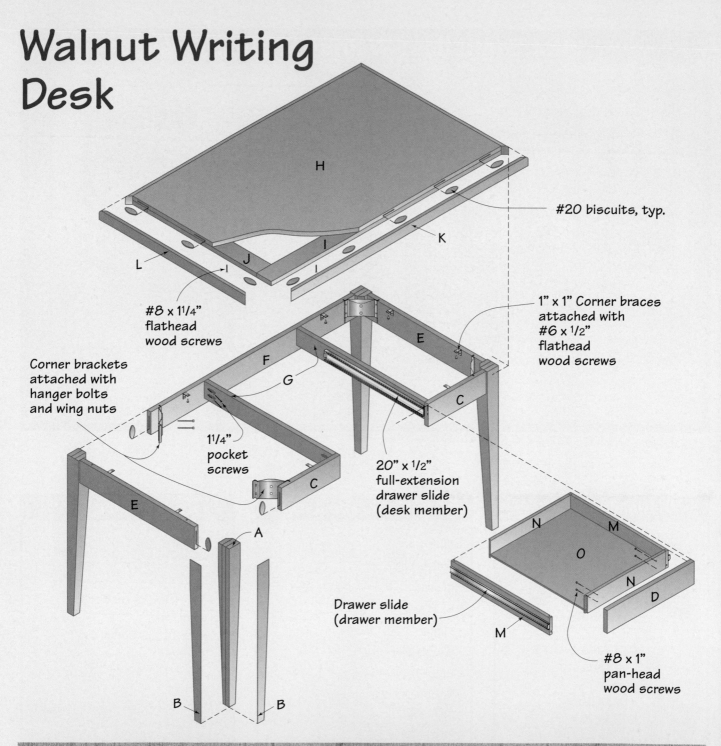

#20 biscuits, typ.

#8 x 1¼" flathead wood screws

1" x 1" Corner braces attached with #6 x ½" flathead wood screws

Corner brackets attached with hanger bolts and wing nuts

1¼" pocket screws

20" x ½" full-extension drawer slide (desk member)

Drawer slide (drawer member)

#8 x 1" pan-head wood screws

Walnut Writing Desk Cutting List

Part	No.	Size	Material
A. Leg blanks	12	¾ × 2½ × 29 in.	MDF
B. Leg veneer	16	1/64 × 2½ × 29 in.	Walnut veneer
C. Front apron	2	¾ × 4 × 11¾ in.	Walnut plywood
D. Drawer front	1	¾ × 3⅞ × 17¹¹⁄₁₆ in.	"
E. Side apron	2	¾ × 4 × 23½ in.	"
F. Back apron	1	¾ × 4 × 41½ in.	"
G. Spreader	2	¾ × 3 × 26 in.	"
H. Tabletop	1	¾ × 28½ × 46½ in.	"

Part	No.	Size	Material
I. Front/back build-up	2	¾ × 3 × 16½ in.	MDF
J. Side build-up	2	¾ × 3 × 22½ in.	"
K. Front/back edge	2	¾ × 1½ × 48 in.	Solid walnut
L. Side edge	2	¾ × 1½ × 30 in.	"
M. Drawer side	2	½ × 3 × 20 in.	Birch plywood
N. Drawer front/back	2	½ × 3 × 16½ in.	"
O. Drawer bottom	1	¼ × 19½ × 16½ in.	"

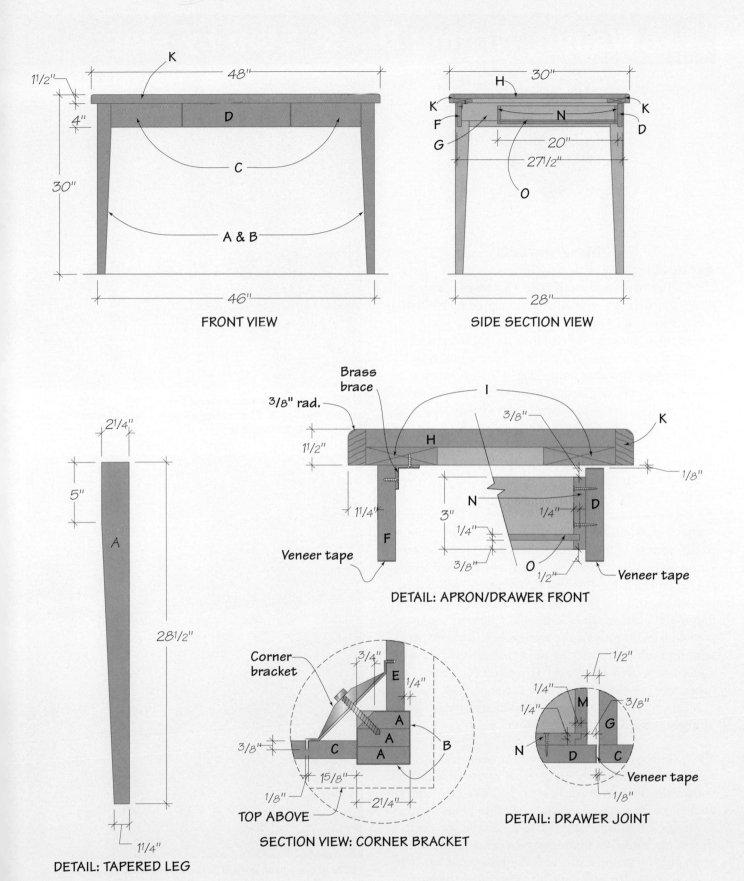

K

1 1/2"
4"
48"
D
C
A & B
30"
46"

FRONT VIEW

30"
H
K
K
F
D
G
N
20"
27 1/2"
O
28"

SIDE SECTION VIEW

2 1/4"

5"

A

28 1/2"

1 1/4"

DETAIL: TAPERED LEG

Brass
brace
3/8" rad.
I
3/8"
K
H
1 1/2"
1/8"
1 1/4"
N
D
3"
1/4"
F
1/4"
O
1/2"
Veneer tape
3/8"
Veneer tape

DETAIL: APRON/DRAWER FRONT

Corner
bracket
3/4"
E
1/4"
A
A
A
B
C
3/8"
1/8"
15/8"
2 1/4"

TOP ABOVE

SECTION VIEW: CORNER BRACKET

1/2"
1/4"
M
1/4"
G
3/8"
N
D
C
Veneer tape
1/8"

DETAIL: DRAWER JOINT

MAKE THE LEGS

1 Cut 12 leg blanks to size from ¾-in. MDF. The blanks are oversized so the legs can be cut to size after they are face-glued into four, three-board assemblies. Spread glue on the faces of the blanks and clamp up a stack of three blanks for each leg. Use plenty of evenly spaced clamps spaced about 6 in. apart to hold the glue joints closed. After the glue dries, scrape off glue squeeze-out with a paint scraper (wear safety glasses to protect your eyes from flying glue chips).

2 Rip-cut the legs to a finished width of 2¼ in. and crosscut each leg to 28½ in.

3 Taper two adjacent faces of each leg. The taper starts 5 in. down from the top of the leg and extends to the bottom of the leg, reducing it to 1¼ in. square. Draw layout lines to mark the tapers and use a tapering jig on the table saw to cut the tapers. Adjust the jig's angle and the saw's rip fence so the blade will follow the marked taper line as the jig and leg are pushed together along the rip fence. Cut the tapers, holding each leg tightly against the tapering jig with a pushstick **(See Photo A)**. Once you've cut the first taper, turn the leg in the jig so the taper side faces up and taper a second leg face. Sand away any surface unevenness left by the saw blade.

4 Cover the leg faces with walnut veneer. Use a veneer saw or a utility knife to cut strips of walnut veneer for the four faces of each leg. When cutting the veneer, guide your veneer saw or knife blade against a straightedge, especially when slicing in the direction of the grain, as blades have a tendency to follow and split the grain. Cut the veneer strips about ¼ in. oversize in width and length to overhang the leg faces. Spread a thin layer of glue evenly over two opposite leg faces (not on the veneer), and clamp the

PHOTO A: Cut tapers on two adjacent sides of each leg using a table saw and tapering jig. When cutting MDF, wear a particle mask—sawing MDF generates fine sawdust.

PHOTO B: Use a band saw and a shop-made V-block support cradle to cut a stopped chamfer on the top inside corner of each leg. Make the long chamfer cuts first, then swivel the jig 90° to cut the wastepieces free, creating recesses for the leg hardware.

PHOTO C: Cut the front apron pieces and the drawer front from one piece of walnut plywood so the grain will match on all three parts.

Lag screw side   Bolt side

PHOTO D: Tighten two nuts against each other on the "bolt" side of the hanger bolts to serve as a "head." Use a wrench to twist the "lag screw" side of each hanger into its hole in the legs. Then remove the nuts.

veneer in place, using scrap-wood cauls between the clamp jaws and the veneer. The cauls should cover the veneer on the leg faces completely to press the entire sheets of veneer flat. NOTE: *Line the cauls with wax paper to keep any glue that migrates through the veneer from bonding the cauls to the veneer.* The tapered faces of the legs will need two separate cauls—one for the leg portion above the taper and the other to cover the taper. After the glue dries, trim off excess veneer carefully with a router and flush-trimming bit, a block plane or a sharp chisel. Try to cut with the grain rather than against it, so any grain that splits will fracture away from, rather than into, the veneer covering the leg face. Then veneer the remaining two faces of each leg in the same way.

❺ Cut a stopped chamfer along the top inside corner of each leg (the corner that separates the tapered faces of the legs). The chamfers provide clearance for metal corner braces that will be used to attach the legs and table aprons. To lay out the chamfers, draw a pair of 3-in.-long layout lines ¾ in. from, and parallel to, the inside leg corner along the adjacent leg faces. Cut the chamfers on a band saw using a "V-block" cradle to hold the leg at a 45° angle to the blade (**See Photo B**). To make the cradle jig, joint the edges and faces of a 2 × 4 straight and square. On the table saw, make two passes with the blade set to 45° to cut a 1-in.-deep, V-shaped notch along the face of the 2 × 4.

Make your bevel cuts so the V-notch is positioned next to a long edge. Attach the cradle to a piece of plywood long enough to clamp to the saw table and flush with one edge of the plywood. Set a leg in the V-notch so the chamfer layout extends beyond the edge of the plywood and lines up with the saw blade. Clamp the jig in place on the saw table. Slide all four legs along the cradle, cutting the chamfer up to the chamfer stop line. Then unclamp the cradle setup, swivel it perpendicular to the blade and use it to support the legs in order to crosscut the chamfer wastepieces free.

ASSEMBLE THE LEGS & APRON

❻ Cut the front apron, drawer front, side aprons, back apron and stretchers to size from ¾-in. walnut plywood. Cut the front apron pieces and the drawer front from one long, 4-in.-wide strip of plywood so the grain on the parts will match all the way across the front of the table (**See Photo C**). Trim ⅛ in. off the top long edge of the drawer front to allow for edge-banding and clearance space under the tabletop.

❼ Cut #20 biscuit slots into both ends of the back and side aprons and the ends of the front aprons opposite the drawer front. Center the slots on the apron ends. Inserting biscuits at these locations will help align the aprons with the legs during assembly. Then cut a #20 biscuit slot into both chamfered faces

PHOTO E: Assemble the legs and apron parts by attaching the legs to the corner brackets and aprons with wing nuts. Tighten the wing nuts to close the joints—no glue is required.

PHOTO F: Attach the tabletop to the apron assembly with brass L-braces and ½-in. screws. Adjust the brackets so the screws pull the tabletop snugly against the apron assembly.

of each leg but not in the chamfered areas. Position these slots 9/16 in. from the edge opposite the chamfer, and center the slots 2 in. below the top of the leg. This way, you'll create a ¼-in. decorative reveal between the legs and aprons. Glue biscuits into the slots in the ends of the aprons and clean off excess glue.

❽ Fit the aprons and legs together upside down on the workbench and set the corner brackets in place in the leg chamfers. Mark bracket hanger bolt hole locations on the legs in the chamfered areas. Also mark the insides of the aprons where grooves will need to be cut to receive the metal "lips" on either end of each bracket. Disassemble the apron. Drill straight holes for the hanger bolts into each leg using a right-angle drilling guide or by clamping the V-block to the drill press table. Install the hanger bolts by threading two nuts onto the bolt and tightening the nuts against one another. Then grip the top nut with a wrench and screw the bolt into the wood (See Photo D). Remove the nuts.

❾ Cut ¼-in.-deep grooves following your bracket layout lines to house the bracket lips. Apply iron-on walnut veneer edge tape to the bottom edges of the back, side and front aprons. Edge-band the ends of the front aprons that will face the drawer, as well as all four edges of the drawer front. For more information on applying edge banding, see page 20.

❿ Reassemble the apron parts on the workbench and square up the assembly by measuring diagonally between the legs. Use wing nuts to fasten the legs to the corner brackets and aprons (See Photo E). NOTE: *It isn't necessary to glue the apron biscuits into the leg slots for strength. The corner brackets will hold the legs securely and make leg removal easy in the future, should you need to disassemble the table for transport.*

⓫ Cut the spreaders to size. Drill holes for pocket screws on the ends of the spreaders and screw them to the front and back aprons. Position each spreader 11 in. from the closer leg pair, and be sure that the top edges of the spreaders are flush with the tops of the aprons.

CONSTRUCT & ATTACH THE TABLETOP

⓬ Cut the tabletop to size from ¾-in. walnut plywood. Cut the front, back and side build-ups from ¾-in. MDF. Attach the build-ups to the underside of the tabletop with glue and countersunk 1¼-in. flathead wood screws, keeping the build-up edges flush with the outside edges of the tabletop.

⓭ Cut the front, back and side tabletop edging from ¾-in. solid walnut, leaving the ends long. Miter-cut the ends of the edging so the pieces fit snugly around the tabletop. Cut #20 biscuit slots about every 12 in. to aid in aligning the edging. Spread glue on the

PHOTO G: Glue and clamp up the drawer parts with the drawer bottom captured in its groove. Use short wood cauls to apply clamping pressure along the whole wood joint.

PHOTO H: With the drawer mounted in place on metal slides, clamp the drawer front temporarily in position with spring clamps. Then attach the drawer front to the drawer box with screws.

mating surfaces and the mitered corners and clamp the edging in place. Use pads between the clamp jaws to protect the edging. After the glue dries, remove the clamps and rout a roundover around the top edge of the tabletop using a ⅜-in.-dia. roundover bit.

14 Center the apron assembly on the bottom of the tabletop and attach the aprons to the tabletop build-ups with brass L-braces. Screw two braces to each apron, fastening them in place with ½-in. screws **(See Photo F)**. Position the braces on the front aprons near the spreaders to anchor the spreaders and aprons where they bear the weight of the drawer. Since the metal L-braces are slotted to allow for adjustment, position them slightly below the top edge of each apron. This way, when you fasten each bracket to the tabletop build-ups, the screws will pull the tabletop tight against the apron.

BUILD THE DRAWER

15 Cut the drawer front, back and sides to size from ½-in. birch plywood. Cut the drawer bottom from ¼-in. birch plywood. Use a table saw and dado-blade set or a router table and straight bit to construct inter-locking ¼ × ¼-in. rabbet joints on the ends and edges of the drawer parts. (See *Detail: Drawer Joints,* page 113, to configure the joints). Cut a ¼ × ¼-in. groove along the inside faces of all four drawer parts, ⅜ in. up from the bottom edges, to capture the drawer bottom. Finish-sand the interior faces of all drawer

parts. Apply glue to the joint rabbets (use no glue in the drawer bottom groove), slide the drawer bottom into place and secure the drawer box parts with clamps and cauls **(See Photo G)**. Wipe away any excess glue with a damp cloth. Check the drawer for squareness by measuring across the diagonals, and reposition the clamps as needed to correct for square.

FINISHING TOUCHES

16 Finish-sand all table parts and apply the finish of your choice. We used two coats of satin polyurethane varnish, rubbing between each dry coat with 0000-fine steel wool. If you like, you can stain the birch drawer parts to match the rest of the walnut before applying the varnish.

17 Attach metal drawer slide hardware to the table spreaders and drawer box according to the manufac-turer's instructions. Center the drawer in the opening so the bottom edges of the front aprons and the drawer face align.

18 Slide the drawer into the apron and attach the drawer front to the drawer box. Adjust the position evenly beneath the tabletop and the front aprons using small spring clamps to temporarily hold the drawer front in place from below. Once you are satis-fied with the position of the drawer front, drill pilot holes and install 1-in. pan-head screws from inside the drawer box **(See Photo H)**.

Desktop Console

A dd a new dimension to a desk or tabletop by building this handsome desktop storage console. Designed to match the walnut writing desk (pages 110-117), this simple project converts little-used space into useful storage with five cubbies and an upper shelf. The project can be built from one sheet of walnut plywood in less than a day's time.

For companion desk plans, see pages 110-117.

Vital Statistics: Desktop Console

TYPE: Desk console

OVERALL SIZE: 13D × 46L × 18H

MATERIAL: Walnut plywood

JOINERY: Butt joints

CONSTRUCTION DETAILS:

· Simple butt joints reinforced with biscuits & nails

· Plywood edges taped with iron-on veneer

FINISH: Two coats of satin polyurethane varnish; match your finish to the walnut writing desk if you are building this project as a companion piece

Building time

 PREPARING STOCK
2 hours

 LAYOUT
1 hour

 CUTTING PARTS
2-3 hours

 ASSEMBLY
2-3 hours

 FINISHING
1 hour

TOTAL: 8-10 hours

Tools you'll use

· Combination square
· Bevel gauge
· Jig saw
· Straightedge
· Biscuit joiner
· Clamps
· Deep clamp extenders (optional)
· Hammer
· Nailset

Shopping list

☐ (1) ¾ in. × 4 ft. × 8 ft. walnut plywood
☐ Walnut edge banding
☐ #20 biscuits
☐ 2-in. finish nails
☐ Wood glue
☐ Finishing materials

Desktop Console

2" finish nails

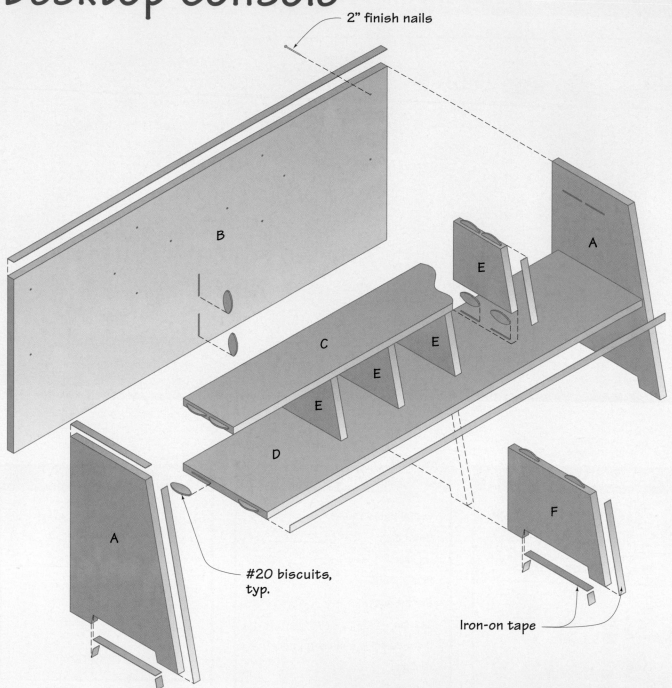

B

A

E

E

E

C

E

D

A

F

#20 biscuits, typ.

Iron-on tape

Desktop Console Cutting List

Part	No.	Size	Material
A. End	2	$\frac{3}{4} \times 13 \times 18$ in.	Walnut plywood
B. Back	1	$\frac{3}{4} \times 44\frac{1}{2} \times 18$ in.	"
C. Top shelf	1	$\frac{3}{4} \times 6 \times 44\frac{1}{2}$ in.	"
D. Bottom shelf	1	$\frac{3}{4} \times 10 \times 44\frac{1}{2}$ in.	"
E. Middle divider	4	$\frac{3}{4} \times 7 \times 6$ in.	"
F. Bottom divider	1	$\frac{3}{4} \times 11\frac{5}{8} \times 8\frac{1}{2}$ in.	"

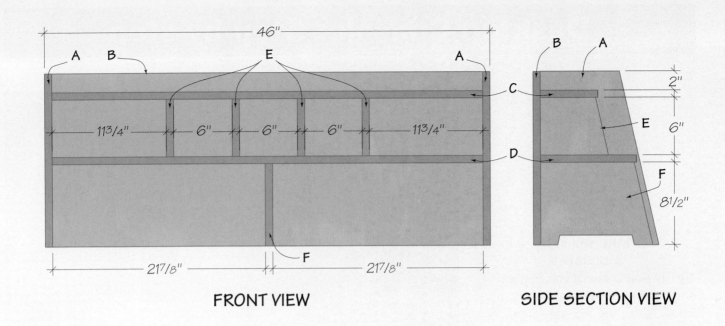

46"

A B E A

C

11³/4" 6" 6" 6" 11³/4"

D

21⁷/8" F 21⁷/8"

FRONT VIEW

B A

2"

E

6"

F

8¹/2"

SIDE SECTION VIEW

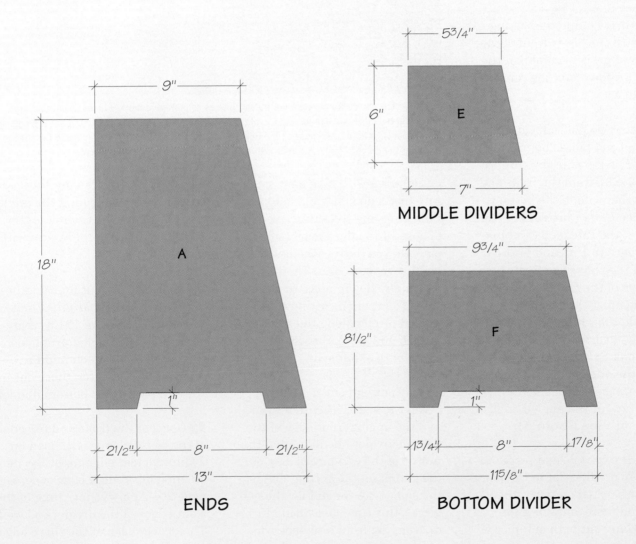

9"

A

18"

1"

2¹/2" 8" 2¹/2"

13"

ENDS

5³/4"

6" E

7"

MIDDLE DIVIDERS

9³/4"

8¹/2" F

1"

1³/4" 8" 1⁷/8"

11⁵/8"

BOTTOM DIVIDER

MAKE THE ENDS & DIVIDERS

1 Rip and crosscut the console ends to size from ¾-in. walnut plywood. Along the top edge of one of the end pieces, measure over 9 in. from the back edge and make a reference mark. Use a straightedge to draw a line connecting this point with the lower front corner of the end piece to establish the angled profile along the console's front edge.

2 Lay out the bottom cutout on the same end piece you marked in Step 1. Mark a pair of reference points 2½ in. from the front and back corners along the bottom edge (See *Ends* illustration, page 121). Set the rule on a combination square to 1 in. and butt the head of the square against the bottom edge of the end piece. Hold a pencil against the end of the rule and slide the square along the bottom edge to draw the top edge of the cutout. Set a bevel gauge to match the angle on the front edge of the end piece and use this setting to lay out the angled ends of the cutout (**See Photo A**).

3 Cut the console end pieces to shape. To do this, clamp the piece you just marked on top of the other end piece, aligining the edges. Gang-cut both end pieces. First, remove material in the

PHOTO A: Lay out the front angle on the end pieces by making a mark 9 in. out from the back along the top edge and connecting the mark with the bottom front corner. Use a bevel gauge set to this angle to lay out the ends of the bottom cutout, and a combination square to lay out the depth of the cutout. Make the cuts with a jig saw against a straightedge guide.

cutout area with a jig saw, using a fine-toothed jig saw blade to minimize chipping the surface veneer. (These sawn edges need to be smooth; you'll cover them with walnut veneer later.) Then clamp a straightedge in place to guide the jig saw when cutting the angled profile along the front edge of each end piece. Smooth all cut edges with sandpaper.

4 Lay out and cut the bottom divider to size. The cutout area and the angled front edge of the bottom divider should match the profile of the end pieces. Lay out the cutout on the bottom divider the same way you did for the end pieces, this time measuring in 1⅞ in. from the front and back corners. Use one of the console ends

as a pattern for drawing the cutout and establishing the angled front edge profile. Complete the cutout and front profile cuts with a jig saw.

5 Measure and cut four middle dividers using the *Middle Divider* illustration on page 121 as a layout guide. The angled profile on the front edge of each middle divider should match those cut in the end pieces and bottom divider.

6 Conceal the front and top edges of the console ends with iron-on walnut veneer edge tape (For more on applying veneer edge tape, see page 20). Apply veneer tape to the front edges of the dividers as well. Then cover each of the three edges of the bottom cutouts on the end pieces and bottom divider with veneer tape. When veneering the cutouts, apply veneer tape to the long sections first, then install the short end pieces of tape, butting the tape into the cutout corners. TIP: *The veneer tape will fit more tightly in the cutout corners if you first cut a small bevel along the ends of the tape with a sharp chisel.* Trim off any overhanging tape with a chisel, edge-banding trimmer or utility knife.

CUT THE SHELVES & BACK

❼ Cut the console back and top and bottom shelves from ¾-in. walnut plywood. Apply veneer tape to the top edge of the console back and the front edges of the shelves. The rest of the edges on the shelves and back can be left untaped—they'll be concealed when you assemble the console.

CUT THE BISCUIT SLOTS

Since the desktop console bears little weight, we used #20 biscuit slots and glue for assembling all the console parts. TIP: *When cutting biscuit joints, lay one part faceup on the workench and clamp the mating part flat on top of it, aligning the layout lines of both halves of the joint. With the fence set at 90°, butt the biscuit joiner base against the end of the mating part to cut the joint. Then flip the biscuit joiner around with its base flat against the face of the first part to cut the joint in the end of the mating part.*

❽ Start by marking slot locations for the middle dividers on the appropriate faces of the top and bottom shelves (See *Front View*, page 121). With the back edges of the dividers and the shelves flush, lay out biscuit joints in these parts and cut the slots. Mark lines for the bottom divider location on the

PHOTO B: Lay out and cut biscuit slots in all console parts. Mark the joint locations with chalk to make them easier to see. Use one of the workpieces as a straightedge to align the fence of the joiner when cutting slots on the face sides of parts. Where possible, cut both slots for a joint one after the next to keep part orientation clear.

PHOTO C: Protect the mating surfaces with tape, then brush on finish to all the interior surfaces. The cubbyholes in the console would be difficult to finish thoroughly if the console were assembled first.

PHOTO D: Glue the middle dividers to the top and bottom shelves. Use scrap-wood cauls or deep clamp extenders to apply even clamping pressure across the joints. We used both homemade scrap-wood cauls and store-bought clamp extenders.

PHOTO E: Glue and clamp the ends to the shelves and back panel. Drive finish nails through the back into the shelves and the middle dividers, and use a nailset to sink the nailheads below the surface.

lower surface of the bottom shelf, and cut two biscuit slots in each part.

9 Mark and cut slots for biscuits that will join the shelves to the console end pieces (**See Photo B**). The bottom edge of the bottom shelf is 8½ in. up from the bottom edges of the end pieces. The top edge of the top shelf is 2 in. down from the top edges of the ends. Since the back panel fits between the end pieces, be sure to account for the thickness of the back panel when positioning slots for the shelves.

10 Cut slots for a joint along the back edge of the bottom divider and the front face of the back panel. Assemble all console parts without glue to check the fit, then disassemble the parts for further preparation.

FINISH INTERIOR SURFACES
11 Once the console is glued up, the cubby areas and inside corners are difficult to reach for applying finish. Instead, finish all the interior surfaces of the console parts before assembly. Sand smooth all surfaces that will face into the console and ease sharp edges where the veneer edging meets the faces of the plywood. Remove all sanding dust with a brush, followed by a careful rubdown with a tack cloth. Cover joint areas with strips of masking tape to keep the biscuit slots dry. Lay out all parts and apply your desired finish, being careful not to get finish on any exposed, biscuited ends (**See Photo C**). We used two coats of satin polyurethane varnish.

ASSEMBLE THE CONSOLE
12 Start by gluing and clamping the middle dividers between the top and bottom shelves (**See**

Photo D). Use cauls or deep clamp extenders to spread clamping pressure evenly across the biscuit joints. Be sure the back edges of the dividers and shelves remain flush as you clamp. The biscuit slots will allow some play between the parts if you need to make minor adjustments. Use wax paper to protect the benchtop and keep from inadvertantly gluing the console assembly to the bench. Clean up any glue squeeze-out with a damp rag.

13 Use a combination square and tape measure to draw lines on the outside of the back panel, marking locations for the dividers and shelves. These lines will guide you when nailing the back in place. The centerline of the top shelf is 2⅜ in. from the top edge of the back. The centerline of the bottom shelf is 8⅞ in. from the bottom edge.

14 After the glue has dried on the first assembly, glue and clamp the shelves and back in place between the ends, keeping the top edge of the back flush with the top edges of the ends. Drive finish nails through the back into the shelves and middle dividers, using the reference lines you drew to position the nails **(See Photo E).** Set the nailheads below the surface with a nailset.

15 Attach the bottom divider to the back panel and the underside of the bottom shelf using biscuits. Clamp the bottom divider in place **(See Photo F).**

16 Sand the outside surfaces of the console, and ease any remaining sharp edges. Apply finish to all remaining surfaces.

PHOTO F: Attach the bottom divider to the bottom shelf and the back with glue and biscuits, clamping it in place. Use scrap blocks to pad the clamps. Make sure the front of the bottom divider is square to the shelf.

Attaching the desktop console to a desk

If you are building this desk console as a companion piece to the writing desk featured on pages 110-117, here's a tip for securing the console to the desktop: Attach 1½-long brass mending plates, available at any hardware store, between the back of the console's back panel and the back edge of the desktop. Mending plates will keep the console from shifting, should the desk get jarred or moved.

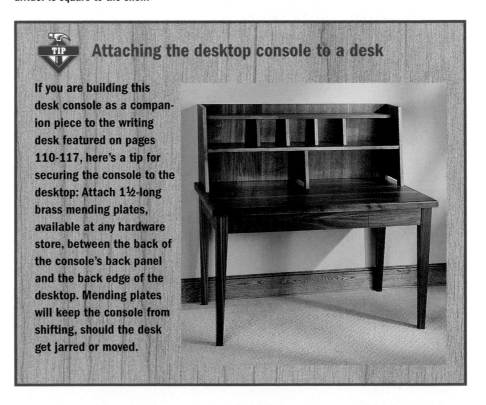

Corner Booth

Create an intimate dining sanctuary in a corner of your kitchen with this two-person corner booth. The Oriental-inspired design is highlighted by a glossy black finish, which gives the impression of black lacquer. The seating portion of the booth measures 4 ft. long in each direction, with the backs extending up to about 40 in. The 32 × 32-in. triangular table is large enough to support a pair of dinner plates, yet trim enough that it doesn't project too far out from the corner. And the easy-to-clean plastic laminate tabletop complements the dark burgundy seat upholstery.

Vital Statistics: Corner Booth

TYPE: Corner dining booth and table

OVERALL SIZE: Benches, 4 ft. × 4 ft. × 40H

MATERIALS: Maple plywood, MDF, plastic laminate, vinyl upholstery

JOINERY: Biscuits, mechanical fasteners, screws

CONSTRUCTION DETAILS:
· Mechanical "knockdown" fasteners at the miter joint in the seat assembly permit the bench to be disassembled into two easy-to-handle sections
· Tabletop is edged and surfaced with plastic laminate
· Vinyl upholstery over foam cushions
· Template used to "pattern-rout" identical legs

FINISH: Glossy enamel paint or black lacquer

Building time

PREPARING STOCK
1-2 hours

LAYOUT
3-5 hours

CUTTING PARTS
4-6 hours

ASSEMBLY
4-6 hours

FINISHING
4-6 hours

TOTAL: 16-25 hours

Tools you'll use

· Jig saw
· Table saw
· File
· Drum sander (optional)
· Clamps
· Router with piloted flush-trimming bit
· Laminate trimmer (small router)
· Drill/driver
· Circular saw
· Biscuit joiner
· Dowel drilling jig
· Drill press
· Compass
· Staple gun
· Combination square
· Framing square
· Trammel points (optional)
· J-roller
· Cloth tape measure
· Heat gun

Shopping list

☐ (2) ¾ in. × 4 ft. × 8 ft. maple plywood

☐ (1) ¾ in. × 4 ft. × 8 ft. MDF

☐ (1) ¾ in. × 4 ft. × 4 ft. MDF

☐ (1) ½ in. × 4 ft. × 8 ft. construction-grade plywood

☐ (1) ½ in. × 4 ft. × 8 ft. foam

☐ Vinyl upholstery (3 sq. yards)

☐ (1) ⅟₃₂ × 36 in. × 8 ft. plastic laminate

☐ (2) ½-in. *Tite-Joint* fasteners

☐ #8 flathead wood screws (1-, 1¼-, 1½-, 2-in.)

☐ #20 biscuits

☐ Wood glue

☐ Staples

☐ Finishing materials

Corner Booth

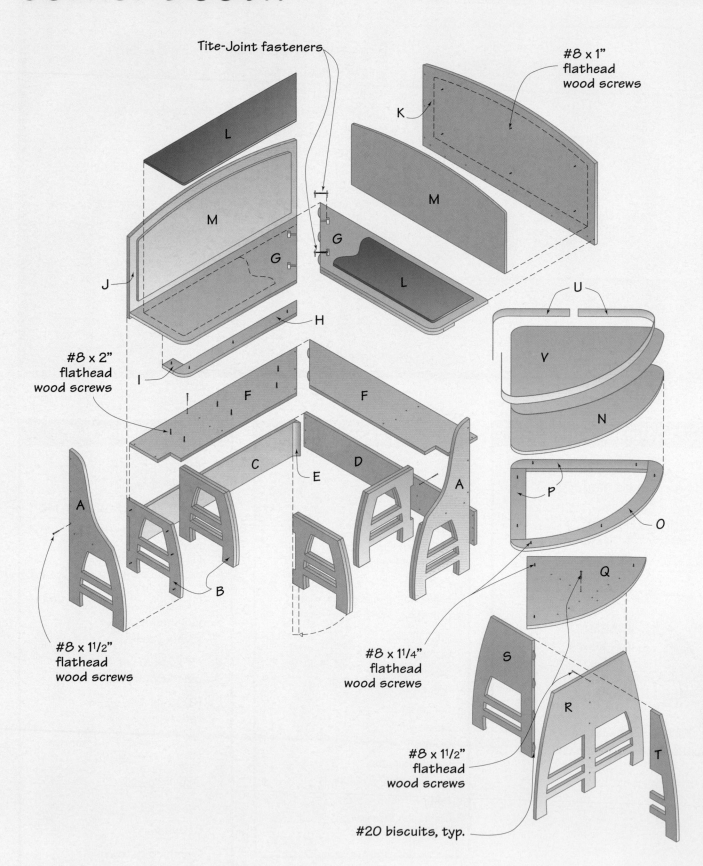

Tite-Joint fasteners

#8 x 1"
flathead
wood screws

L

K

M

M

G

G

J

L

H

#8 x 2"
flathead
wood screws

I

U

V

N

F

F

C

E

D

A

P

O

A

Q

#8 x 1½"
flathead
wood screws

B

#8 x 1¼"
flathead
wood screws

S

R

T

#8 x 1½"
flathead
wood screws

#20 biscuits, typ.

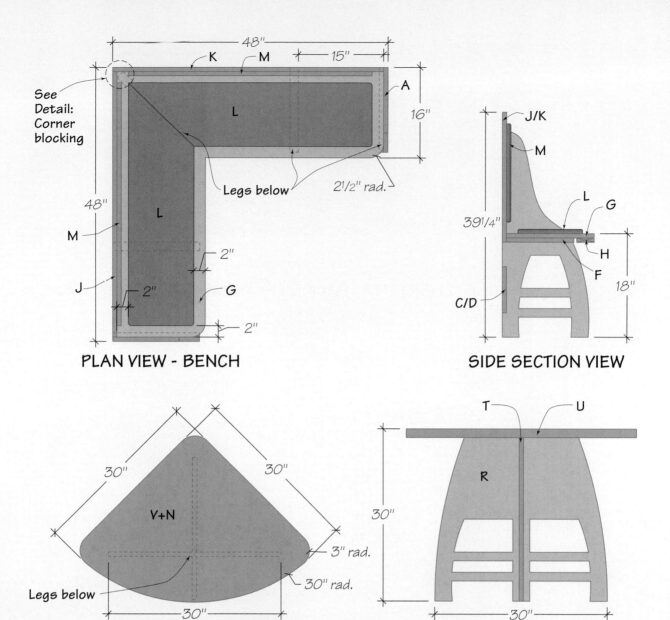

PLAN VIEW - BENCH

See Detail: Corner blocking

48"

K   M   15"

A

16"

48"

M

L

L

Legs below

2 1/2" rad.

J

2"

2"

G

2"

SIDE SECTION VIEW

J/K

M

L   G

39 1/4"

H

F

C/D

18"

PLAN VIEW - TABLE

30"   30"

V+N

30"

3" rad.

30" rad.

Legs below

30"

FRONT VIEW - TABLE

T   U

R

30"

30"

Booth Cutting List			
Part	No.	Size	Material
A. Outside leg	2	3/4 × 15 × 36 in.	Plywood
B. Inside leg	8	3/4 × 15 × 16 1/2 in.	"
C. Short stretcher	1	3/4 × 8 × 46 1/2 in.	"
D. Long stretcher	1	3/4 × 8 × 47 1/4 in.	"
E. Corner blocking	1	1 1/2 × 2 1/8 × 8 in.	Solid wood
F. Seat subbase	2	3/4 × 11 1/4 × 47 1/4 in.	MDF
G. Seat base	2	3/4 × 15 1/4 × 47 1/4 in.	"
H. Front build-ups	2	3/4 × 3 × 34 1/4 in.	"
I. End build-ups	2	3/4 × 3 × 3 in.	"
J. Short backrest	1	3/4 × 22 3/4 × 46 1/2 in.	Plywood
K. Long backrest	1	3/4 × 22 3/4 × 47 1/4 in.	"
L. Seat board	2	1/2 × 11 1/4 × 42 1/2 in.	Plywood
M. Backrest board	2	1/2 × 17 1/4 × 42 1/2 in.	"

Table Cutting List			
Part	No.	Size	Material
N. Tabletop	1	3/4 × 30 × 30 in.	MDF
O. Curved build-up	1	3/4 × 9* × 43* in.	"
P. End build-up	2	3/4 × 3 × 30* in.	"
Q. Table subbase	1	3/4 × 23 1/2 × 23 1/2 in.	"
R. Front leg	1	3/4 × 30 × 28 1/2 in.	Plywood
S. Inner leg	1	3/4 × 16 1/2 × 28 1/2 in.	"
T. Outer leg	1	3/4 × 7 1/2 × 28 1/2 in.	"
U. Edging	2	1/32 × 1 3/4 × cut to fit	Laminate
V. Top surface	1	1/32 × 31 × 31 in.	"

* Oversized dimensions

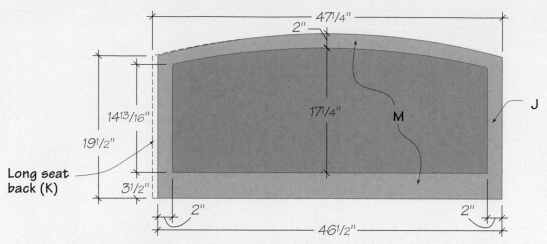

47¹/₄"

2"

14¹³/₁₆"

17¹/₄"

M

J

19¹/₂"

Long seat
back (K)

3¹/₂"

2"

2"

46¹/₂"

LONG/SHORT SEAT BACK & BACK CUSHION BLANK

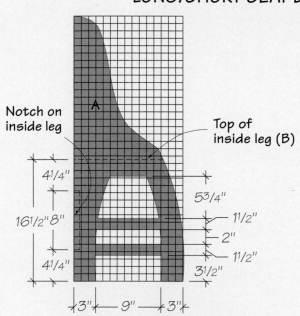

Notch on
inside leg

A

Top of
inside leg (B)

4¹/₄"

5³/₄"

16¹/₂" 8"

1¹/₂"

2"

1¹/₂"

4¹/₄"

3¹/₂"

3"   9"   3"

INSIDE/OUTSIDE LEGS

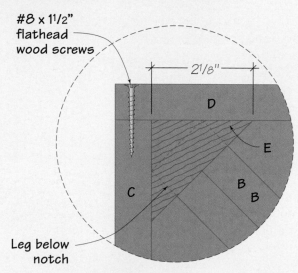

#8 x 1¹/₂"
flathead
wood screws

2¹/₈"

D

E

C

B

B

Leg below
notch

DETAIL: CORNER BLOCKING

Grid squares are 1" x 1"

20"

R

5³/₄"

1¹/₂"

2"

1¹/₂"

3¹/₂"

10¹/₂"   3"   10¹/₂"   3"

30"

TABLE FRONT LEG

11¹/₂"

2¹/₂"

S

T

3"   10¹/₂"   3"

16¹/₂"

3"

7¹/₂"

TABLE INSIDE LEG   TABLE OUTSIDE

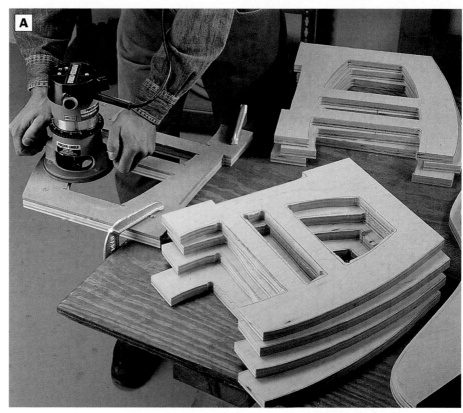

PHOTO A: After rough-cutting the legs so they're close to the traced template lines, screw the template to a leg and trim the leg flush to the template with a router and a flush-trimming router bit. Either shim the parts up or overhang them to avoid cutting into the worksurface.

MAKE THE BENCH FRAMEWORK

To make sure the profiles of the bench legs are identical, use hardboard templates and a router with a flush-trimming bit. To make the templates, draw a full-scale version of the grid pattern for *Inside/Outside Legs* on page 130, using the pattern as a reference. Attach the drawing to a piece of ¼-in. tempered hardboard, using spray adhesive (we chose to make the template in two sections, as indicated by the dotted line in the grid drawing). Cut along the template cutting lines (both the outside profile and the interior shapes) with a jig saw. You may want to use a straightedge to guide your cuts on the straight sections. Use a file or sanding block to smooth out the edges. A drum sander can help on the inside curves.

❶ Cut the rough blanks for the outside and inside bench legs to size (See *Cutting List,* page 129) from ¾-in. plywood (we used "C-3" paint-grade maple plywood with a veneer core).

❷ Trace the shapes of the legs onto the rough blanks, using the template discussed at the top of this page. *NOTE: Do not include the rear notch cutout on the outside leg pattern; this is only for the inside legs.* Make sure the outer edges of the templates are flush with the outer edges of the blanks. After tracing shapes onto all the blanks, cut out the shapes close to the lines (about ¹⁄₁₆ in. away), using a jig saw (drill starter holes for internal cuts). Then, screw the template to each leg blank in succession and trim the profiles to follow the template, using a router and

Top-mounted pilot bearing

Pattern routing

We used a top-bearing flush-trim bit to pattern-rout the edges of the bench legs. This bit is used with the template on top of the blank. The bearing rides along the template and the blades trim the blank to the exact shape of the template edges. A bottom-bearing bit would be used with the package flipped over, so the template is below the blank. The ball-bearing collar is the same diameter as the cutters.

PHOTO B: After attaching the outside leg unit to the stretcher with glue and screws, fasten the middle inside leg in the same way, but alternate the screws in a zigzag manner to hit both pieces of plywood.

PHOTO C: Screw the seat subbases to the inside bench legs (screw the corner leg to the left sub-base only). Screw through the outside faces of the outside legs to attach them to the ends of the subbase. Clamp on temporary spacers to set the subbases back from the back edges of the legs enough to allow for the backrests that will be added later.

pattern routing bit (**See Photo A and *Tip*, page 131**). *NOTE: The router bit probably will protrude all the way through the template and the blank, so remember to shim up the workpieces or over-hang them to protect your work-surface.* After all the legs are trimmed to shape, square out the inside corners with a sharp chisel or a file.

❸ Double-up the legs to create 1½-in.-thick supports for the bench. Glue and screw an inside leg to the inside surface of each of the outside legs (clamp them first to keep the edges flush while you drive the screws). Next, assemble three double-thick inside legs by gluing and screwing the remaining legs together. Clean up excess glue. When the glue has dried, smooth the edges with a sanding block.

❹ Cut the short and long leg stretchers to size. Cut the corner blocking from 2 × 4 lumber (the corner blocking is triangular, and the 2⅛-in. dimensions refer to the sides of the triangle). To make the blocking, set your table saw blade to 45° and bevel-rip a 2 × 4 on both edges. It's helpful to reattach the first cutoff edge with double-sided tape before bevel-ripping the other edge. Glue and clamp the corner blocking to the short stretcher, flush with the end that will mate with the long stretcher.

❺ Lay out lines on the front sur-face of each stretcher to mark the location of the two middle inside legs. They should be placed 15 in. from the outer end of each stretcher. Also, draw reference lines on the back sides of the stretchers to aid in screw location. Insert the outer end of the short leg stretcher into the notch on the back of the left outside/inside leg, with its end butted against the inside face of the outside leg, and glue and screw it in place with countersunk screws driven from the back. Attach an inside leg to the stretcher at the middle leg reference marks. Alternate the screws from side to side to hit both pieces of plywood. Repeat the procedure to assemble the other leg/stretcher assembly (**See Photo B**). You can now screw the stretchers together with countersunk screws driven through the overlapping long stretcher and into the end of the short stretcher. Do not glue this joint (you may want to disassemble and move the corner booth in the future). Complete the assembly by gluing and clamping the corner, inside leg to the corner blocking.

❻ Cut the seat subbases to size from ¾-in. MDF. Cut a precise 45° miter on the inside end of each board, using a circular saw and a straightedge. Cut a 3¼-in.-wide × 3-in.-deep notch into the front outside corner of each subbase with a jig saw. Then, cut three slots for #20 biscuits in the mitered end of each subbase. Glue biscuits into the slots in one of the subbases, but don't glue the joint together. Remember, the two halves of the bench come apart along this joint.

❼ Fit the subbases together and place the assembly onto the leg assembly. To allow for the seat backs, the back edges of the seat subbases should be inset ¾ in. from the back edges of the legs. Using a scrap piece of plywood as a spacer, butt the ends of the subbases up tightly against the insides of the outside legs. Use a framing square to make sure the leg assembly and the subbases are square. Screw the seat subbases to

PHOTO D: Use a doweling jig as a guide for drilling holes that will accept the shaft of the *Tite-Joint* fasteners in the seat base joint (follow the hardware manufacturer's instructions). Drill the large holes in the faces of the panels with a Forstner bit on the drill press.

the inside legs with countersunk screws driven down from above (**See Photo C**). Stagger the screws so they catch both pieces of plywood. Since the corner leg is glued to the corner block that's attached to the short stretcher, attach the corner leg to the left subbase by running screws down into the leg along the left side of the joint. Also drive countersunk screws through the outside legs and into the ends of the subbases.

MAKE & ATTACH THE SEATS & BACKRESTS

❽ Cut the seat bases, front build-up strips and end build-up strips to size. Cut a 45° miter on one end of each seat base, using a circular saw and a straightedge guide. Lay out marks along the top and the inside edges of the miters for the two *Tite-Joint* fasteners. The fas-

teners will be accessible for adjustment from the top surface of the seat bases, so square the layout lines out at 4 in. from the front inside corner of the joint and 4 in. from the back corner so the fasteners will be covered by the seat cushions. Use a doweling jig and a drill press to drill the holes in the edges and faces of the seat tops for the *Tite-Joint* fasteners, according to the manufacturer's instructions (**See Photo D**).

❾ Miter-cut the mating ends of the front build-up strips. Attach the front and end build-ups to the underside of each seat base with glue and screws. The build-up strips should be flush with the edges and ends of the seat bases. Use a compass to draw a 3-in.-radius curve at both of the front, outside corners of the seat bases.

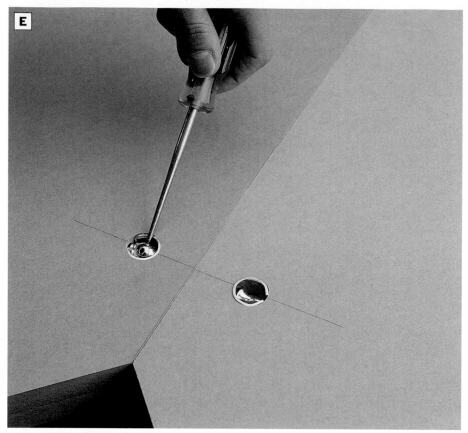

PHOTO E: *Tite-Joint* fasteners are loosened or tightened by using the tiny bar included in the kit or a scratch awl (shown) to turn the threaded ball.

PHOTO F: Staple the edges of upholstery to the backer boards, starting with the longer edges. Tuck and fold the corners of the upholstery neatly and staple them down.

Cut the curved corners with a jig saw and sand smooth.

10 Fit the seat bases together and tighten the *Tite-Joint* fasteners **(See Photo E)**. Place the seat on the leg assembly. It should fit into place easily, with the build-up strips dropping down into the notch in the front of the seat sub-base. Align the back edges of the seat bases with the subbases, and butt the ends of the seat bases tightly against the inside faces of the outside legs. Make any adjustments necessary and screw the base to the subbase from underneath. Also drive screws through the outside leg into the ends of the seat base.

11 Cut the short backrest and long backrest to size. To lay out the top curve, make marks 3¼ in. down from the top edge at each end of the long backrest. Mark the centerpoint of the back along the top edge. Use a batten (a thin flexible strip of solid wood or hardboard sprung to form the curve and tacked in place) to draw a curved line that intersects these three marks. Cut the curve with a jig saw and clean it up with a sander or hand plane. Use the long backrest as a pattern for laying out the curve on the short backrest. First, make your marks 3¼ in. down from the top edge at each end of the short backrest. Then, center the long backrest on top of the short backrest with the marks aligned, and trace the cutting line. Cut close to the line with a jig saw. Then, clamp or screw the long backrest to the short backrest and trim the short backrest to match using a router and flush-trimming bit (See *Tip,* page 131).

12 Spread glue on the back edges of the left seat base and subbase, and on the outer end of the left backrest where it will fit against the outside leg. Clamp the short backrest to the seat assembly, keeping the bottom edge of the backrest flush with the underside of the seat subbase. Fasten the backrest by driving countersunk screws through the outside leg and into the end of the backrest. Also drive screws through the backrest into the back edges of the seat base and subbase. Repeat this process with the right side of the bench and the long backrest. Do not glue the miter joint between the seat backs.

13 Prime and paint the bench assembly. We used two coats of black gloss enamel paint applied with a paint roller.

MAKE & INSTALL THE CUSHIONS

14 Cut the seat boards and backrest boards from ½-in. plywood. Use the shape of the seat backs as an aid in tracing the curved tops on the backrest boards. Cut the curved shapes with a jig saw and smooth the cuts with a sanding block or file. Cut 45° miters at the ends of the seat boards. Round over the corners and soften the edges of the board to eliminate any sharp edges that might penetrate the upholstery.

15 Cut the ½-in.-thick foam batting to match the shapes of the seat boards and backrest boards. An electric carving knife works well for cutting foam. If you don't have one, use a utility knife, shears or scissors. Next, trace the shapes of the boards onto the back side of the upholstery fabric you will be using, leaving a border of 2 to 3 in. Cut out the upholstery pieces with scissors or shears. Lay

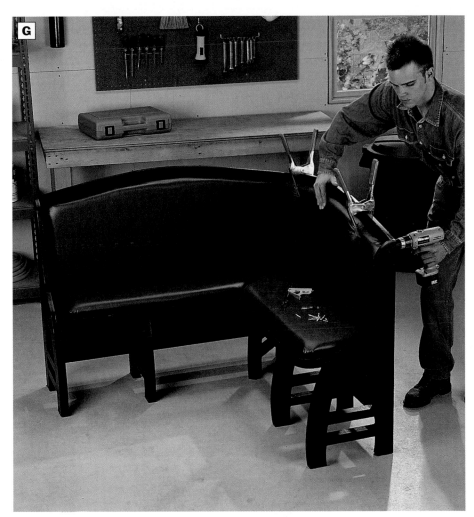

PHOTO G: Attach the cushions to the bench seat and backrests.

a piece of upholstery upside down on a clean worksurface, and place a piece of foam batting on top of the upholstery. Then, lay a seat board or backrest board on the foam. Align the edges of the foam with the board, and center them on the fabric. Wrap one long edge of the upholstery up and staple it down securely. Then, pull the opposite long edge tight and staple it down, starting in the middle and working your way toward the ends. Staple the ends of the upholstery down in the same way, then tuck and fold the corners neatly and staple them down to complete the cushion **(See Photo F)**. Repeat to upholster the remaining cushions.

16 Clamp the seat cushions in place with large spring clamps. Adjust them so there is a consistent 2-in. reveal around the edges of the cushions and the miters are butted up tightly against each other. Attach the cushions to the seats from below. Clamp the back cushions in place similarly with a 2-in. reveal all around, and screw them to the seat backs with countersunk screws **(See Photo G)**.

MAKE THE TABLETOP

17 Cut the tabletop to rough size. The curved edge of the tabletop is an arc with a 30-in. radius. Locate the centerpoint of the arc by measuring up ³⁄₁₆ in. from one corner along the two adjoining edges. Use a combination square to extend

PHOTO H: Lay out the curves on the tabletop. Swing the large (30-in.-radius) arc with trammel points (note the centerpoint is not at the corner of the square). Use a compass to swing the small (3-in.-radius) arcs at the corners.

PHOTO I: Make a hardboard template of the inside leg shape, and use it to outline all three legs. On each leg the template gets positioned differently.

the lines across until they intersect. Set your trammel points to 30 in. If you don't have trammel points, cut a strip of thin scrap wood about 1 in. wide and drive a brad through the scrap near one end. Drill a ¼-in.-dia. hole in the strip. The centerpoint of the hole should be 30 in. from the point of the brad. Insert a pencil into the ¼-in. hole. Set the pivot point of your trammel at the point where the reference lines on the tabletop intersect, then swing an arc across the panel. Lay out the rounded corners by setting a combination square to 3 in. and drawing intersecting lines near each of the three corners as radius centerpoints. Set a compass to three inches and swing arcs at the corners from these centerpoints (**See Photo H**). Use a jig saw to cut out the shape of the tabletop. Then, smooth the cut edge with a sanding block, taking care not to round over or angle the edge since you'll be applying plastic laminate to them (if you have a vertical belt or disc sander with a table, it would make this smoothing step easier and more accurate).

13 Trace the curved shape of the tabletop onto a piece of ¾ × 9 × 43-in. MDF to make a cutting line for the curved tabletop build-up strip. Cut along the outline with a jig saw or a band saw. Screw the build-up to the underside of the tabletop, allowing the build-up to overhang the top's curve a little. Use a router with a flush-trimming bit to trim the build-up flush with the tabletop. Use a compass or combination square to draw a cutting line parallel to the curved edge, 3 in. inside it. Remove the build-up and cut the new arc with a jig saw or band saw, then attach the build-up to the underside of the tabletop with glue and countersunk screws. Cut the end build-ups to size. To fit them to the tabletop, first butt one end build-up against the inside curve of the curved build-up and align its edge flush with the straight edge of the top. The other end will overhang the top; trace the outline of the top corner on the build-up. Cut the end of the build-up close to the line, then glue and screw it in place and flush-trim it even with the top. Cut the remaining build-up piece to fit between the two that are already attached, and glue and screw it to the tabletop.

MAKE THE TABLE BASE

19 Cut the table subbase to rough size. Trace the curved profile of the tabletop onto the edge of the subbase and cut the subbase to finished size.

20 Cut the front, inside and outside table legs to size. Measure and mark centerpoints along the 30-in. lengths of the front leg, and connect them with a straightedge to draw centerlines up the width (height) on both sides of the leg. Make a template for the legs from a piece of ¼ × 16½ × 28½-in. hardboard. Use the pattern provided on page 130 as a guide for laying out the shapes and profiles of the table legs. Cut out the template with a jig saw and smooth with a file or sanding block. *NOTE: The pattern is used a bit differently on each table leg. The inside leg is the exact shape and size of the template. The front leg is a mirror image of the template, so you will need to flip the template over. On the outside leg, let the template overhang the workpiece and create a leg that is open on one end.* Outline each leg **(See Photo I)** and cut them to rough shape with a jig saw. Screw or clamp the template to each leg and trim the legs flush

PHOTO J: After the outside table leg has been screwed to the front leg, attach the inside leg with glue and biscuits.

to the template with a router and a flush-trim bit. Square inside corners with a chisel or a file.

21 Mark centerpoints at the open ends of the outside leg, and position the outside leg against the front leg so the centerpoints are aligned with the vertical centerline on the front leg. Clamp the outside leg temporarily in place and drill pilot holes for attaching the legs with screws. Apply glue to the edge of the outside leg and screw it to the front leg, keeping the top edges flush. The inside leg is attached to the front leg with #20 biscuits and glue. To machine for the biscuits, offset the front leg's centerline by ⅜ in. in one direction. Clamp the inside leg to the front leg, face to face, with the straight edge of the inside leg

along the line you just offset. The top edges should be flush. Now you can make marks and machine for #20 biscuits, registering the biscuit joiner base against the edge to cut the face slots, and against the face to cut the edge slots. Avoiding the screws, cut four biscuit joints into the parts. Glue biscuits into the slots on the inside leg and dry-fit the parts together. Work out how you are going to clamp the legs together. Quick-action clamps attached to the inner straight upright of the inside leg will hold the lower half, but the top half requires some creativity. We used a band clamp. You could also clamp a block to each face at the top of the inside leg, and clamp these down to the top of the front leg. When you've worked this out, apply glue to the

PHOTO K: Drill screw clearance holes in the table subbase for attaching it to the leg assembly. Place the subbase on the legs and extend the clearance holes into the legs. Attach the subbase with glue and screws.

PHOTO L: Glue plastic laminate edging to the edge of the tabletop with contact cement. Use a J-roller to press it tight. A heat gun on low setting can be used to soften the laminate so it can be bent around the corners without breaking.

edge of the inside leg and to the slots on the front leg. Clamp the parts together, keeping the top edges flush (**See Photo J**).

㉒ Draw a diagonal centerline on the table subbase, then offset the line ⅜-in. in each direction. Set the subbase on your worksurface with the lines facing up. Remove the clamps, then set the leg assembly upside down on the subbase. The outer edge of the inside leg should be 5½ in. from the corner of the subbase. Trace the outline of the legs onto the subbase. Remove the leg assembly and drill screw clearance holes so you can screw the subbase to the legs (**See Photo K**). Use only a regular drill bit, not your countersink bit, since this is the underside. Make sure to get two screws into the short edge of the outside leg. Set the leg assembly on the floor, right side up, and place the subbase on the assembly, referencing the traced outlines to ensure proper location. Countersink the screw holes from above. Remove the subbase, apply glue to the top edges of the legs, and screw the subbase to the tops of the legs. Paint the table base to match the bench.

LAMINATE THE TABLETOP
㉓ Start with the edging. Rip two 1¾-in.-wide strips of plastic laminate (clamp an auxiliary plywood rip fence to your table saw fence if the laminate slips underneath it). The circumference of the tabletop is about 104 in., so if you cut one laminate strip to 74 in. and the other (slightly oversize) to 32 in. you can cover the edge, with the joints located midway along the straight sections. Make sure the ends of the laminate are cut clean and square. Using a combination square, draw a line across each straight edge of the tabletop

where you want the joints in the edge-stripping to be located. Apply contact cement to the edge of the tabletop and the long piece of edging. After the glue has dried so it's no longer tacky (see manufacturer's directions), attach the long piece of edging to the tabletop. Align the end of the edging precisely with one of the reference lines you drew on the tabletop edge. Keeping the edging strip straight and pulled tight, gradually press it firmly down against the edge of the top, applying pressure with a J-roller. You'll need to soften the laminate a bit with a heat gun to get it to bend around the corners. Keep the heat gun moving to avoid burning or melting the plastic. Work your way around the tabletop, keeping the overhang equal at the top and bottom. When you've finished, use a cloth tape measure to measure the required length for the second piece of edging. Cut it ⅓₂ in. longer than this distance. Apply contact cement to this piece and reapply a fresh coat to the top if the previous coat has dried too long (refer to manufacturer's directions). After the cement has dried properly, apply the short edging strip to the edge, butting it tightly against the end of the strip you already attached. Work your way around the corner and butt the edging against the other end of the edging already applied. Use your J-roller to press the edging against the tabletop edge **(See Photo L)**. Use a router or a

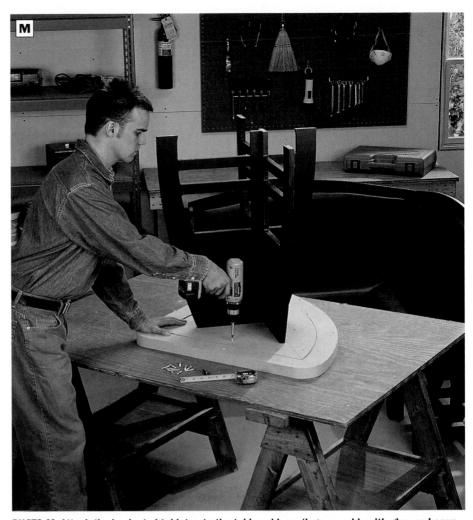

PHOTO M: Attach the laminated tabletop to the table subbase/leg assembly with glue and countersunk wood screws.

laminate-trimmer with a flush-trim bit to remove the overhanging laminate.

24 Cut the top laminate to size. Apply contact cement to both the tabletop and the laminate. Wait for the cement to dry and set the top laminate on the top, making sure it overhangs all edges of the tabletop. Press the laminate to the tabletop, starting at one straight edge and working your way across the surface with your J-roller. Use a flush-trimming bit in your router to remove the excess laminate. File the edges so they are not sharp.

25 Attach the leg assembly to the tabletop with countersunk screws driven up through the bottom of the table subbase **(See Photo M)**.

Changing Table / Dresser

Y ou'll be the toast of the baby shower when you produce this striking and efficient baby changing table for your loved one. Clean lines and contemporary styling create a little design flair that will enhance baby's room. And the easy-clean plastic laminate surfaces will be much appreciated by the new parents. NOTE: if you're giving this changing table as a gift, the new parents will also appreciate it if you throw in a changing pad to go with it. When baby no longer needs the changing table, it can be easily converted to a dresser or linen cabinet for bedrooms and bathrooms.

Vital Statistics: Changing Table/Dresser

TYPE: Changing table with storage

OVERALL SIZE: 40L × 20W × 32H

MATERIAL: Maple or birch plywood, solid mahogany or birch, particle-board, plastic laminate

JOINERY: Biscuit joints, pocket screws, tongue-and-groove drawer joint

CONSTRUCTION DETAILS:

· Top surface, door and drawer fronts covered with easy-to-clean plastic laminate
· Cabinet sides and front rails/legs taper outward.
· Left side has free-floating drawers, right side has interior cabinet with adjustable shelves.
· Tabletop mounts with corner braces.

FINISH: Satin polyurethane on maple parts

Building time

PREPARING STOCK
2-4 hours

LAYOUT
2-4 hours

CUTTING PARTS
2-4 hours

ASSEMBLY
6-8 hours

FINISHING
4-6

TOTAL: 16-26 hours

Tools you'll use

· Table saw
· Corner-beading bit
· Drum sander
· Circular saw
· Jig saw
· Square
· Router and router table
· Dado blade set
· Flush-trim bit
· Small level
· Straightedge
· Laminate trimmer (router)
· Straightedge guide
· J-roller
· Band saw (optional
· Laminate file
· Biscuit joiner
· ¼-in-radius roundover bit
· Bar or pipe clamps
· Belt sander
· Drill/driver
· Pocket screw drilling jig

Shopping list

- [ ] (1) ½ in. × 4 ft. × 4 ft. maple plywood
- [ ] (1) ¾ in. × 4 ft. × 8 ft. maple plywood
- [ ] (1) ¾ in. × 4 ft. × 8 ft. particleboard
- [ ] ¾ × 4 × 40 in. maple
- [ ] ⅟₃₂ in. × 4 ft. × 4 ft. laminate
- [ ] (1) maple edge banding (8 ft.)
- [ ] (2) European face-frame hinges
- [ ] (4) 1¼ in. door/drawer knobs
- [ ] (6) 16 in. low-profile drawer slides
- [ ] (6) 3 in. drawer mounting sockets
- [ ] (8) 1¼ in. shelf supports
- [ ] (4) 9½ in. corner braces
- [ ] 1¼ in. pocket screws
- [ ] #20 biscuits
- [ ] Wood glue, finishing materials

Changing Table

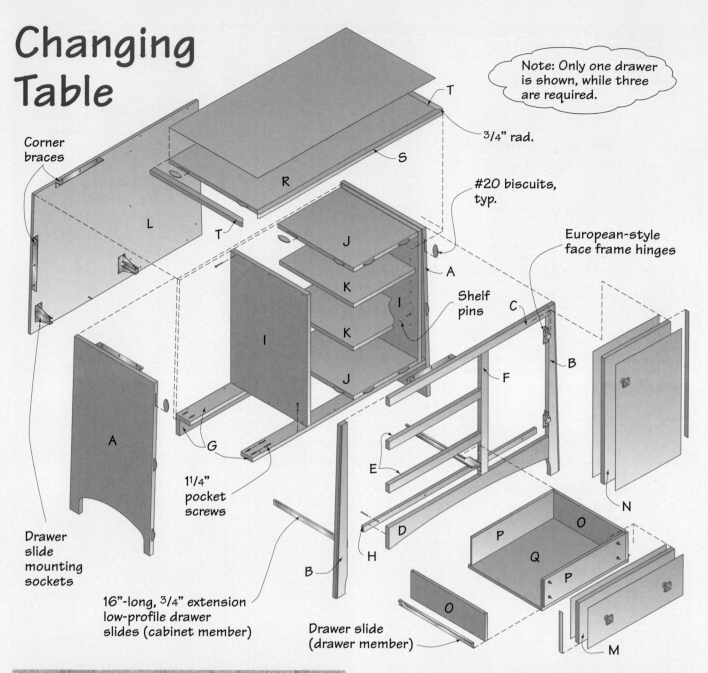

Corner braces

Note: Only one drawer is shown, while three are required.

3/4" rad.

T

S

R

#20 biscuits, typ.

European-style face frame hinges

J

K

K

J

A

I

Shelf pins

C

B

F

L

T

I

N

A

G

1 1/4" pocket screws

E

D

H

P

O

Q

P

Drawer slide mounting sockets

B

16"-long, 3/4" extension low-profile drawer slides (cabinet member)

H

D

O

Drawer slide (drawer member)

M

Cabinet Cutting List

Part	No.	Size	Material
A. End panel	2	$3/4 \times 17^7/_{16} \times 31^1/_4$ in.	Maple plywood
B. Stiles	2	$3/4 \times 2^1/_2 \times 31^1/_4$ in.	Solid maple
C. Top rail	1	$3/4 \times 1^1/_2 \times 34$ in.	"
D. Bottom rail	1	$3/4 \times 4 \times 34$ in.	"
E. Drawer rail	2	$3/4 \times 1^1/_2 \times 19^1/_2$ in.	"
F. Divider	1	$3/4 \times 1^1/_2 \times 22^1/_4$ in.	"
G. Blocking	3	$3/4 \times 3 \times 37$ in.	Maple plywood
H. Front cleat	1	$3/4 \times 1 \times 37$ in.	Solid maple
I. Side panels	2	$3/4 \times 16^7/_{16} \times 24^1/_2$ in.	Maple plywood
J. Fixed shelf	2	$3/4 \times 16^7/_{16} \times 13^3/_8$ in.	"
K. Adj. shelf	2	$3/4 \times 16 \times 13^1/_8$ in.	"
L. Back panel	1	$1/2 \times 37^1/_8 \times 25^1/_2$ in.	"

Drawers/Door Cutting List

Part	No.	Size	Material
M. Drawer core	3	$3/4 \times 7^7/_{16} \times 20^7/_{16}$ in.	Particleboard
N. Door core	1	$3/4 \times 13^{15}/_{16} \times 23^7/_{16}$ in.	"
O. Side	6	$1/2 \times 5 \times 16$ in.	Maple plywood
P. Front/back	6	$1/2 \times 5 \times 17^{15}/_{16}$ in.	"
Q. Bottom	3	$1/2 \times 16 \times 18^7/_{16}$ in.	"

Top Cutting List

Part	No.	Size	Material
R. Top panel	1	$3/4 \times 19 \times 38$ in.	Particleboard
S. Front edge	1	$1^3/_{16} \times 1 \times 40$ in.	Solid maple
T. Side edge	2	$1^3/_{16} \times 1 \times 20$ in.	"

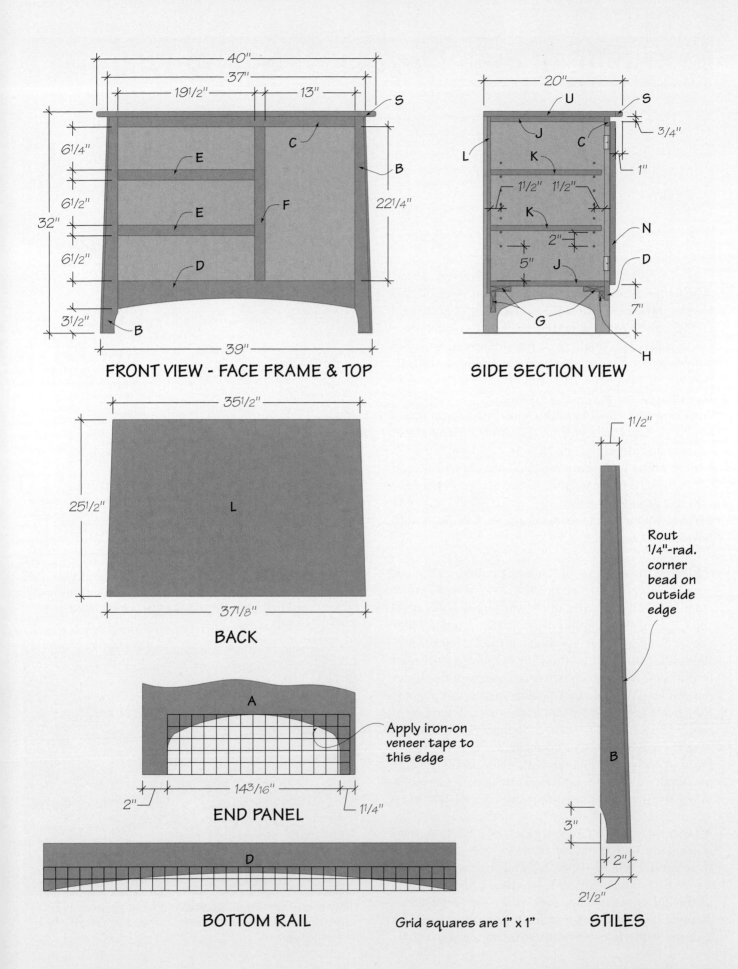

FRONT VIEW - FACE FRAME & TOP

40"
37"
19¹/2"   13"
S
C
6¹/4"
E
B
6¹/2"
E
F
22¹/4"
32"
6¹/2"
D
3¹/2"
B
39"

SIDE SECTION VIEW

20"
U
S
J
C
3/4"
L
1"
K
1¹/2"   1¹/2"
K
N
2"
5"
D
J
7"
G
H

BACK

35¹/2"
25¹/2"
L
37¹/8"

END PANEL

A
Apply iron-on veneer tape to this edge
2"   14³/16"   1¹/4"

BOTTOM RAIL

D

Grid squares are 1" x 1"

STILES

1¹/2"
Rout 1/4"-rad. corner bead on outside edge
B
3"
2"
2¹/2"

BUILD THE CARCASE

1 Cut the two end panels to size from ¾-in. birch or maple plywood. Since the ends will angle outward slightly, their top and bottom edges will need to be cut at a bit of an angle to be parallel to the floor. Set your table saw blade at a 2° angle and lower it so it just barely protrudes from the table. Attach an auxiliary plywood or particleboard fence to your rip fence with clamps or double-stick tape. Using scrap pieces of plywood (preferably from the same plywood sheet) to test the cut, adjust the rip fence and the blade height so the blade cuts into the auxiliary fence at just the right point to cut a bevel on the plywood edge without reducing its overall length. Bevel both ends of each finished end with this setup, making sure the bevels are parallel.

2 Using the drawing of the lower cutout on the end panel as a guide (See page 143), make a template from ¼-in. hardboard. Cut out the shape and smooth the edges of the template with a drum sander. Label the front and back leg sections of the template, as they differ in width to allow for the added thickness of the face frame in front. Trace the template shapes onto the outside faces of the end panels, making sure the beveled top and bottom edges are aligned correctly **(See Photo A)**. Cut close to the lines with a jig saw; then clamp, nail or double-stick tape the template to each end panel, in succession. Trim the end panels flush to the template outlines using a router and a flush-trim (pattern-cutting) bit (See page 131).

3 Cut the cabinet face frame parts, including the stiles, top rail, bottom rail, drawer rails and divider from solid birch. Also cut the birch front cleat to size. Taper the outside edges of the stiles from 2½ in. wide at the bottoms to 1½ in. wide at the top. We used a straightedge template and flush-trim bit mounted in a router table to cut the tapes. You could also use a

PHOTO A: Make a hardboard template of the cutout shape for the bottoms of the end panels. Trace the shape onto the lower portions of each end panel (make sure the beveled bottom edge is facing in the correct direction).

PHOTO B: Glue the face frame joints and clamp the parts together, making sure all faces are flush. Drive pocket screws to hold the face frame parts together.

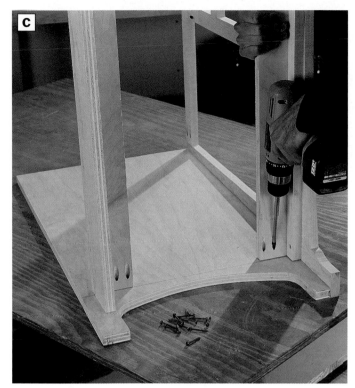

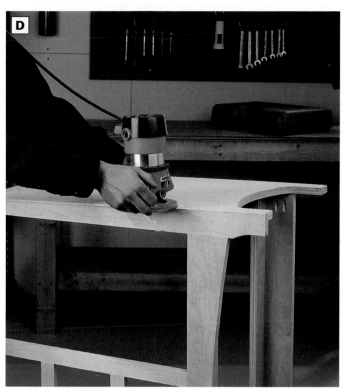

PHOTO C: Attach the blocking to the inside of the cabinet with pocket screws. Mount the blocking so its lower faces ride on lines drawn 6 in. up from the bottom edges of the end panels.

PHOTO D: To create a decorative bead on the outer corners of the cabinet, rout a corner bead along the front outside edge of each stile.

taper-cutting jig and a table saw. Using the measurements on page 143 and a French curve or flexible spline curve as references, draw the decorative cutout on the bottom inside edge of each stile. Make the cuts with a band saw or jig saw and sand the edges smooth with a drum sander.

❹ Draw the arc on the bottom edge of the bottom rail using a flexible strip of thin scrap wood to form the arc (or, you can simply plot out the arc using the drawing on page 143 as a guide). Cut the arc with a band saw or jig saw and smooth the cut edges with a drum sander.

❺ Lay out the joints on the face frame parts, and drill pocket screw holes on the inside surfaces of all the rails and the center divider (See page 19). Machine for two pocket screws at each joint.

❻ Assemble the face frame using glue and pocket screws (See Photo B). Hold the parts together with clamps while you insert the screws. Wipe up excess glue squeeze-out with a damp cloth.

❼ The end panels get attached to the face frame by biscuit-joining the front edges of the panels to the stiles. Butt the parts together, then mark out and cut

slots for #20 biscuits in the joint area. Glue biscuits into the backs of the stiles, spread glue on the edges of the end panels, and clamp the end panels to the face frame with padded bar or pipe clamps. Make sure the top and bottom edges are all flush, and that the joints are square (you can use a combination square, or measure across the front and the back of the assembly—the distances should be equal). Wipe up glue squeeze-out.

❽ Use glue and countersunk screws to attach the front cleat to the inside face of the bottom rail, 1½ in. below the top edge of the rail.

❾ Cut the three blocking strips to size from ¾-in. plywood. On the inside face of each end panel, measure up and make marks 6 in. from the bottom edge, at the front and back of each. Use a straightedge to draw a line connecting the two points, creating a reference line across each end panel. This is the height at which the blocking will be mounted. Machine for pocket screws at both ends of each blocking strip. Attach the front blocking with countersunk screws driven down into the front cleat, and with pocket screws driven into the end panels. The lower face of the blocking should ride against the lines on the end panels. Using glue and clamps and/or screws, make

PHOTO E: Use a square and a straightedge to draw a line down the right side of the back panel. The line should be perpendicular to the top and bottom edges and it should cut off the angled edge. This will create a reference for attaching the internal cabinet to the back panel.

PHOTO F: Cut biscuit joints for attaching the top and bottom front edges of the internal cabinet to the inside of the face frame.

an L with the two remaining blocking strips in the configuration shown in the *Side Section View,* page 143. Fasten the L to the end panels with pocket screws, aligning the lower face of the top member with the lines drawn on the end panels (**See Photo C**). The back edge of the "L" should be inset 1 in. from the back edges of the end panels to allow room for the cabinet back. Because the internal cabinet structure will rest on the blocking, the upper face of the cabinet bottom should be flush with the top edge of the bottom rail.

⑩ With a corner-beading bit mounted in your router, rout a decorative corner bead profile along the front outside corner of each stile (**See Photo D**).

CONSTRUCT THE INTERNAL CABINET

To simplify assembly of the changing table, we designed it as essentially a cabinet within a cabinet. The internal cabinet structure is squared up and assembled separately, then mounted inside the larger cabinet carcase.

⑪ Cut the side panels, fixed shelves and adjustable shelves to size from ¾-in. plywood. Also cut the back panel from ¾-in. plywood. The back panel will be angled on both ends to fit between the angled ends of the cabinet. Lay out the angled lines with a straight-edge, according to the cutting diagram labeled *"Back"* on page 143. Make the cuts with a circular saw and a straightedge guide. Then, use a square and a straightedge to square a line down from the top right corner of the back (**See Photo E**). This will give you a reference for positioning the internal cabinet against the back panel.

⑫ Cut slots for #20 biscuits used to assemble the internal cabinet (the top and bottom will be captured between the sides). Then, drill ¼-in.-dia. shelf pin holes in the sides (make sure the holes are even and are sized to fit your shelf pins). Use a drill press or a portable drill with a right-angle drilling guide.

⑬ Glue and clamp up the internal cabinet, reinforcing the joints with biscuits. Adjust the clamps as needed to square up the cabinet. Clean up glue squeeze-out.

⑭ Attach the back panel to the internal cabinet with countersunk screws, following the reference line drawn on the inside face of the back panel. The back panel can help ensure the cabinet is squared correctly. The back panel will overhang the internal cabinet by 1 in. at the bottom.

15 Apply iron-on veneer tape to the front edges of the adjustable shelves, and trim off excess with a hand edging trimmer or a sharp chisel (See page 20).

JOIN THE INTERNAL & MAIN CABINETS

16 Lay out and cut slots for #20 biscuits to join the top front edge of the internal cabinet to the inside face of the top rail, and the bottom front edge of the interior cabinet to the inside face of the bottom rail **(See Photo F)**. Glue biscuits into the slots in the face frame, and dry-fit the assembly. The back panel should fit snugly in between the end panels.

17 Disassemble the construction and apply glue to the front edges of the internal cabinet. Clamp the internal cabinet to the face frame with bar or pipe clamps. Use wood cauls to spread the clamping pressure. Using the screws provided with the hardware, attach metal corner braces at the left end/back panel joint, as well as along the top edges of the end panels, the back, and the top rail in the drawer section of the cabinet **(See Photo G)**.

BUILD & HANG THE DOORS & DRAWERS

18 Cut the drawer sides, fronts/backs and bottoms to size from ½-in. plywood. The drawers will be constructed with tongue-and-groove drawer joints. Install a dado-blade set adjusted to ¼ in. in your table saw, and cut ¼ × ¼-in. grooves in the drawer sides ¼ in. from each end **(See Photo H)**. Then, cut matching tongues in the drawer fronts and backs by cutting ¼ × ¼-in. rabbets in the end of each board **(See Photo I)**.

19 Finish-sand the interior faces of the drawer parts. Spread glue on the mating parts and clamp the drawer sides to the fronts and backs with bar or quick-action clamps. Make sure the boxes are square during assembly. Wipe up any glue squeeze-out with a damp rag.

20 Attach the drawer bottoms with 1-in. countersunk screws **(See Photo J)**, making sure the edges of the drawer and bottom are flush all around.

21 Mount the drawer slides to the face frame, according to the manufacturer's directions. Use mounting sockets to attach the back end of each slide to the cabinet back so the slide is level. Attach the mating

PHOTO G: Glue the internal cabinet to the inside of the face frame with biscuit joints, using wood cauls to spread the clamping pressure. Through a metal corner brace, screw the back panel to the left-hand end panel. Also attach corner braces along the top edges of the drawer compartment to serve as mounting brackets for the cabinet top.

PHOTO H: The first step in machining the drawer joints is to cut a ¼ × ¼-in. dado into the drawer sides, ¼ in. from the ends.

PHOTO I: Cut ¼ × ¼-in. rabbets in the ends of the drawer fronts and backs to form matching tongues.

PHOTO J: Use countersunk 1-in. screws to fasten the bottoms to the drawers. If the bottoms are cut square, they can be used to square up the drawers by keeping the drawer box outer faces flush with the edges of the bottoms.

drawer slide members to the drawers and make sure they operate properly. The slides should be mounted so each drawer hangs in its face frame opening with ½ in. above and ½ in. below.

㉒ Cut the drawer front cores and door cores to size from ¾-in. particleboard. Cut plastic laminate to cover the cores, at least ¼ in. larger than the cores in each direction (See page 23). Attach an auxiliary plywood fence to your table saw's rip fence when cutting the thin laminate to keep it from sliding under the rip fence.

㉓ Laminate the edges of the drawer fronts and the door first, then laminate the faces. Start by rolling contact cement on the vertical edges of the parts and their mating laminate edging strips. When the adhesive has dried so it's no longer tacky, apply the edging and roll it firmly with a J-roller. Trim overhanging laminate with a laminate trimmer and a piloted flush-trim bit. Repeat this procedure with the horizontal edging on all parts. Then laminate the back

faces of the parts and finally the front faces, trimming the overhanging laminate each time with the laminate trimmer or router and flush-trim bit. File all laminate edges so they're flush, and soften any sharp edges.

㉔ Install the adjustable hinges according to the manufacturer's instructions and hang the doors on the cabinet.

㉕ Slide the bottom drawer into the cabinet. Use double-sided tape to fit a drawer front onto the drawer box. It should be ½ in. from the door, with its bottom edge flush with the bottom of the door. Put the other drawer fronts in position similarly, with ½-in. spaces between them. Remove the drawers from the cabinet and drill pilot holes from inside the drawer boxes, then attach the drawer fronts permanently with pan-head screws (over-size the guide holes through the fronts of the drawer boxes slightly so the position of the drawer fronts can be adjusted). Drill holes and mount knobs on the drawer fronts and the door.

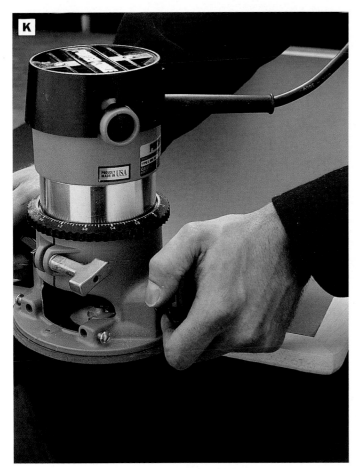

PHOTO K: After rounding the sharp corners of the top, round over the top and bottom edges of the wood all around with a ¼-in.-radius roundover bit in the router.

PHOTO L: After the finish has dried, rehang and adjust the door and the drawer fronts for proper alignment.

Adjust the door and drawer fronts as necessary so they are straight and aligned properly.

BUILD & MOUNT THE TOP

26 Cut the top core to size from ¾-in. particleboard. Cut a piece of plastic laminate slightly larger than the core. If it's more convenient than cutting on the table saw, you can cut laminate by scoring it against a steel straightedge and breaking it along the scored lines. Glue the laminate onto the top core as with the drawer and door cores, and trim the excess.

27 Cut the front and side edging to size from solid wood. Miter the front corners so the edging wraps around the core. Machine the edging and the edges of the top core for #20 biscuit joints, and glue the edges to the core. Remember to glue the edging miters.

28 Round the front corners of the top to a ¾-in. radius, using a belt sander. Then run a router with a ¼-in.-radius roundover bit around the top and bottom edges **(See Photo K)**.

29 Mount the top on the cabinet and center it so the overhang is even all around. Attach it to the internal cabinet with countersunk screws driven up from inside the cabinet. Drive them in only until the heads are flush with the surface. Attach the left side of the top to the cabinet with the metal corner braces in the top of the door compartment.

FINISHING TOUCHES

30 Remove hardware and finish-sand all surfaces. Apply finish of your choice. We used clear satin polyurethane.

31 When the finish has fully cured, reassemble and rehang the door and drawers **(See Photo L)**. Install the knobs. Attach bumpers to the back faces of the drawer fronts and the door. Insert the shelf pins and install the adjustable shelves.

Country Cupboard

Add a touch of rural charm to any kitchen or dining area with this pine country cupboard. Our design features a beadboard back panel, sides made of glue-up pine panels (see the description on page 13) and arched accents to mimic traditional styling for storage cupboards of this kind. Both shelves are fully adjustable, and the cupboard is hung securely with concealed French cleats.

Vital Statistics: Country Cupboard

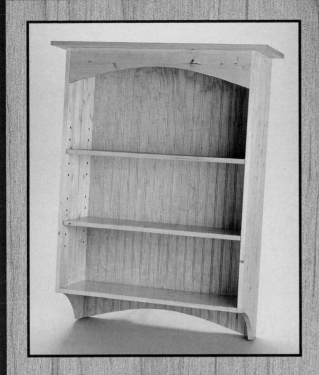

TYPE: Wall-hung country cupboard

OVERALL SIZE: 48H × 36W × 14D

MATERIAL: Glue-up pine panels & plywood beadboard

JOINERY: Dado, rabbet and biscuit joints; butt joints reinforced with pocket screws

CONSTRUCTION DETAILS:
· Decorative arch cutouts on valance, sides and back panel
· Beadboard back panel fits into dadoes machined in cupboard sides
· Fully-adjustable shelves
· Cupboard mounts to wall with interlocking French cleats

FINISH: Two coats of orange or amber natural shellac

Building time

 PREPARING STOCK
3-4 hours

 LAYOUT
2-3 hours

 CUTTING PARTS
3-5 hours

 ASSEMBLY
2-3 hours

 FINISHING
1-2 hours

TOTAL: 11-17 hours

Tools you'll use

· Compass or trammel points
· Table saw
· Jig saw
· Band saw (optional)
· Drum or pad sander
· Biscuit joiner
· Drill/driver
· Pocket-hole jig
· Router table with ⅜-in. straight bit
· Hammer
· Clamps
· Chisel
· Combination square

Shopping list

☐ (1) ¾ × 24 × 48 in. glue-up pine panel
☐ (2) ¾ × 16 in. × 6 ft. glue-up pine panels
☐ (1) 11⁄32 in. × 4 ft. × 8 ft. pine beadboard
☐ (20) brass shelf pin grommets
☐ (8) ¼-in. brass shelf pins
☐ #20 biscuits
☐ 1¼-in. pocket screws
☐ #8 flathead wood screws (1-, 1½-, 3-in.)
☐ Wood glue
☐ Finishing materials

Country Cupboard

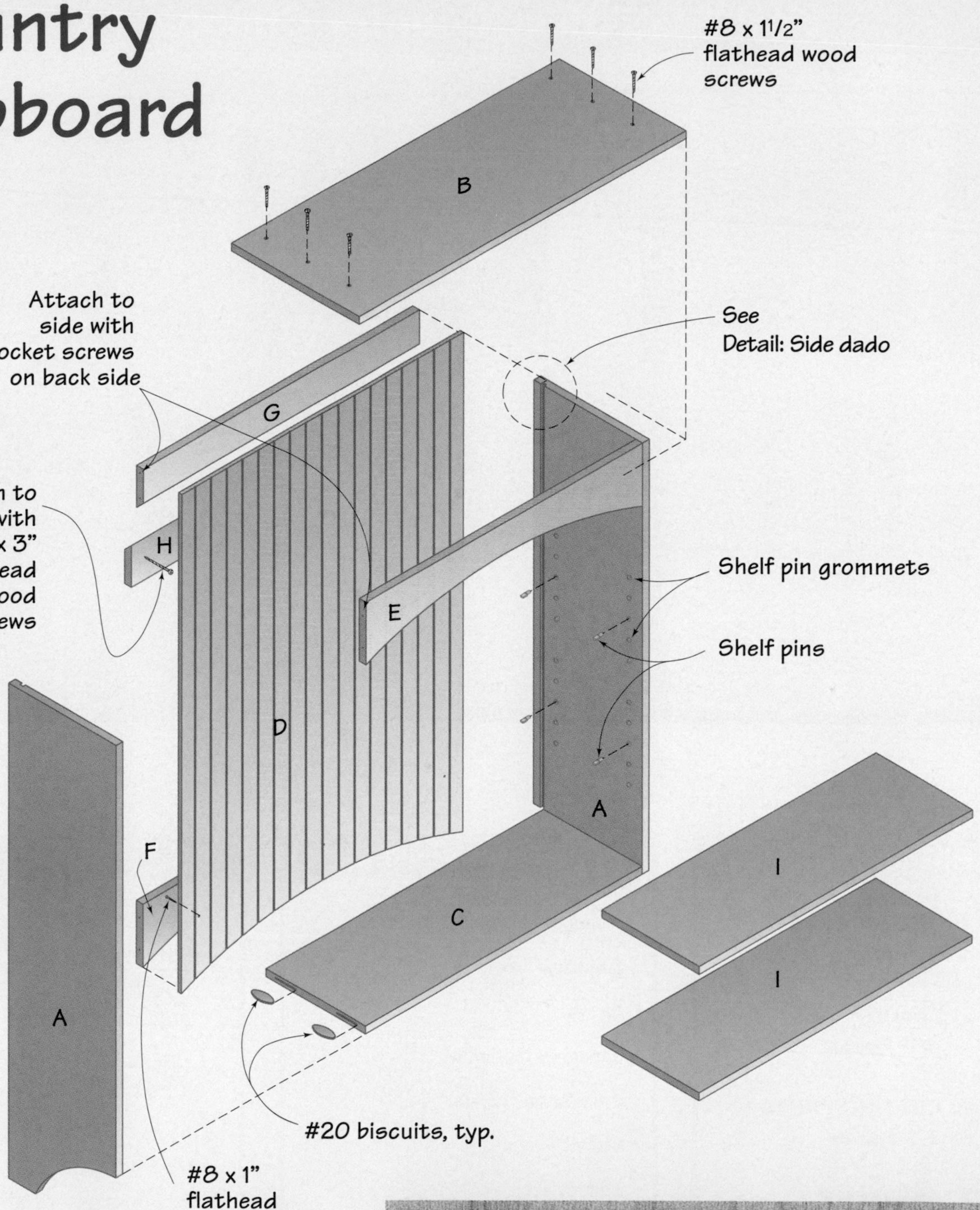
#8 x 1 1/2"
flathead wood
screws
B
Attach to
side with
pocket screws
on back side
See
Detail: Side dado
G
Attach to
wall with
#8 x 3"
flathead
wood
screws
H
E
Shelf pin grommets
Shelf pins
D
A
F
C
I
I
A
#20 biscuits, typ.
#8 x 1"
flathead
wood screws

Country Cupboard Cutting List

Part	No.	Size	Material
A. Sides	2	¾ × 12 × 47¼ in.	Glue-up panel (pine)
B. Top	1	¾ × 14 × 36 in.	"
C. Bottom	1	¾ × 10⅞ × 30½ in.	"
D. Back	1	11⁄32 × 31 × 47⅝ in.	Pine beadboard
E. Valance	1	¾ × 6 × 30½ in.	Glue-up panel (pine)
F. Blocking	1	¾ × 6 × 30½ in.	"
G. Cabinet cleat	1	¾ × 4 × 30½ in.	"
H. Wall cleat	1	¾ × 4 × 28½ in.	"
I. Shelves	2	¾ × 10¾ × 30½ in.	"

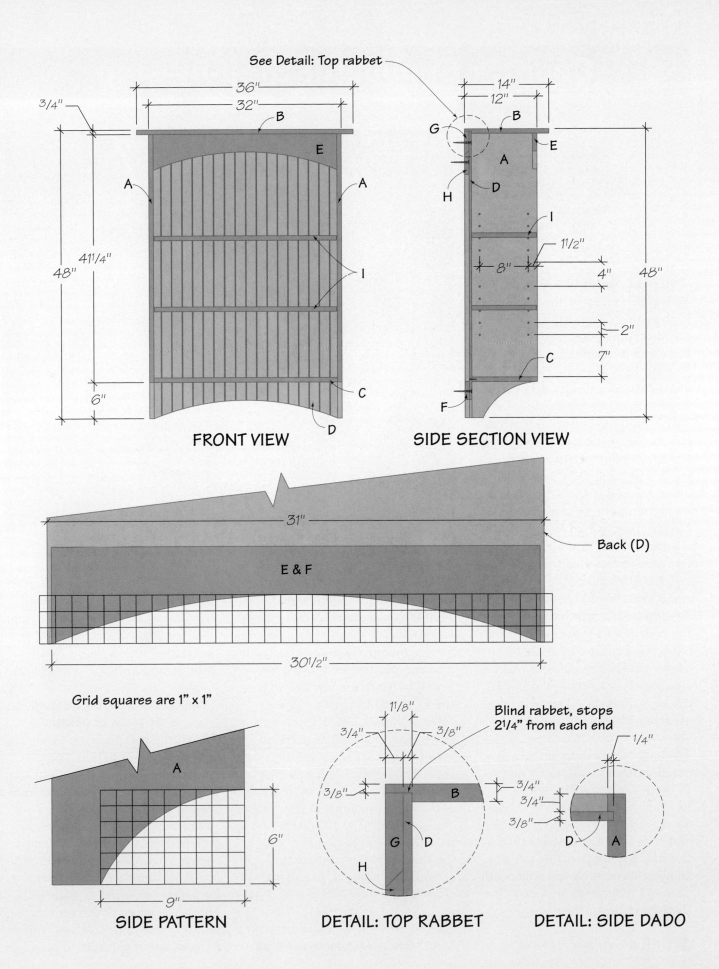

See Detail: Top rabbet

36"

32"

3/4"

B

E

A

A

48"

41 1/4"

I

6"

C

D

FRONT VIEW

14"

12"

G

B

A

E

H

D

I

11/2"

8"

4"

48"

2"

C

7"

F

SIDE SECTION VIEW

31"

Back (D)

E & F

30 1/2"

Grid squares are 1" x 1"

A

6"

9"

SIDE PATTERN

11/8"

3/4"

3/8"

Blind rabbet, stops
2 1/4" from each end

1/4"

3/8"

B

3/4"

3/4"

G

D

3/8"

H

D

A

DETAIL: TOP RABBET

DETAIL: SIDE DADO

PREPARE THE SIDES & SHELVES

1 Rip and crosscut the sides and shelves to size from 12-in.-wide glued-up pine panels, according to the measurements given in the *Cutting List*. The sides feature a decorative arc cutout in the lower front corners. To lay out the arcs, make a reference mark 6 in. from one corner of one side panel along the edge and a second reference mark 9 in. from the same corner along the end of the panel. Make an arc template from ¼-in. scrap hardboard or plywood. Start with a square about 11 × 11 in. Use a compass or trammel points to swing a 10⅜-in.-radius arc from one corner. We attached white paper over the hardboard to see the pencil marks more clearly. Cut out the template and smooth the edges. Set the template on one side panel, aligning the arc with the layout marks. Then trace the arc (**See Photo A**).

2 Gang-cut the arcs on both side panels with a band saw or jig saw. To do this, clamp both panels together so that the panel marked for the arc is on top and the edges and ends of the panels are flush. Cut along the layout line to form identical arcs. With the panels still clamped, sand both arcs smooth. Unclamp the panels.

3 Drill two rows of holes in each

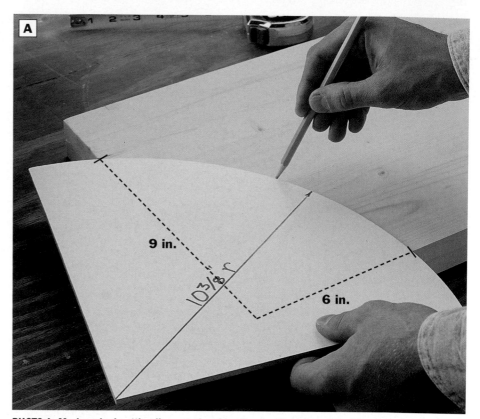

PHOTO A: Mark arched cutting lines on the side pieces using a template. The arc should intersect points measured from one corner—6 in. along one edge and 9 in. along the adjacent end of the panel.

side panel to house the adjustable shelf pin grommets. NOTE: *Grommets will keep metal shelf pins from widening the holes as they are inserted and removed.* Draw two long lines that are parallel with the front and back edges of the sides and inset 1½ in. from each edge. Make a reference mark on both layout lines, 13¾ in. from the bottom edge of the sides, for the first holes. Then, mark off the rest of the holes as shown in the *Side Section View*, page 153. Drill 9/32-in.-dia. holes at each mark, gauging the depth according to the grommets you buy. Use a depth stop on your drill bit.

4 Rout a ⅜-in.-wide dado on the inside face of each side panel for

the back panel. Make each dado ¼ in. deep and locate it ¾ in. from the back edge of each panel. Cut the dadoes with a router and a ⅜-in. straight bit.

MAKE THE BOTTOM, VALANCE & BOTTOM BLOCKING

5 Cut the bottom, valance and bottom blocking to size. The valance and bottom blocking have arc cutouts that are gang-cut and sanded simultaneously. Use a ¼-in.-thick strip of wood about 1 in. wide and about 42 in. long or a scrap piece of tempered hardboard to form a flexible batten for determining the arc curve. Measure and mark the centerpoint (both lengthwise and widthwise) of either the bottom blocking or the valance and tack a long finish nail ¼ in. below this spot. Set the workpiece on a scrap board to use as a tacking surface for marking the ends of the arc, and nail a finish nail at each of these two locations. Flex the batten over the centerpoint nail and under the nails at each end to form a gentle arc. Reinforce the batten's curve by adding a few more nails next to the batten. Draw a line along the batten to mark the curve (**See Photo B**).

6 Clamp the bottom blocking and valance together with the curve layout on top and gang-cut the curves in both workpieces. Smooth the curves with a sander (**See Photo C**).

7 Drill three pocket screw holes in each end of the valance and bottom blocking in order to attach these pieces to the side panels later. (For more on pocket screws, see p. 19.) Drill the holes on the back side of each piece so the screws won't show once the cupboard is assembled.

8 Lay out and cut #20 biscuit slots for attaching the ends of the bottom panel to the sides. Use one end of the bottom as a straight-edge to help align the biscuit joiner as you cut slots in the side panels. Glue biscuits into the ends of the bottom now to make assembly easier later, and wipe up excess glue around the biscuits.

PREPARE THE BACK & TOP PANELS

9 Cut the back panel to size from 11⁄32-in. pine beadboard. Using the bottom blocking or valance as a pattern, trace the decorative arc onto the bottom of the back. Cut the back with a jig saw and sand the edge smooth.

PHOTO B: Mark the arc cutout on the valance or bottom blocking by springing a thin, flexible wood or hardboard batten between nails to connect the centerpoint with the corners. The batten creates a smooth arc for tracing.

PHOTO C: We used spring clamps to stack the valance and bottom blocking so they could be gang-cut and sanded smooth together.

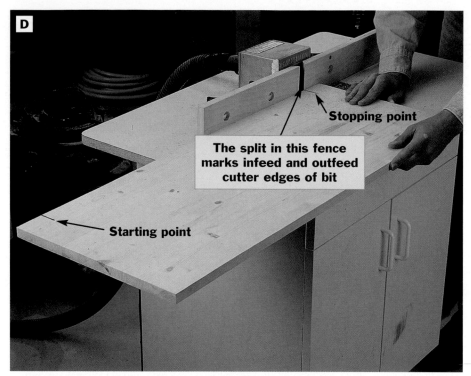

PHOTO D: Machine a stopped rabbet in the back bottom edge of the top. Make stop marks on the workpiece to locate where to start and end the cut, and make a second set of marks to locate the edges of the bit. Use the workpiece and bit marks in tandem to cut the rabbet.

⓾ Cut the top to size. Rout a ⅜-deep rabbet along the back, bottom edge of the top. This stopped (also called blind) rabbet should stop 2 in. from either end. Mark the workpiece to indicate starting and stopping points for the rabbet. Also mark the fence to show the left (outfeed) and right (infeed) edges of the bit. Then, install a ½- or ¾-in. straight bit for cutting the rabbet. To prepare for the first cut, attach a scrap-wood fence to your router table fence. Set the scrap fence as close as possible to the blade, without touching it. Raise the blade to ⅜-in. cutting depth. Start the router and slide the router fence forward until the bit cuts into the scrap fence about ⅛ in. NOTE: *If your router fence splits into two pieces as ours does, simply set the fence halves slightly over the edge of the bit instead of cutting into a scrap-wood fence.* Begin the rabbet by starting the router with the workpiece clear of the bit. Pivot the workpiece slowly into the bit and against the fence so the starting mark on the workpiece aligns with the outfeed blade mark on the fence. Then feed the workpiece along the fence until the stop mark on the workpiece aligns with the infeed blade mark **(See Photo D)**. Since the rabbet is 1⅛ in. wide, you'll need to make multiple side-by-side passes in this fashion to cut the rabbet to full width, sliding the fence ¼ in. or so back from the bit with each pass, removing progressively more material. Once you are finished routing, square up the ends of the rabbet with a chisel.

ASSEMBLE THE CUPBOARD

⓫ Dry-assemble the cupboard. Set and clamp the valance and bottom pieces into place between the side panels, with the front of the cupboard facing down on a

PHOTO E: Dry-assemble the carcase with clamps and pocket screws to check the fit. Start by installing the valance and bottom panel temporarily with screws and clamps.

PHOTO F: Glue and clamp up the sides, bottom, valance, and top. Slide the back in place and screw it to the cupboard bottom with 1-in. flathead wood screws. Check the cupboard for square by measuring the diagonals before driving the screws.

PHOTO G: Attach the cabinet hanging cleat and bottom blocking to the cupboard sides with glue and pocket screws. Be sure the cabinet hanging cleat bevel faces the right direction (See page 27).

suitable worksurface. Drive pocket screws into the valance pocket holes, stopping short of seating the screw heads (**See Photo E**). Mark the centerline of the cupboard bottom on the back inside edge of each side panel, behind the dado. Slide the back into the dado. Set the top into position over the side panels. Screw the top temporarily to the sides using 1½-in. flathead wood screws. Slide the back in the dado; the bottom of the back should sit flush with the bottom of the sides. Draw a line across the back to connect the bottom panel centerline marks.

⓬ Disassemble the cupboard and apply glue to the ends of the bottom, valance and top edges of the sides. Reassemble and clamp up the cupboard carcase, wiping up any glue that squeezes out with a damp cloth. Slide the back into the dado and attach it to the bottom with 1-in. flathead wood screws (**See Photo F**). Attach the bottom blocking piece to the cupboard sides with glue and pocket screws, aligning the bottom blocking and back panel arcs.

⓭ Cut the hanging French cleats to size and rip a 45° bevel along one long edge of each cleat. Attach the cabinet hanging cleat to the cupboard sides with glue and pocket screws, orienting the cleat as shown in *Detail: Top Rabbet,* page 153 (**See Photo G**).

FINISHING TOUCHES

⓮ Plug the screw holes in the top if you like, and trim the plugs flush when the glue dries. Sand the cupboard with 120-grit sandpaper and apply the finish of your choice. Traditionally, country pine furnishings are finished with natural shellac, so we applied two coats of amber shellac flakes dissolved in alcohol.

⓯ Push metal grommets into the shelf pin holes in the sides. If it's difficult to drive them in fully, tap the grommets home with a hammer and block of wood.

⓰ Attach the wall hanging cleat to the wall with 3-in. countersunk flathead wood screws. NOTE: *The wall cleat is 2 in. shorter than the cabinet cleat so you have some leeway from side to side when hanging the cupboard.* Make sure you hit two wall studs when you drive the screws to anchor the cleat solidly. Mark stud locations on the wall so you can drive screws into the studs from inside the cupboard after hanging it on the wall cleat.

⓱ Hang the cabinet on the wall and drive 3-in. screws into the wall studs at the top and bottom of the cabinet (through the cabinet hanging cleat and bottom blocking). Install the shelf pins and adjustable shelves.

Index

A

African Padouk sheet veneer, 21
APA grading system, 8
Arc, scribing, 66, 68, 87, 134, 135, 154, 155

B

Band clamp, 137
Battens, 66, 68, 134, 154, 155
Bending plywood, 7
Bevel gauge, 122
Bi-fold doors, installing, 90
Birch veneer, 9
    edge banding, 20
Birdseye maple sheet veneer, 21
Biscuits, 59, 85, 115, 116, 123, 124, 137, 146
Blades,
    laminate, 12
    sheet goods, 17
Blum-brand fasteners (see *Ready-to-assemble fasteners*)
Butt hinges, mounting, 51, 90
Butt joint, 18

C

Cabinet,
    door types, 27
    drawer hanging, 26
    hanging with French cleats, 27
Carbon paper (see *Transferring patterns*)
Carcase,
    assembling, 39, 48, 49, 86, 87
    squaring up, 22
Casters, installing, 78, 79
Cauls, 115, 117, 124, 125, 147
Chamfer, stopped, 114, 115
Cherry veneer, 9
Chisel, as mortising tool, 51
Circular saw, 67
Clamp holder, 78, 79
Clamping technique, 49, 117, 124, 125, 147, 157
Combination square, 66, 67, 69, 96, 122
Compass jig, 104
Core types, plywood, 7
Corner bead, routing, 145
Corner bracket, 116
Cove, routing, 59, 60
Cross-dowel fasteners, 19

Cutting,
    circle with router, 104
    compound angles, 107, 108
    dadoes on router table, 41, 67
    dadoes on table saw, 39, 147
    dadoes with router, 76, 77
    kerfs in plywood, 67
    medium-density fiberboard, 96
    melamine board, 12, 38
    rabbets, 50, 97, 148
    sheet goods, 16, 17
    slots, 85, 86
    stopped chamfer on bandsaw, 114, 115
    stopped rabbet, 156
    tapers, 114
    veneer, 114

D

Dado,
    cutting on table saw, 39, 48, 147
    hand-held routing, 76, 77
    joint, 18
    routing on router table, 67, 89
    shelf supports, 25, 78
Dado/rabbet joint, 18
Deep clamp extenders, 124, 125
Defects, filling, 28
Dolly, sheet goods, 15
Doors (cabinet),
    frame assembly, 50
    hanging, 149
    hardware installation, 43
    panel construction, 42
    types, 27
Dowel,
    joints, 50, 42
    setting, 107, 108
Doweling jig, 133
Dowel pin shelf support, 25
Drawers,
    assembling, 40, 41, 90, 91, 117, 148
    false face attachment, 40, 41, 91
    glide options, 26
    hanging, 26
Drill press, 96-98, 108
Drum sander, 155

E

Edge banding,
    applying, 20
    common types, 20
Edging, solid stock, applying, 42, 43
Embossed molding, cutting &

attaching, 58, 59
European hinges, installing, 60, 61
Exterior-rated plywood, 7

F

Face frame,
    assembling, 87, 144
    attaching, 87, 88
Face-gluing blanks, 114
Filing, 106
Finishing,
    country pine furnishings, 157
    plywood, 28, 29, 123, 124
Finish nailing, 124, 125
Flush-mounted cabinet door, 27
French cleat, 27, 157
Full-overlay cabinet door, 27
Furnishings from sheet goods, 5

G

Gang-cutting, 96, 122, 154
Gang-sanding, 155
Gel stain, 28
Glass stops, making, 52
Glue-up panels, 13
Grade stamps, sanded plywood, 8
Grommets, 25, 154, 157

H

Half-overlay cabinet door, 27
Handling sheet goods, 14, 15
Handy panels (see *Glue-up panels*)
Hanger bolts, installing, 108, 109
Hardboard,
    perforated, 13
    tempered, 13
HPVA grading system, 8
HVLP sprayer, 60, 61

J

Jig,
    circle-cutting, 104
    kerf-cutting plywood, 67
    pocket-screw, 19
    taper, 114
Joinery, 18, 19
    reinforcing, 76
Jointing lumber, 49
J-roller, 23, 43, 138

K

Kerf-cutting plywood, 67, 68
Knockdown fasteners (see *Ready-to-assemble fasteners*)

L

Laminate,
  applying, 23, 42, 43, 138, 139,
    148
  around corners, 138
Laminating tools, 23
Layout techniques,
  battens, 66, 68, 134, 154, 155
  bevel gauge, 122
  combination square, 66, 67, 69,
    96, 122
  straightedge, 85, 146
  template, 131, 136, 144, 154
L-braces, 115, 116
Liquid stain, 28

M

Madrone burl sheet veneer, 21
Mahogany veneer, 9
Maple burl sheet veneer, 21
Maple veneer, 9
  edge banding, 20
Mechanical fasteners, 18, 19
Medium-density fiberboard
    (MDF), 11
  cleaning up glue on, 58
  cutting, 96
  manufacturing, 11
  weight chart, 14
Melamine board, 12
  cutting, 12, 38
Mela-quinella, 12
Minifix-brand fittings, 19
Miscellaneous sheet goods types,
    13
Miter saw (power), 76, 77, 107
Mortising, hinges, 51

O

Oak veneer, 9
  acceptance of common wood
    stains, 29

P

Painting furniture, 60, 61, 71, 108
Panel cutter, 17
Particleboard, 10, 11
  manufacturing, 10
  weight chart, 14
Pattern routing, 131
Pegboard (see *Perforated
    hardboard*)
Perforated hardboard, 13
  as shelf pin hole guide, 38, 48
Pine veneer, 9

acceptance of common wood
    stains, 29
Plywood, 6-9
  anatomy diagram, 6
  common veneer species, 9
  core types, 7
  face grades, 8
  grade stamps, 8
  manufacturing, 6
  sanding, 28
  selecting, 8, 9
  special-purpose types, 7
  surface preparation, 28
  textured, 13
  thickness guide, 7
  veneer grain patterns, 8
  weight chart, 14
  wood stain tone chart, 29
Pocket screws, 19, 99, 144, 145,
    155-157
Polyurethane glue, 107
Purpleheart sheet veneer, 21

R

Rabbet joints, 50, 97, 117, 148
  stopped, 156
Ready-to-assemble (RTA)
  fasteners, 19, 97
  installing, 96-99
Right-angle drill guide, 107, 108
Rotary-cut plywood veneer, 6, 8
Router compass jig, 104
Router table, 41, 67, 85, 86, 89, 156
Routing,
  corner bead, 145
  coves, 59, 60
  dadoes on router table, 41, 67
  dadoes with handheld router,
    76, 77
  patterns, 131
  rabbets, 50
  roundover, 97, 149
  slot, 85, 86

S

Sanding tips, 28
Sheet goods,
  common joints, 18, 19
  cutting, 16, 17
  handling & storage, 14, 15
Sheet veneer,
  applying, 21
  types, 21
Shelf,
  construction & installation, 24,
    25, 78

edge construction, 24
edge options, 24
standards, installing, 61
support options, 25
Slot-cutting, 85, 86
Spacers, 76-78
Squaring up carcase, 22
Stain application, 28, 29
Straightedge,
  cutting guide, 16, 77
  layout tool, 85, 146

T

Table saw extension, 16
Taper jig, 114
Tee nuts, 108, 109
Tempered hardboard, 13
Textured plywood, 13
Tile, installing, 61
Tite-Joint brand fasteners, 19
  installing, 133
Toekick, assembling, 38
Tote, sheet goods, 15
Trammel point, 135, 136
Transferring patterns, 106

U

Upholstering, 134, 135

V

V-block, chamfer cutting, 114, 115
Veneer,
  applying, 40, 88, 114, 115
  common plywood species, 9
  edge-banding application, 20,
    122, 123
  edge-banding types, 20
  grain patterns, plywood, 8
  sheet types & application, 21
  trimming, 39
Vermillion sheet veneer, 21
Vix bit, 90
Voids, filling, 28

W

Walnut veneer, 9
  edge banding, 20
Wire brads, 53
Wood putty, applying, 28
Wrap hinges, 90

Z

Zebrawood sheet veneer, 21

Index of Projects

Base Cabinet, 34-43
building time, 35
cutting list, 37
detailed drawings, 36, 37
shopping list, 35
step-by-step, 38-43
tools needed, 35
vital statistics, 35

Changing Table/Dresser, 140-149
building time, 141
cutting list, 142
detailed drawings, 142, 143
shopping list, 141
step-by-step, 144-149
tools needed, 141
vital statistics, 141

Corner Booth, 126-139
building time, 127
cutting list, 129
detailed drawings, 128-130
shopping list, 127
step-by-step, 131-139
tools needed 127
vital statistics, 127

Country Cupboard, 150-157
building time, 151
cutting list, 152
detailed drawings, 152, 153
shopping list, 151
step-by-step, 154-157
tools needed, 151
vital statistics, 151

Desktop Console, 118-125
building time, 119
cutting list, 120
detailed drawings, 120, 121
shopping list, 119
step-by-step, 122-125
tools needed, 119
vital statistics, 119

Entertainment Center, 80-91
building time, 81
cutting list, 83
detailed drawings, 82-84
shopping list, 81
step-by-step, 85-90
tools needed, 81
vital statistics, 81

Hallway Bookcase, 92-99
building time, 93
cutting list, 94
detailed drawings, 94, 95
shopping list, 93
step-by-step, 96-99
tools needed, 93
vital statistics, 93

Plant Stand with Hidden Storage, 54-61
building time, 55
cutting list, 56
detailed drawings, 56, 57
shopping list, 55
step-by-step, 58-61
tools needed, 55
vital statistics, 55

Play Table & Chairs, 100-109
building time, 101
cutting list, 102
detailed drawings, 102, 103
shopping list, 101
step-by-step, 104-109
tools needed, 101
vital statistics, 101

Sailboat Sandbox, 62-71
building time, 63
cutting list, 64
detailed drawings, 64, 65
shopping list, 63
step-by-step, 66-71
tools needed, 63
vital statistics, 63

Sheet Goods Cart, 72-79
building time, 73
cutting list, 74
detailed drawings, 74, 75
shopping list, 73
step-by-step, 76-79
tools needed, 73
vital statistics, 73

Wall-hung Cabinet, 44-53
building time, 45
cutting list, 46
detailed drawings, 46, 47
shopping list, 55
step-by-step, 48-53
tools needed, 45
vital statistics, 45

Walnut Writing Desk, 110-117
building time, 111
cutting list, 112
detailed drawings, 112, 113
shopping list, 111
step-by-step, 114-117
tools needed, 111
vital statistics, 111